A DIGEST AND INDEX
OF THE
MINUTES OF THE GENERAL SYNOD
OF THE
REFORMED CHURCH IN AMERICA
1958–1977

The Historical Series of the Reformed Church in America
No. 7

A DIGEST AND INDEX OF THE MINUTES OF THE GENERAL SYNOD OF THE REFORMED CHURCH IN AMERICA 1958–1977

by
Mildred W. Schuppert

Wm. B. Eerdmans Publishing Co.
Grand Rapids, Michigan

Library of Congress Cataloging in Publication Data
Main entry under title:

Digest and Index of the Minutes of the General Synod of the Reformed Church in America, 1958-1977.

(The Historical series of the Reformed Church in America; v. 7)
Includes index.
1. Reformed Church in America. General Synod—Indexes. I. Schuppert, Mildred W. II. Reformed Church in America. General Synod. III. Series.
BX9518.A2 262'.5'5732 79-10043
ISBN 0-8028-1774-2

Gratefully dedicated
to the memory of my parents
Mr. and Mrs. I. Thomas Schuppert

CONTENTS

The Historical Commission	ix
Foreword	xi
Preface	xv
Abbreviations	xvii
Digest and Index	1

THE HISTORICAL COMMISSION

The Historical Series of the Reformed Church in America

This series has been inaugurated by the General Synod of the Reformed Church in America, acting through its Commission on History, for the purpose of encouraging historical research and providing a medium wherein this knowledge may be shared with the academic community and with the members of the denomination in order that a knowledge of the past may contribute to right action in the present.

General Editor

The Rev. Donald J. Bruggink, Ph.D.
Western Theological Seminary

The Commission on History

Professor John Beardslee III
New Brunswick Theological Seminary
The Rev. Arie R. Brouwer
General Secretary, R.C.A.
The Rev. Elton J. Bruins, Ph.D.
Hope College
Professor Gerald F. De Jong, Ph.D.
University of South Dakota
Professor Barbara Fassler, Ph.D.
Central College
The Rev. Norman J. Kansfield
Western Theological Seminary
The Rev. Joseph A. Loux, Jr.
Helderberg Reformed Church, Guilderland Center, New York
The Rev. Sharon T. Scholten
Reformed Church of Keyport, Keyport, New Jersey

FOREWORD

Within recent decades the Reformed Church in America has been suffering from a progressively worsening case of amnesia. While the output of the General Synod with her committees and commissions steadily increased, and while her administrative offices underwent radical alteration, the memory of the church increasingly faltered. This breakdown of memory was the result not of intellectual incompetence, but rather the lack of basic information retrieval. Without any means of recalling what the General Synod of the Reformed Church with her myriad agencies, committees, and commissions had done, the amnesia of the church has gotten progressively worse, with the usual difficulty of the victim: a failure to know oneself.

The cure is now in our hands, and we are all deeply indebted to Mildred Schuppert, who has undertaken the task of being the memory of the church. Her accomplishment has been possible through finely-honed skills developed as head of the Beardslee Library of Western Theological Seminary. As a result, the church once again has a memory, for it is to Mildred Schuppert that we are indebted for this *Digest and Index of the Minutes of the General Synod of the Reformed Church in America, 1958–1977.*

The excellence with which this *Digest and Index* has been executed has resulted in the request of the Historical Commission that work be begun on the period between the publication of Corwin's *Digest and Index* in 1906 and the present volume.

As indicated in the preface, not since 1906 has the church had available a memory of its actions. It was then that Edwin Tanjore Corwin published his *Digest of Synodical Legislation.* This, together with five editions of his *Manual of the Reformed Church in America,* which was both a church history and a historical directory, constituted the very massive erudition of Edwin Tanjore Corwin that intimidated anyone from taking his place.

Since 1906 the church has lived through a world war, a depression, another world war, and after the pacific 50s, the turbulent 60s with the movement for civil rights, the Vietnamese conflict, a new round of women's liberation, and radical alterations of the familiar fabric of society. The church has tried to speak to these affairs moral, political, and economic, as well as being in ecumenical conversations with other denominations, all within the context of theology and polity, but without ever bringing its information retrieval system up to date.

During this period the church of necessity lived from personal memory—often that of long-tenured servants. The Rev. James M. Martin served as permanent clerk of General Synod from 1920 to 1954, the Rev. Dr. James E. Hoffman served as Stated Clerk of General Synod from 1943 to 1961, and the Rev. Dr. Marion de Velder served first as Stated Clerk and then in the continuance of that office as General Secretary from 1961 to 1977. Personnel of the Boards were also known for longevity, as indeed were members of the Boards. However, in 1960 a rule was passed "that no member shall serve for more than two consecutive terms" (it should be noted that I found this information by checking the *Digest and Index* under "Committees, Rules concerning membership on: 1960: 302"—and it worked!). As a member of General Synod's Board of Education in 1960 we honored a retiring member who had served for over twenty years. The new six-year maximum was intended to give greater numbers opportunity to serve—but throughout the denominational structures, it served also to sever the cords of personal memory, and there was no other information retrieval system to take its place.

No one will be able to assess how much wasted effort has resulted from this inability to remember what we have done; for like a person with failing memory, we don't know when we are retelling a story (or considering again the same proposed legislation). Earlier this year, while reading the manuscript for the *Digest and Index,* a request for information came from denominational headquarters. A classis was overturing that the number of elders voting at classes be equal to the number of ministers and it was hoped that as a professor of historical theology I might be able to shed some light on the subject. Armed with the invaluable *Digest and Index,* and finding "Classes, Representation in," it became immediately apparent that this question had appeared before the General Synod in 1969. Other facets of representation at classes had also been considered in 1968, 1970, 1976, and 1977. While an awareness of the previous actions of Synod would in no way guarantee satisfaction, it would nonetheless make a more mature consideration of the issue possible, with discussion building on actions of the past, rather than merely repeating them. Hopefully, classes, as well as the members of classes, will avail themselves of this denominational memory, the *Digest and Index,* to research what has been done in the past, before repetitive overtures are placed before Synod.

Even as the life of an amnesia victim is deprived of the cohesiveness given by memory, so the life of our denomination has lacked wholeness. In part, issues have divided us, but our lack of memory, the inability to retrieve what has been said and done in the past, has contributed to a failure to understand the issues as well as to remember what we have said and done.

It will become immediately obvious to anyone using this work that it requires the availability of the *Minutes of General Synod* to be fully intelligible. However, not only are these volumes available at every library affiliated with the Reformed Church, but they are sent to each church/minister after each General Synod. Hopefully, the presence of the *Digest and Index* will give convincing answer to the otherwise intelligent minister who was overheard to ask concerning the General Synod *Minutes:* "What would one want to save those for?" They are the annual history of the church, and Miss Schuppert has given us the memory, the *Digest and Index,* to make that history available. We are in her debt.

Donald J. Bruggink, General Editor
Historical Series of the
Reformed Church in America

PREFACE

Seventy-one years ago Edward Tanjore Corwin's *Digest of Constitutional and Synodical Legislation of the Reformed Church in America* was published. It was a large 851 page volume done by a Reformed Church historian who had lived close to the workings of the denomination with a wealth of historical material at his fingertips. His digests of the various subjects are expertly done.

Since that time (1906) no digest has been published. There have been typed copies covering brief periods, which were helpful, and offices of the church have sometimes prepared indexes in order to help them in the work of their offices, but only a few such typed copies exist. There has been a real need for this kind of information. Three years ago the former General Secretary, Dr. Marion de Velder, asked me to undertake the job of making an index of the last twenty years of the Minutes of General Synod. The thought was that it would then be published in the 350th year of the history of the Reformed Church in America. As the first year's index began to take shape it was easy to see that an index was not enough. Although I knew that I could not hope to produce an exhaustive work like Dr. Corwin's it became evident that a digest of some sort was needed. After the initial request, the work came under the aegis of the Historical Commission. In the fall of 1975 I took my one-year index-digest for 1958 to a meeting of the Commission in New Brunswick, and there it was decided that it should be more than an index. Thus the pattern for this work fell into shape—a digest-index in alphabetical order. This *is* a digest. Year and page references are given for each entry. Full information may be found in the *Minutes of General Synod* by referring to the volume indicated.

It has been my aim to try to touch on almost every subject mentioned in the Minutes. I come to the job with the skill of a librarian—not a church historian. Unlike Dr. Corwin, I have never attended a General Synod meeting. I have done the best I could with the assignment. I am haunted by the thought that there are errors lurking where I have not been able to spot them. I hope the volume will be helpful. I would echo Dr. Corwin's words, "The preparation of it, often interrupted, has been a lengthy, but an interesting and pleasant labor."

Mildred W. Schuppert

Holland, Michigan
Christmastide, 1977.

ABBREVIATIONS

ABC	American Bible Society
AIC	American Indian Council
AIM	Adventure in Mission
App.	Appendix
BC	Black Council
BCO	Book of Church Order
BCWM	Board of Christian World Mission
BD	Board of Direction
BDM	Board of Domestic Missions
BE	Board of Education
BLMS	Bi-level Multi-site
BNAM	Board of North American Missions
BP	Board of Pensions
BTE	Board of Theological Education
BWM	Board of World Missions
CAC	Christian Action Commission
CAF	Contributory Annuity Fund
CC	Commission on Chaplains
CCU	Committee on Church Unity
C18	Committee of Eighteen
CH	Church Herald
CHE	Committee on Higher Education
CIR	Committee on Interchurch Relations
CJB	Committee on Judicial Business
CLC	Covenant Life Curriculum
CNPM	Committee on Next Place of Meeting
COCG	Committee on Church Government
COCU	Consultation on Church Union
COH	Commission on History
COR	Committee of Reference
CPT	Clinical Pastoral Training
*CRC	Christian Reformed Church
*CRC	Committee on the Revision of the Constitution

*The abbreviation CRC refers to the Christian Reformed Church only where the context makes that reference obvious.

CRL	Committee on the Revision of the Liturgy
CTE	Committee on Theological Education
C12	Committee of Twelve
CWCC	Committee on the World Council of Churches
CWM	Christian World Mission
CWS	Church World Service
DAVARCA	Department of Audio Visual Aids, RCA
DAW	Department of Adult Work
DE	Department of Evangelism
EC	Editorial Committee
ECCG	Editorial Committee on Church Government
ECRC	Editorial Committee on the Revision of the Constitution
GPC	General Program Council
GS	General Synod
GSEC	General Synod Executive Committee
HC	Historical Commission
HR	Human Resources
IRC	Interchurch Relations Committee
JC24	Joint Committee of Twenty-four
JED	Joint Educational Development
LC	Liturgy Committee
LDA	Lord's Day Alliance
MGS	Minutes of General Synod
NAE	National Association of Evangelicals
NBEDC	National Black Economic Development Conference
NBTS	New Brunswick Theological Seminary
NC	Nominating Committee
NCC	National Council of Churches
NDWW	National Department of Women's Work
OAF	Office of Administration and Finance
OAVS	Office of Adult Voluntary Services
OHR	Office of Human Resources
OPC	Office of Promotion and Communications
PC	Promotion and Communications
PCP	Permanent Committee on Professorate
PCTE	Permanent Committee on Theological Education
PCUS	Presbyterian Church in the United States
PR	President's Report
PS	Particular Synod
PSC	Particular Synod of Chicago
PSNJ	Particular Synod of New Jersey
PTR	Preaching-Teaching-Reaching Mission
RCA	Reformed Church in America
RCBP	Review Committee on the Board of Pensions
RCGPC	Review Committee on the General Program Council
RCHE	Review Committee on Higher Education
RCPR	Review Committee on President's Report
RCTE	Review Committee on Theological Education
RCW	Reformed Church Women
RIAL	Religion in American Life
SC	Stewardship Council
SCBE	Standing Committee on the Board of Education
SCBWM	Standing Committee on the Board of World Missions
SCDS	Standing Committee on Denominational Structure
SCHE	Standing Committee on Higher Education

SCIR	Standing Committee on Interchurch Relations
SCO	Standing Committee on Overtures
SCSC	Standing Committee on Stewardship Council
SCSM	Standing Committee on Synodical Minutes
TC	Theological Commission
TRAVARCA	Television, Radio, Audio Visuals, RCA
UPCUSA	United Presbyterian Church, U.S.A.
WARC	World Alliance of Reformed Churches
WBFM	Women's Board of Foreign Missions
WC	Worship Committee
WCC	World Council of Churches
WRC	Western Regional Center
WHBL	World Home Bible League
WTS	Western Theological Seminary

A DIGEST AND INDEX
OF THE
MINUTES OF THE GENERAL SYNOD
OF THE
REFORMED CHURCH IN AMERICA
1958–1977

ABELARD, FRANK
Dispensation requested, but incomplete.
1971: 31. No action.

ABORTION
CAC statement on.
1967: 209–210.
CAC recommends laws be changed to allow abortion: (1) if the pregnancy would gravely impair the physical or mental health of the mother; (2) if the child would likely be born with physical or mental defects; (3) if the pregnancy resulted from rape or incest.
1968: 217–218, 220. Adopted.
CAC recommends GS go on record urging various state legislatures to abolish all abortion laws and make it a matter of individual conscience to be experienced within the context of one's faith with proper medical counsel.
1969: 243, 249. Lost.
CAC report: (1) the decision re legal abortion is every person's right under Christian freedom; (2) to use or not use legal abortion should be considered carefully and prayerfully; (3) no person should be forced or encouraged to undergo abortion if it is against the person's moral beliefs; (4) the Christian community should play a supportive role for persons making a decision to utilize abortion.
1971: 220. Adopted.
Six overtures urging revising or rescinding action of 1971—that no statement at all would be better.
1972: 82–86, 102–103. No action. To be referred to the TC and CAC for a comprehensive study.
Overture requesting a revision of the 1971 statement: that the RCA teaches the sanctity of human life and that in principle abortion ought not be practiced at all, however, in this complex society where rape or incest has been the cause of pregnancy that it be allowable, or where the life of the mother is in danger, abortion would be permitted; that we stand against any legislation that liberalizes the abortion law.
1973: 105–106. Adopted, but GS awaits further judgment by the CAC and TC.
TC and CAC are preparing study papers which will be presented in 1974.
1973: 194.
Overture requesting GS to urge the President of the U.S. to repudiate the Supreme Court "Black Monday" decision.
1973: 103. No action, since the President has no authority to repudiate a Supreme Court decision.
Overture requesting the GS to declare the official position of the RCA to be in favor of life, therefore in opposition to the Supreme Court ruling.
1973: 103. No action.
Overture requesting the TC to make a study of abortion and provide guidelines for churches.
1973: 104–105. No action.
Overture requesting GS to deplore the Supreme Court decision and affirm again the Christian position upholding the right to life of unborn children.
1973: 104. No action.
Overture requesting that GS call upon the President of the U.S. to urge the Supreme Court to reconsider their decision and to urge Congress to adopt a constitutional amendment.
1973: 104. No action.
TC sets forth a study of Scripture passages that might be pertinent to the issue.
1974: 207–208.
CAC continues study "in conjunction with" TC.
1974: 212–213.
Overture requesting reaffirming of the 1973 action with these additions: (1) we support the adoption of "conscience clauses" to free medical personnel and agencies from any legal penalties or limitations of employment due to unwillingness to be involved in performing abortion; (2) that GSEC review ways in which the RCA programs can assist in publicizing, encouraging, and if possible, assisting financially in providing alternatives to abortion.
1974: 100–101. Adopted.
GSEC has taken action: (1) to ask the Church Herald to continue articles on programs and agencies providing alternatives; (2) has requested CAC to assist in ways in which RCA programs, personnel, and agencies can if possible assist financially in providing alternatives.
1975: 96–97.
CAC recommends: a) the ability to make a decision on abortion is every person's right and should not be abridged because of financial difficulties or the imposed moral opinion of other persons; b) to use or not to use legal abortion should be carefully considered by all persons involved, decision made prayerfully in the love of Jesus Christ; c) no person should be forced or encouraged to undergo or participate in an abortion when it is against the person's moral beliefs; d) churches are called upon to make alternatives known to those who are contemplating abortion; e) Christians

and the Christian community should play a supportive role for persons making a decision about or utilizing abortion.
1975: 191-193. a) defeated (yes 107, no 135); b) adopted (yes 120, no 113); c) adopted; d) adopted; e) adopted.
CAC minority report on the above: believe in principle that there should be no abortions and that GSEC review ways in publicizing alternatives to abortion.
1975: 201.
Action of 1973 reaffirmed.
1975: 202.

ABSENT MEMBERS
Overture regarding follow-up procedure when members leave. Elders to follow-up.
1960: 93-94. Adopted.

ACKERMAN, ROY
Dispensation from professorial certificate requested.
1973: 33, 36. Granted.

ADAM, HISTORICITY OF
Overture in opposition to TC report.
1961: 138-140, 142. No action. See GENESIS, HISTORICITY OF.

ADMINISTRATION AND FINANCE, OFFICE OF
To be constituted.
1966: 167-168.
Proposals for.
1966: 177-180, 182-183.
Administrative Chart.
1966: 180.
Progress toward.
1968: 352-353.
Duties of.
1969: 178-179.
Report.
1970: 161.
1971: 153.
1972: 121-122.
1973: 154-155.
Name changed to OFFICE OF FINANCE, see also FINANCE, OFFICE OF.

ADULT WORK, DEPARTMENT OF
Report.
1958: 76. 1963: 59.
1959: 76. 1964: 56.
1960: 69. 1965: 51.
1961: 86. 1966: 54.
1962: 75-76.

ADULT VOLUNTARY SERVICES
A new office.
1971: 141, 154. 1975: 147.
1972: 59-60, 123. 1976: 83.
1973: 156. 1977: 91.
1974: 67, 161.

ADVANCE IN MISSION
1973: 59, 69.
1974: 58, 74.

ADVENTURE IN MISSION (AIM)
1967: 92, 93, 96, 144. 1975: 58.
1968: 74, 81. 1977: 91.
1972: 59.

AFRICA, SOUTH
See SOUTH AFRICA.

AGRICULTURAL AND MIGRANT WORKERS
Recommended: (1) that RCA approve the right of agricultural and migrant workers to organize labor unions; (2) minimum wage laws to apply to migrants; (3) support efforts of farm workers.
1972: 216. Adopted. See also BOYCOTTS, ECONOMIC.

AID TO AREAS OF ACUTE HUMAN NEED
1961: 161.
See also CHURCH WORLD SERVICE and WORLD HUNGER.

AINSWORTH, ELDER JAMES H.
Overture requesting admission of candidate to NBTS without college training.
1959: 53-54, 57. Granted provided he passes certain examinations.
Dispensation from study of original languages requested.
1961: 66, 68-69, 74. Granted.

ALBANY, PARTICULAR SYNOD OF
Realignment of
1961: 327.

ALCOHOL
Voluntary total abstinance recommended.
1960: 186, 187. 1962: 224.
1961: 213. 1965: 217.
President expresses concern about liquor traffic
1965: 335, 345, 348. Referred to CAC to prepare a positive statement against the abuse of alcoholic beverages.
CAC study recommends a Christian position of moderation or voluntary total abstinence, educational program, etc.
1966: 215-218, 234. Adopted. CAC authorized to select someone to administer the program.
"Alcohol and Traffic Safety," a CAC study paper
1973: 219-220.
Recommended that seminaries have seminars on this subject.
1974: 40. Adopted.
BTE reports a member of NBTS faculty has special training in this field and is available if students encounter the problem. WTS

has recently brought Rev. Herman Kregel, an authority on the subject, for a student seminar.
1975: 32. see also DRUGS.
ALCOHOLISM, SUB-COMMITTEE ON
Report.
1958: 202, 204.
Statement concerning.
1959: 209.
ALLIANCE OF REFORMED CHURCHES CHURCHES HOLDING THE PRESBYTERIAN SYSTEM
Committee report.
1958: 173–176.
1959: 183–186.
1960: 157–159.
1961: 186–188.
1962: 179–180.
1963: 171–174.
1964: 275–276.
North American Area.
1960: 154–156.
1961: 189–191.
1962: 181–184.
1963: 169–171.
1964: 283–286.
1965: 258–260.
1966: 242–243, 274–278.
1967: 247–251.
General Secretary's report.
1964: 276–282.
1965: 253–257.
1966: 242, 267–274.
1967: 225–226, 239–247.
Proposal to unite the Alliance with the International Congregational Churches.
1968: 266–268.
Name changed to WORLD ALLIANCE OF REFORMED CHURCHES, which also see.
1968: 267.

AMENDMENTS
Overture requesting that some amendments be voted on by seriatim votes instead of one vote for questions of some magnitude.
1972: 93. No action since each synod has a right to decide the method.
Overture requesting amendments to the BCO be made only every third year.
1974: 106. No action.
Overture requesting amendments be considered only every third year.
1975: 92. No action.
Overture asking for an amendment in the BCO declaring that any amendment that has been defeated may not be recommended again to the classes without a 2/3 vote of GS.
1976: 103–104. No action.
Overture concerning revision of the procedure of amending the BCO: a) GS shall approve an amendment at a stated meeting; b) if approved it shall be referred to COCG to be presented to GS the next year; c) if approved it will be recommended to classes; d) a 2/3 vote of classes will allow the declaration resolution and it will become effective.
1977: 116–117. No action, since it would take an additional year.
See also, CONSTITUTION, AMENDMENTS.

AMERICAN BIBLE SOCIETY
Report.
1958: 179–186.
1959: 188–192.
1960: 164–169.
1961: 193–197.
1962: 187–191.
1963: 301–304.
1964: 296–299.
1965: 260.
1966: 278–279.
1967: 251–253.
1968: 257–259.
1969: 284–286.
1971: 233, 242–246.
1972: 243–248.
1973: 246–250.
1974: 241–246.
1975: 219–224.
1976: 127–128.
1977: 137–138.
AMERICAN INDIAN COUNCIL
Report.
1972: 75–76.
1973: 75–78.
1974: 85–86.
1975: 72–74.
1976: 170–171.
1977: 191–192.
Overture asking for an Indian representative on the GPC.
1971: 103, 114. Adopted.
Request that two Indian Americans be appointed on the GPC.
1972: 75. Referred to GPC.
Other references.
1973: 66, 71, 74, 119.
1974: 68.
Only one congregation is served by an Indian pastor. None are in schools, colleges or seminaries preparing for the ministry.
1977: 191–192.
Formerly INDIAN CAUCUS, which also see.

AMNESTY
CAC recommends that churches use the resources of the CAC so that they become aware of this serious human problem and that we come to terms with the moral issues which cause young people to become war resistors or exiles.
1973: 203–208. Adopted.
Restatement of action taken in 1973.
1974: 294–295. Adopted.
CAC recommends a) GS urge the church to support congressional legislation which may lead to broad general amnesty for all victims of the Vietnam war; b) that GS en-

courage the churches to make use of the resources of the National Interreligious Service Board for Conscientious Objectors in order to better continue education and counsel of its membership.
1975: 193. Adopted.

ANGUS, MRS. WILLIAM, MISSIONARY TO CHINA
Death.
1975: 64.

ANNUAL CONGREGATIONAL VISIT
Made in 1971 to most congregations.
1972: 133. Comprised of ministers, laymen and some national staff members.

ANNVILLE INSTITUTE
1971: 60-61.
1973: 63.
1974: 66.
1975: 57-58.
1976: 135-136.
See also APPENDIX

ANTIPHONAL PRAYER
Presented by the WARC.
1965: 229, 233, 243. Reaction of churches and pastors to be sent to chairman of PCIR.
TC had no objection to its use. TC sent some suggestions for strengthening the statement.
1967: 187.
The response of the TC was the only one received from the 13 member churches.
1967: 226.

ANUAK TRANSLATION OF THE NEW TESTAMENT
Completed by Rev. Harvey Hoekstra.
1960: 77.

APARTHEID
see SOUTH AFRICA

APOSTLES' CREED
Overture regarding alternate reading of.
1959: 125. Not approved.
Overture requesting the words "universal Christian" be substituted for "Catholic."
1966: 118-119, 142. No action.

APPEALS AND COMPLAINTS
Overture suggesting the time limit for filing be changed from 10 days to 20 days.
1961: 128, 142, 152. Approved and referred to CRC.
COCG amendments will be presented in 1974.
1973: 181.
Recommended that GS request COCG to study procedural sequence in BCO.
1976: 62. Adopted.
COCG reports one judicatory can lodge a complaint against another under certain conditions. In order to lodge a complaint the judicatory (or communicant member) must be subject to the immediate administrative authority of the judicatory against which the complaint is lodged.
1977: 314.
COCG recommends the following amendment to the BCO: A complaint is a written statement alleging administrative error. a. A complaint may be filed only by (1) a communicant member in good and regular standing against the consistory or board of elders having superintendence over that person; (2) a member of an assembly against that assembly of which the person is a member; (3) an assembly against the assembly having immediate superintendence over the complaining assembly. b. Complaints may be filed only with the assembly that has immediate superintendece of the assembly against which the complaint is filed. c. No complaint can be taken against any action of GS. The CJB shall be notified of the complaint.
1977: 316-317. Adopted.
COCG recommends that GS adopt and recommend to the classes for their approval the following amendment to the BCO: that "30 days" be substituted for "20 days."
1977: 318. Adopted and sent to classes for approval.

APPENDIX
Annual reports of.
BOARD OF THE CHRISTIAN WORLD MISSION
BOARD OF DOMESTIC MISSIONS
BOARD OF EDUCATION
THE BOARD OF PENSIONS
KIRKSIDE, INC.
REFORMED CHURCH WORLD SERVICE (added in 1967)
1958: Bound in after MGS.
1959: Bound in after MGS.
1960: Bound in after MGS.
1961: Bound in after MGS.
1962: Bound in after MGS.
1963: Appendix 1 bound separately.
1964: Appendix 1 bound separately.
1965: Appendix 1 bound separately.
1966: Appendix 1 bound separately.
1967: Appendix 1 bound separately.
1968: Appendix 1 bound separately.
After 1968, the first three boards listed became part of the GPC. The reports of the others appear in the MGS.

APPROACHES TO UNITY, COMMITTEE ON
Report.
1958: 352-356.

APPROACHES TO UNITY, SPECIAL COMMITTEE ON
Report.
1958: 357-358.
Name changed to COMMITTEE ON CONFESSIONAL INTERPRETATION.
1958: 357.
See also CONFESSIONAL INTERPRETATION, COMMITTEE ON

ARCHIVES, DENOMINATIONAL
Reorganization of at NBTS.
1961: 394-396.
Growth of.
1962: 410-412.
Microfilming of.
1963: 334. Copies being sent to WTS.
Boards and agencies urged to deposit archival materials in the archives at NBTS.
1972: 268.
Detailed archival program proposal.
1977: 239-242.

ARCOT SEMINARY FUND
See INDIA.

ARMED FORCES MESSENGER
Magazine for the Armed Forces.
1958: 146-147.
1959: 152.
1960: 128-129.
1961: 156 (edited by Rev. Norman Thomas)
1962: 145.
1963: 155.
1964: 446.
1965: 409.
1966: 364.
1967: 317.
Publication discontinued after a decade.

ARMSTRONG, PAUL
Dispensation from professorial certificate requested.
1959: 53, 57. Should apply to WTS for a professorial certificate after additional study and apprenticeship.
Request for dispensation withdrawn.
1960: 52.

ASKINGS
See ASSESSMENTS, ASKINGS, OFFERINGS

ASSESSMENTS, ASKINGS, OFFERINGS
Discussion on assessable funds and non-assessable funds.
1968: 179-180.
1973: 124.
Definitions: a) assessment—a specified dollar amount levied by a judicatory, payment of which is mandatory; b) asking—a specific dollar amount approved by a judicatory as an assigned share; c) offering—a voluntary gift in response to a specific appeal.
1973: 124.
Overture requesting that there be no assessments for anything beyond the operating expenses in the budget; that other requests be in the nature of "askings."
1972: 90. No action, since it is difficult to separate some benevolences from operating expenses.
GS to request GSEC to make a study of the definitions of "askings" and "assessments" and that they be included in the BCO.
1976: 62. Adopted.
GSEC proposes no changes. The definitions of 1973 remain in effect.
1977: 42.

ASSESSMENTS OF GENERAL SYNOD
1958: 32 (46¢ per member).
1959: 31 (50¢ per member).
1960: 29 (58¢ per member).
1961: 30 (68¢ per member).
1962: 27 (70¢ per member).
1963: 28 (75¢ per member).
1964: 29 (78¢ per member).
1965: 29 (86¢ per member).
1966: 30 (92¢ per member).
1967: 33 ($1.08 per member).
1968: 36 ($1.20 per member).
1969: 34 ($1.26 per member).
1970: 159 ($1.26 per member).
1971: 190 ($1.26 per member).
1972: 160 ($1.32 per member).
1973: 169 ($1.35 per member).
1974: 179 ($1.40 per member).
1975: 151 ($1.70 per member).
1976: 84 ($2.00 per member).
1977: 93 ($2.12 per member).

ASSISTANT MINISTERS
see MINISTERS, ASSISTANT

ASSOCIATE MINISTERS
see MINISTERS, ASSOCIATE

ASSOCIATES IN MISSION
1972: 271.
See also ADVENTURE IN MISSION

ATTENDANCE AT WORSHIP
Gallup Poll taken in years 1940-1958.
1959: 234.

ATWOOD, REV. DONNER B.
Elected Vice President of General Synod.
1964: 7.
Elected President of General Synod.
1965: 8.

AUDIO VISUAL AIDS, DEPARTMENT OF
Report.
1959: 319-320. Joined with the

BROADCASTING AND FILM COMMISSION OF THE NCC, which see.
DAVARCA (Department of Aduio Visual Aids, R.C.A.)
1969: 180–181. Films available from the Grandville, Michigan Office; Filmstrips from the Albany, N.Y.; Lansing, Illinois; and Anaheim California offices. See also TRAVARCA.

"AUTHORITY AND CONSCIENCE IN THE CHURCH"
Paper submitted by TC on the right of authority of the NCC and the Church. Pronouncements of a Council are only advisory. Pronouncements by agencies of the Church, approved by GS, carry authority. GS speaks for the church and to the church.
1976: 233–235. Adopted.

AUTHORITY (EXECUTIVE)
The right is either explicitly given by the constitution, or it is implied in the right to legislate.
1965: 154–157.

BAHR, FRANK J.
Dispensation from A.B. degree requested.
1965: 46. Suggest Mr. Bahr apply for admission to one of our seminaries.
Overture requesting dispensation from biblical languages and the professorial certificate.
1966: 46. Granted.

BAHRAIN
1970: 60–61.
1971: 60.
See also entry under APPENDIX.

BAKER, EDWARD
Dispensation from professorial certificate requested.
1970: 32. Tardy request; conditional requirements not met. Not granted.
Request for dispensation repeated.
1971: 31, 36. Approved.

BAKKER, RICHARD
Dispensation from the professorial certificate requested. A graduate of Union Seminary. Examination by NBTS.
1966: 46. Granted.

BAPTISM (BELIEVERS BAPTISM, OR REBAPTISM)
Overture requesting TC to give guidance to churches on the matter of baptism, especially for RCA ministers who have reservations regarding infant baptism and/or are willing to "rebaptize" those who seek "believer's" baptism.
1973: 102–103. No action, since this has already been treated in 1967 by "A Statement on Infant Baptism" by Dr. M. E. Osterhaven.
1973 Overture repeated since guidelines of 1967 do not adequately cover this problem.
1974: 102. Adopted.
A paper on rebaptism presented by TC, and TC recommends: (1) that the paper be adopted since it provides pastoral counsel to churches faced with this question; (2) that GS request the Liturgy Committee to examine the liturgical and theological advisability of creating new forms or orders which may serve to affirm, celebrate and express a new experience of revitalized faith and which, hopefully, will alleviate the need for any recourse to repeated baptism.
1975: 172–180. Both adopted.
Overture requesting the TC to study and report on the validity of a baptism that takes place in youth or adulthood when the person has already been baptized as an infant.
1974: 97. Adopted.

BAPTISM, INFANT
CRL recommends the following be added to the Constitution: "The Sacrament of Baptism shall be administered to a child only if at least one of the parents, natural or otherwise, be a member of the Christian Church and that parents, natural or otherwise, of the child must in some way be amenable to the Board of Elders of the church in question."
1966: 213,214. Adopted.
TC making an in-depth study. Will report later.
1966: 206.
TC statement.
1967: 187–188, 189–196.
Amendment to the Constitution recommended: "The Sacrament of Infant Baptism may be administered only to a child, at least one of whose parents or guardians is a communicant member of the church and is amenable to the Board of Elders of the church in which the sacrament of baptism is to be administered."
1967: 182, 185. Adopted. Referred to classes for approval.
The above statement not approved by classes.
1968: 169.
Three overtures opposing above statement
1968: 97–99, 118, 123. No action.

Overture asking TC to clarify position of RCA with regard to pre-requisites of non-communicant parent or parents who seek baptism for their children.
1974: 101. Adopted.
Overture requesting a sentence be added in the Government: "They shall consider requests for infant baptism, providing at least one parent or guardian is a communicant member of the Christian Church."
1975: 82–83, 161. Adopted and referred to EC.
Classes approve above statement
1976: 46.
President suggests and it is recommended that the GPC produce an instructional booklet on infant baptism to be used by pastors with parents before baptism.
1976: 30, 34. Adopted.
Overture requesting an addition in the BCO to the effect that elders may grant permission for the baptism of a child when the parent or parents, guardian or guardians are Christian and members of the congregation over which the elders have oversight. If the parent(s) or guardian(s) are members of another Christian church it must first be approved by the judicatory of that congregation.
1976: 101–102. Referred to TC for study as they are already dealing with this issue.
GPC announces production of a "Manual on Infant Baptism" in the *Heritage and Hope* series under supervision of Arthur O. Van Eck.
1977: 140.
TC has presented three studies in the last decade and believes another study would make no further contribution. TC favors the statement in the BCO but further finds no fault with the recommendation that when a parent or guardian from another Christian church requests baptism for their infant, the request may be granted, only when the proper judicatory of the parents' own congregation first authorizes it.
1977: 306. Referred to COCG.

BAPTISM (SPIRIT BAPTISM)
TC recommends the RCA encourage the development of a biblical understanding of the "baptism in the Holy Spirit" and gifts of the Spirit by approving distribution of the TC report to the churches of the RCA and requesting responses to provide material for possible revision and future study.
1975: 180–188. Approved.
TC paper indicates that the "baptism in the Holy Spirit" and the "fullness of the Spirit" are closely related and sometimes even identified in Neo-Pentecostal literature. Paper includes a study of all Scriptural references (both Old and New Testament) to the filling of the Holy Spirit. Recommended that the study be made available to the churches.
1977: 284–293. Adopted.

BAPTIZED CHILDREN AND THE LORD'S SUPPER.
See LORD'S SUPPER AND BAPTIZED CHILDREN.

BAPTIZED NON-COMMUNICANTS
Overture requesting study of.
1968: 99, 118, 123. Referred to CRC for study.
COCG gives a detailed report of duties of Elders, rewording Part I, Article 5, Section 2 of the *Government.*
1969: 211–213, 229. Adopted.
Meaning of Baptized Non-Communicant Member, presented by TC.
1977: 296–297.

BARMEN DECLARATION
Thanksgiving for this witness to the sole Lordship of Christ, and urging the RCA to be aware of the temptations that threaten the church today.
1974: 213. Adopted.

BARNY, MRS. MARGARET RICE, MISSIONARY TO ARABIA, 1898–1939
Obituary.
1961: BWM Annual Report, APPENDIX, 49.

BAST, REV. HENRY
Elected Professor of Practical Theology at WTS.
1958: 59, 62, 64.
Elected Vice President of General Synod.
1959: 6.
Elected President of General Synod.
1960: 6.
Resigned as Professor at WTS. Resolution.
1963: 42–43, 50.
Resolution upon his retirement as radio minister of Temple Time.
1973: 291–292.

BATTLESON, ROSE NYKERK
Honored by Synod for missionary work.
1976: 134–135.

BATTS, MARTIN
Dispensation from professorial certificate requested.
1973: 33, 36. Denied.
Recommended that dispensation from professorial certificate be granted.
1974: 37, 38. Granted.

BEARDSLEE, REV. JOHN WALTER, JR.
Resolution for service to the Church and NBTS.
1962: 36-37.

BEARDSLEE, REV. JOHN WALTER III
Nominated to be elected Professor of Theology at NBTS in the field of Church History.
1965: 44, 47. Approved.

BECKER AMENDMENT
To overrule the Supreme Court decision outlawing public school sponsored prayer and Bible reading.
1964: 229-230. Study document requested from CAC.
See also BIBLE READING AND PRAYERS IN THE PUBLIC SCHOOLS.

BECKERING, REV. RAYMOND E.
Elected Vice President of GS.
1965: 8.
Elected President of GS.
1966: 7.

BELGIC CONFESSION
Proposed changes in and opposition to, studied by TC.
1962: 399-402. No action.
Overture requesting Article 36 be removed into a footnote since RCA holds to separation of Church and State.
1972: 99-100. No action since the Confession is an historical document and not subject to revision.

BENES, REV. LOUIS H., SR.
Resolution on his retirement after 29 years as Editor of the Church Herald.
1973: 292.
Elected Vice President of GS.
1975: 16.
Elected President of GS.
1976: 17.

BENEVOLENCE BUDGET OF GENERAL SYNOD
1967: 160-165. 1971: 184-189.
1968: 147-151. 1972: 151-159.
1969: 175-177. 1973: 162-168.
1970: 135-137, 150-158.
Overture requesting amendment of the BCO to read, "Is your church fulfilling its stewardship obligations by contributing annually to the benevolent program of the RCA on all levels?"
1972: 95. Adopted and sent to classes for approval.
Above statement approved by classes.
1973: 128.
Benevolence Budget changed to MISSION BUDGET, which see.

BENEVOLENCE RECEIPTS
1963: 344-366. 1967: App. 2, 23-55.
1964: 361-368. 1968: App. 2, 25-57.
1965: 303-331. 1969: App. 1, 125-159.
1966: 409-441.

BENEVOLENCES, ASSESSMENTS FOR
Overture regarding.
1959: 126-127, 128. Contrary to spirit and practice of RCA.

BENEVOLENCES, GENERAL SYNOD
Comparison of 1967, 1968, 1969.
1968: 165-166.

BENEVOLENT ASKINGS (GENERAL SYNOD)
1966: 167, 176, 182. Adopted.

BENEVOLENT FUNDS
Overture regarding submitting of budget to Mission Boards.
1959: 124. No action.

BENEVOLENT SOCIETIES
See BIBLE CAUSE.

BENGSTON, WILLIAM
Dispensation from the professorial certificate requested.
1971: 31, 36. Granted.

BENNINK, REV. RICHARD J.
Appointed Director of Field Education and Assistant Professor of Christian Ministry at WTS.
1977: 165.

BERGEN, CLASSIS OF
Complaint filed regarding certain items in the budget of the PSNJ.
1965: 130-131. Not filed within 20 days.
Report of CJB concerning complaint.
1966: 157-161. Stated Clerk directed to make a study and define "assessments." Recommendation also sent to GSEC for follow-up.
Discussion of complaint by COR.
1966: 186. Sub-Committee to study matter and report to GSEC.
PSNJ appeals action of Synod of 1966.
1967: 132-138. Referred to GSEC.
GSEC report on complaint.
1967: 134.
GSEC reports "benevolences" should not be regarded as an assessment but as an asking.
1967: 147-148. SC to make further study.
Rehearing of the complaint by CJB. Committee is of the opinion that the article provides for the authority of PS to assess classes for such items.
1968: 128-130. Complaint dismissed.

BERKENPAS, MISS ANNA G., MISSIONARY TO WINNEBAGO
Death
1975: 64.

BEUKELMAN, JAMES
Dispensation from professorial certificate requested
1973: 33, 36. Granted.

BIBLE CAUSE, PERMANENT COMMITTEE ON
Report.
1958: 179-191. 1962: 187-195.
1959: 188-196. 1963: 300-310.
1960: 164-173. 1964: 296-303.
1961: 193-201.
Committee discontinued.
1964: 175.

BIBLE READING AND PRAYERS IN THE PUBLIC SCHOOLS
Overtures regarding.
1964: 116, 117, 127, 151-152. Referred to CAC.
See also BECKER AMENDMENT and RELIGION AND THE PUBLIC SCHOOLS

BI-LEVEL MULTI-SITE SEMINARY PROGRAM
See entry under SEMINARIES.

BIOLOGICAL ENGINEERING
Overture requesting a special committee of scientists, doctors, and theologians to give continuing study to startling advances in science.
1968: 116, 122, 124. Referred to TC.
At the request of TC, Dr. Donald Mulder (M D.) prepared a paper on Heart Transplants, which appeared in the May 2, 1969 issue of The Church Herald.
1969: 233-235. Study continuing.

BIRTH CONTROL-DEATH CONTROL
"The Size of the Family of Man," a paper by CAC
1973: 213-216
See also PLANNED PARENTHOOD and POPULATION CONTROL.

BLACK COUNCIL
Report.
1971: 79-80. 1975: 69-71.
1972: 72-74. 1976: 168-169.
1973: 72-73. 1977: 185-187.
1974: 76-79.
Establishment of.
1970: 62.
Requested two representatives on the GPC and one on the GSEC.
1970: 184-185. Adopted.
Recommendation of GSEC and GPC: (1) one "at large" representative on the GSEC elected by the Black Council for membership by 1972 with a representative attending until a voting member is elected; (2) that GS elect two Black Council nominations to GPC.
1970: 126-127, 184-185.
1971: 65, 75.
Representation on GSEC. The study of representation of minority groups on GSEC continues.
1976: 37, 38.
See BLACK MANIFESTO.

BLACK MANIFESTO
After a confrontation with members of the National Black Economic Development Conference at "475," Mr. James Forman of the Conference spoke to Synod. The NBEDC made the following demands of the RCA: (1) to implement the demands of the Manifesto which calls for the creation of four major publishing houses inside the United States; (2) to demonstrate good faith in its intentions to help in the implementation of the demands of the Manifesto; (3) a list of assets, real estate holdings, unrelated business items, pension funds and Southern investment policies, and we will negotiate what should be donated to the Conference. An Ad Hoc committee was appointed by the COR to study the demands of the NBEDC.
1969: 98-99.
In a report of Thanksgiving, Confession, and Judgment Out Of Love, for our failure to be aware of these situations, the Committee offered the following recommendations in response to the Black Manifesto: (1) that the black members of GS call a caucus of black leaders of the RCA to develop a continuing "Black Council" for the Program of General Synod; (2) that GSEC and GPC implement ways of sharing an adequate portion of moneys with the "Black Council"; (3) that the total program of the church have special focus on race relations in urban work; (4) that GS immediately set aside $100,000 to be disbursed according to decisions of the "Black Council"; (5) that GS authorize a special appeal for funds for the same purpose; (6) that in programs relating to minority groups every effort be made to give power of decision to minority groups; (7) that the imaginative suggestions made by Mr. Beale be referred to the GPC and the "Black Council"; (8) that GSEC call upon other tenants of the Interchurch Center to cooperate in offering facilities; (9) that GS instruct GPC to supply funding for a black executive staff person to assist in

aforementioned programs and others the Black Council may recommend; (10) that each classical delegation to GS interpret these decisions to the classes; (11) that the President of GS send out a pastoral letter to all congregations interpreting GS action; (12) that GPC proceed immediately to develop guidelines for local churches.
1969: 99-105. All adopted.
Response and recommitment to the Black Manifesto of 1969 reprinted.
1974: 80-84.

BLACK RELIGION
Recommended by BC that GS instruct BTE to take action to include an annual colloquium on Black Religion as a permanent part of RCA's program of Theological Education.
1975: 71. Adopted.

BLAHUT, ERIC
Dispensation from professorial certificate requested.
1971: 31, 36. Granted.

BLAKE, DR. EUGENE CARSON
Reference to his sermon, "A Proposal Toward the Reunion of Christ's Church."
1961: 137.

BOARD OF SECRETARIES
See EXECUTIVE SECRETARIES.

BOARDS AND AGENCIES
Lists of.
1970: App. 2, 8-11.
1971: App. 2, 14-18.
1972: App. 2, 14-18.
1973: App. 2, 14-18.
1974: App. 2, 15-20.
1975: App. 2, 15-20.
1976: App. 1, 15-20.
1977: App. 1, 15-20.
Financial reports.
1970: App. 1.
1971: App. 1.
1972: App. 1.
1973: App. 1.
1974: App. 1.
1975: App. 1.
1976: App. 1, 291-388.
1977: App. 1, 299-392.
Overture regarding PS's nominations to.
1964: 130, 140, 150. No action.
Overture requesting an amendment to the Constitution; that the respective PS's shall nominate, for election by the GS, or for election by the respective boards when required, its members for each such board.
1965: 110, 117, 123. Item 5 to be referred to GSEC for submission to a Sub-Committee on Study of Boards and Agencies. Other items adopted.
Overture requesting a general study of boards and agencies so that they may work more effectively.
1962: 125, 127. Referred to GSEC.
President's report asks for re-examination of the problem.
1962: 280, 341.
President suggests fewer meetings and reduced size of boards.
1963: 374-375, 436, 439, 144-145. To be taken into consideration in reorganization study.
Sub-Committee on Boards and Agencies appointed.
1964: 161.
Outline prepared.
1965: 136-137. Board continues study in two areas—Nominations and Administration.
Name of Sub-Committee changed. See DENOMINATIONAL STRUCTURE, SUB-COMMITTEE ON.
1966: 163.

BOARDS, NAMES OF, COMMITTEE ON
Report.
1960: 330-332. Mission boards renamed. "The Board of the Christian World Mission" becomes "The Board of World Missions, R.C.A." and "Board of Domestic Missions" becomes "The Board of North American Missions."

BOEREMA, FRANK
Dispensation from professorial certificate requested.
1973: 33, 36. Granted.

BOOK OF CHURCH ORDER
Book issued in loose leaf form. Replacement sheets to be distributed from time to time.
1970: 199.

BOOK STORE (RCA) IN GRAND RAPIDS
Overture requesting it remain in operation, since it is more profitable than the Teaneck Store.
1966: 124-125, 142. Referred to SCBE.
Recommended that the BE look into the possibility of having the store relocated, or for it to go completely into the mail order business.
1967: 61. Adopted.

BOOT, MRS. ANNA HENRIETTA, MISSIONARY TO CHINA, 1908-1940.
Obituary.
1960: CWM Annual Report, Appendix, 34.

BOSCH, DR. TAEKE, MISSIONARY TO CHINA, 1915-1931
Death.
1971: 72.

BOSSENBROEK, REV. ALBERTUS G.
Elected Vice President of GS.
1976: 17
Elected President of GS.
1977: 18.

BOSSEY, ECUMENICAL INSTITUTE
1961: 163.

BOVENKERK, REV. HENRY
Resolution regarding many years as Secretary of the BWM.
1961: 97.

BOYCOTTS, ECONOMIC
CAC statement on—especially upholding the California Grape Embargo.
1969: 246-247.
Overture requesting that the CAC be instructed to exercise extreme constraint when it considers endorsing or recommending economic boycotts in the future, and that it diligently seek all facts before making a statement. (Reference to the California Grape Boycott.)
1969: 130-132, 136-137, 145, 152. No action.
CAC recommendations: (1) GS urge membership of RCA to participate in boycott of table grapes; (2) that institutions of the RCA and its suppliers be urged to cooperate in the boycott of table grapes; (3) that RCA express concern to federal and state agencies for the health, safety and welfare of the workers by recommending limitations of pesticides; (4) that GS urge Congress to consider legislation which would give recognition to the United Farm Workers, insuring the full rights of strike and boycott by limiting protracted negotiations by the growers forstalling any signed contracts, thus fatally weakening the union.
1970: 220-221. (1) defeated; (2) defeated; (3) adopted; (4) defeated.
CAC recommends people of our churches lend support to the agricultural workers and their families by refusing to purchase grapes and lettuce not under United Farm Workers' label.
1974: 213. Referred back to CAC for further study.
See also AGRICULTURAL AND MIGRANT WORKERS and entries under CHRISTIAN ACTION COMMISSION.

BREAD FOR THE WORLD
A Christian citizens' movement of people who are concerned about world hunger.
1975: 59.
See CHURCH WORLD SERVICE and WORLD HUNGER.

BREWTON
1970: 59-60.
1971: 60.
1974: 66-67, 73.
1975: 57-58.
See also APPENDIX.

BROADCASTING AND FILM COMMISSION OF THE NCC
Response to 1957 overture regarding a comprehensive statement of policy.
1958: 313.
Overture regarding freedom of the air.
1959: 124, 128. Approved.
Overture regarding insufficient answer to the 1959 overture.
1961: 130.
Report.
1958: 311-318.
1959: 312-318.
1960: 293-297.
1961: 349-358.
1962: 379-388.
1963: 185-199.
1964: 259-262.

BROADCASTING, BOARD OF, R.C.A.
See RADIO BROADCASTING.

BROOKS, STEPHEN ROBERT
Dispensation from professorial certificate requested.
1977: 162, 166, 168. Granted.

BROUWER, REV. ARIE R.
Named Associate General Secretary-Program.
1968: 141
Invited to become President of the Seminaries.
1972: 25. Invitation declined.
Elected General Secretary of the RCA to succeed Rev. Marion de Velder.
1977: 54.
Recommended that appreciation be given for his work with GPC and good wishes be extended as he assumes new responsibility.
1977: 151. Adopted.

BROWER, DAVID
Dispensation from professorial certificate requested.
1976: 146, 148. Granted.

BROWN, REV. WILLARD DAYTON
Congratulations on Rotary Honor.
1961: 90, 91.

BROWNSON, REV. WILLIAM C., JR.
Elected Professor of Theology, Chair of Preaching at WTS.
1967: 44, 53, 56.

Resolution for, upon resignation from position of Professor of Preaching at WTS. Has accepted appointment as Temple Time Preacher.
1974: 34-35, 37, 130.

BRUGGINK, REV. DONALD J.
Elected Professor of Theology (Historical Theology) at WTS.
1966: 47, 49-50.

BRUINS-ALLISON, MARY
Honored by Synod for missionary work.
1976: 134-135.

BRUNSTING, REV. BERNARD R.
Elected Vice President of GS.
1961: 5.
Elected President of GS.
1962: 6.

BUDGET
See specific boards.

BUDGET BUILDING AND PROGRAM EVALUATION, R.C.A.
1966: 166-167.

BUILDING FUND
See REFORMED CHURCH IN AMERICA—EXTENSION FOUNDATION, INC.

BURIAL SERVICES, FORMS FOR
See LITURGY, PROVISIONAL

BURT, DOROTHY
Retiring after 33 years of service to the RCA.
1971: 288.

BUSING FOR QUALITY EDUCATION
Statement of CAC indicating the complexity of the problem and how Christians can help.
1972: 206-207. Adopted.
CAC recommends general approval of voluntary busing for the purpose of achieving quality education and urges those who find themselves opposed to busing to seriously search their consciences before God to determine the true root of their convictions.
1976: 187-190. Adopted.

BUTEYN, REV. JOHN
Elected Executive Secretary of the BWM.
1961: 98.

BYLAARD, GERARD
Dispensation requested, but incomplete.
1971: 31. No action.

CALENDAR OF SPECIAL DAYS
See SPECIAL DAYS, CALENDAR OF.

CALLING OF MINISTERS
See MINISTERS, CALLING OF.

CALLING OF SEMINARY SENIORS
See THEOLOGY, STUDENTS OF.

CALLS, DISAPPROVAL OF BY CLASSIS
Overture asking that guidelines be provided in the case that the classis for one reason or another does not approve of the call.
1971: 105, 115. No action.

CALVIN, JOHN—450TH ANNIVERSARY OF BIRTH
Jubilee in Geneva.
1959: 183-184.
Jubilee in Frankfurt, Germany.
1960: 218.

CALVINISTIC WITNESS IN WASHINGTON, D.C.
1961: 340.
See also UNITED CALVINIST WITNESS IN WASHINGTON, D.C.

CAMP, JOHN THOMAS, JR.
Dispensation from professorial certificate requested.
1977: 162, 166, 168. Mr. Camp requested it not be acted upon at this time.

CAMPUS MINISTRY
Overture requesting establishment of a committee to study a program of ministry to RCA young people on university campuses.
1960: 74. Approved.
RCA involvement.
1962: 285, 342.
Overture requesting appointment of a Commission to study work on non-denominational campuses.
1963: 111, 112. Referred to the BWM, BE, BNAM, and colleges of the RCA.
Special Commission report.
1963: 76-78. Work being done on several campuses.
Suggested that PS's work through Campus Christian organizations already established.
1964: 77-79.
President suggests GPC consider how to obtain, train and support a larger number of RCA ministers on secular campuses.
1969: 328, 330-331. Adopted. Referred to GPC.
University Christian Movement discontinuing work. Recommended GPC study alternate programs.
1969: 301, 302. Adopted.
Overture asking for study of all work on college campuses when there is no organized church. Guidelines for this kind of work.

1972: 106. Adopted and referred to GPC for report.
Lack of funds curtails the program.
1973: 60.
Work in Taiwan especially active.
1973: 60.

CANADA
Classis of Ontario to be formed.
1962: 92, 135.
Report of Special Committee
1963: 271-273. The work in Canada is to receive our prayers and aid.

CANDIDATES FOR MINISTRY
See MINISTRY, CANDIDATES FOR

CAPITAL PUNISHMENT
Report of CAC opposing retention of capital punishment.
1965: 211-214, 219, 221, 222-225. Adopted.
CAC study on biblical background for repeal of capital punishment.
1966: 220-222, 234. Adopted.
Overture requesting rescinding of action of 1965, thus showing approval of capital punishment.
1968: 102, 119, 124. No action.

CAREER DEVELOPMENT PROGRAM
1974: 72.

CATECHISM INSTRUCTION
Very important in the churches because of Supreme Court decision on Prayer and Bible Reading in the schools.
1964: 57.
Intermediate Catechism to be put into modern English.
1967: 60, 61. Adopted.

CENTERS.
GPC paper, "Reformed Church Centers"
1972: 146-147, 274.
Overture requesting delay of at least one year in establishing centers, and that classes be given an opportunity to vote as to whether the church desires this plan.
1972: 99, 68. No action.
"Site must follow function"
1972: 50-51, 67-68. Planning for centers to continue.
Centers are working out well and GS commends GPC and the Executive staff for their leadership in the development of the centers concept.
1973: 68.
Recommended that GS accept seminaries' offer to become partial or complete "centers," rendering training to both clergy and laymen.
1973: 280. Adopted.
Regional centers having many workshops, retreats and other events; a hopeful beginning.
1974: 58-59.
1975: 143.
See also REGIONALIZATION, and also REGIONAL CENTERS.

CENTRAL COLLEGE
Report.
1958: 68-70. 1968: 49-52.
1959: 64-65. 1969: 45-52.
1960: 63-64. 1970: 37-41.
1961: 79-80. 1971: 39-41.
1962: 68-70. 1972: 34-36.
1963: 64-67. 1973: 39-43.
1964: 66-69. 1974: 41-44.
1965: 56-58. 1975: 37-40.
1966: 68-71. 1976: 152-154.
1967: 62-66. 1977: 174-176.

CENTRAL SERVICES COMMITTEE
Committee formed in 1961 to increase efficiency of and reduce costs of Boards.
1961: 342-343. 1965: 416-422.
1962: 362-367. 1966: 374-381.
1963: 288-295. 1967: 324-331.
1964: 455-462. 1968: 353-364.

CHAPLAINS, INSTITUTIONAL
Proposed that a new Commission on Institutional Chaplains be appointed.
1958: 147. Referred to officers of GS.
Report of Study Committee.
1959: 361-362. Commission approved.

CHAPLAINS, INSTITUTIONAL COMMISSION ON
Report.
1960: 328-329.
1961: 389-391.
1962: 404-407.
1963: 156-158. Work to be absorbed by RCA Commission on Chaplains.

CHAPLAINS, RCA COMMISSION ON
Report.
1958: 144-149. 1968: 342-348.
1959: 151-156. 1969: 335-340.
1960: 127-133. 1970: 258-262.
1961: 155-158. 1971: 278-283.
1962: 145-148. 1972: 284-289.
1963: 152-155. 1973: 282-288.
1964: 445-449. 1974: 289-295.
1965: 405-410. 1975: 257-264.
1966: 363-368. 1976: 175-181.
1967: 316-321. 1977: 193-197.
Overture requesting provisions for delegation of chaplains as voting delegates to GS.
1969: 123, 142, 152. Referred to ECRC.
Amendment sent to classes for approval.
1969: 231.
Classes approved above amendment.
1970: 141.

No special status to be given non-military chaplains as far as synodical representation is concerned.
1970: 196. Adopted.
Changes in organization—membership, responsibilities, etc.
1970: 144.
Motion made to abolish the Commission and refer to GSEC for report.
1970: 218. Adopted.
GSEC took action to defer above study until a broader study of GS's permanent committees and commissions is undertaken.
1971: 130.
Recommendation that membership of Commission be reduced from 9 to 6 members.
1975: 161, 264. Adopted.
GSEC recommends the amendment.
1976: 46. Adopted.
Overture requesting GS study ways of strengthening ties with RCA chaplains and that a study be made of the feasibility of annuity support for chaplains.
1976: 99. Adopted.
Recommended that the Commission be disbanded and the mission of military and institutional chaplains be integrated into the mainstream of the mission program of the RCA; that GPC responsibility take place January 1, 1979; that 3 members of the Commission on Chaplains be present at GPC when it deliberates concerning chaplains and their mission through 1982, at which time the transfer of responsibility will be evaluated and if necessary we return to a separate chaplain's commission.
1977: 195. Adopted.

CHARISMATIC MOVEMENT
The TC has initiated a study on the Charismatic Movement. In preparation for the study the following should be read: "Report of the Special Committee on the Work of the Holy Spirit" presented to the 182nd General Assembly of the UPCUSA.
1973: 201.
Observer present at the National Charismatic Conference in Kansas City.
1977: 254.
See BAPTISM (SPIRIT BAPTISM).

CHAVIS, REV. BENJAMIN
Resolution to express concern over the alleged abuse of police power and misuse of the law courts in the conviction of the Reverend Benjamin Chavis and refer the matter to the GSEC for study and appropriate action.
1976: 256. Adopted.
Continued action on the part of the GSEC in writing letters and making provision for a news story in the Church Herald.
1977: 41.

CHICAGO, PARTICULAR SYNOD OF
Complaint of Rev. Harry J. Hager against PSC. After reviewing correspondence and making phone calls GSEC (1) confirmed action of PS and dismissed complaint; (2) commended action of PSC and "requests the Classis of Chicago to give serious consideration to all allegations of slander and to seek reconciliation of all parties concerned."
1976: 61-62. Adopted.
GSEC reviewed papers and evidence submitted, looked into the matter of the handling of the complaint against the Classis of Chicago, and found they followed procedures set forth in BCO. Recommended complaint be dismissed.
1977: 63-64. Adopted.

CHILDREN, ADOPTIVE
Recommended that GPC make information readily available to the churches.
1975: 67. Adopted.

CHILDREN'S HOME
In response to an overture expressing need for. (Although this statement is made, the overture can't be located. M.S.)
1963: 89-90. BNAM will report in 1964. (Neither is there a record of a report.)

CHILDREN'S WORK
1958: 75.
1959: 72-73.
1960: 68.
1961: 86.
1962: 75.
1963: 60.
1964: 56, 57.
1965: 49-50.
1966: 54.

CHINA, FOOD TO MAINLAND
1961: 216

CHINA (RED)
See PEOPLE'S REPUBLIC OF CHINA.

CH'OL EDITION OF THE NEW TESTAMENT
1958: 100

CHOW, BENJAMIN
Dispensation from professorial certificate requested. A graduate of New York Seminary. Examinations at WTS.
1967: 52, 55. Granted.

"CHRIST IN THE CONCRETE CITY"
Presented at Synod
1958: 225.

CHRISTIAN ACTION
Theological basis for.
1959: 210, 211.

CHRISTIAN ACTION COMMISSION
Report.
1958: 201-205.
1959: 208-211.
1960: 179-187.
1961: 208-217.
1962: 205-224.
1963: 312-323.
1964: 218-232.
1965: 206-225.
1966: 215-236.
1967: 204-215.
1968: 202-220.
1969: 240-250.
1970: 213-222.
1971: 219-228.
1972: 203-221.
1973: 203-226.
1974: 212-226.
1975: 191-201.
1976: 182-195.
1977: 198-236.
Overture regarding composition of commission.
1958: 132, 136.
Overture suggesting members of CAC be nominated through NC.
1961: 131, 142.
Changes in organization—membership, responsibilities, etc.
1970: 144-145.
Overture requesting CAC to communicate to the churches their decisions, but also the theological and biblical background contributing to their decisions.
1970: 96, 109. Already their practice. If "time is of the essence" they sometimes act as a commission and not as the RCA.
Overture requesting that CAC be instructed to desist from making public statements of a partisan nature, of different convictions (Vietnam, right to work law, grape issue . . .).
1971: 103, 114. No action, since CAC speaks for itself and not the denomination.
Addendum concerning consciencious objection: (1) that RCA members be informed that they may make contributions to the Legal Defense; (2) that the Defense Fund be the recipient of the Communion Offering; (3) that GS express support to Glenn Pontier of his right to Christian conscience; (4) that an Ad Hoc Committee receive draft cards.
1971: 229-230. (1) Adopted; (2) Lost; (3) adopted; (4) lost.
Two overtures in the nature of a reprimand of the CAC and one member in particular for releasing news to public media recommending a "yes" vote on abortion reform.
1973: 91-93. No action, although it is unrealistic to think that news releases would be possible without giving the impression that the RCA as a whole was speaking rather than just the CAC.
Overture concerning membership—that there be 12 members.
1973: 91. No action.
Overture concerning membership of commission: suggested that there be 18 members—3 from each PS, and that recommendations go only to GS, each accompanied by two position papers.
1973: 89-90. Adopted.
Membership—(3 from each PS)
1974: 122, 200. Adopted.
Overture requesting that the CAC allow at least one full year to elapse between the publication and dissemination of their "study papers" and any official action to be taken on the issues presented to GS.
1974: 99. No action.
Membership and terms of office.
1975: 100. Adopted.

CHRISTIAN EDUCATION, DIRECTORS AND MINISTERS OF
Overture requesting more judicious oversight by classes and consistories.
1962: 76.
Report of Committee on Professorate.
1963: 131-132. No action.
Recommended that certification procedures be worked out and that an Order of Recognition be included in the Liturgy.
1967: 61. Adopted and referred to CRL.
Order already included in the *Liturgy and Psalms.*
1968: 199.
Overture asking GS to give approval for development of procedures making possible the licensing or ordination for an individual to the office of minister of Christian Education.
1973: 107. No action.
Overture requesting ordaining of an individual to this office provided the person has a degree of Master of Christian Education from an accredited theological seminary and is employed in the ministry of Christian Education by a local church.
1974: 109. No action.
Motion made that the BTE make a serious study of the process of licensing ministers of Christian Education, and prepare a plan for licensing.
BTE to continue the study of licensing of, and report to 1977 GS.
1976: 148. Adopted.
BTE reports on certification of directors of Christian Education. Criteria have been worked out for three categories of certification: (1) Certified Director of Christian Education; (2) Certified Minister of Christian Education; (3) Certified Associate of Christian Education; these to be under the supervision of a Committee on Credentials.
1977: 162-165, 167. Adopted.

CHRISTIAN ENDEAVOR AND THE NATIONAL YOUTH ORGANIZATION
Overture regarding.
1959: 78.

CHRISTIAN INTELLIGENCER
Complete run microfilmed by the American Theological Library Association.
1961: 395.

CHRISTIAN REFORMED CHURCH
Overture suggesting conversations with.
1962: 122, 123-124. No action pending outcome of other conversations.
The CIR of the RCA met at Calvin College with the CRC Committee.
1966: 244.
Conversations with at Hope College.
1967: 227-228.
Two all-day meetings.
1968: 232.
Overture asking GS to take steps to be involved in dialogue with the CRC to work toward closer cooperation and possible union.
1969: 133, 139, 146, 152. Approved. Such meetings already being held. Referred to CIR.
Recommendation of the CIR that GS initiate conversations exploring possibility of union with the CRC.
1969: 291, 294. Approved.
The CRC took the following action: (1) that they do not wish to close the door on conversations at a future time; (2) that they do not think this is an opportune time because they don't want to interfere with problems the RCA is having; (3) that after these are clarified they might resume conversations.
1970: 226-227.
Efforts being made to have further joint meetings for discussion of possible means of cooperation.
1971: 234.
Plans drawn up for a three-day formal joint meeting at Ninth Street CRC of Holland.
1972: 233, 256.
Recommendations of the above conference: (1) that a study commission of 10 members (5 from each denomination) prepare a theology of evangelism; (2) that one area be chosen where a cooperative pilot project in church planning can be carried on; (3) the possibility of an overseas mission project; (4) that we choose one area of youth work to do together—camping, conferencing, etc.
1973: 263. Adopted.
The above three-day conference was held to promote "closer fellowship, cooperation and denominational unity."
1973: 232.
Statement of conference.
1973: 260-263.
CRC/RCA committee appointed (5 from each denomination) to prepare a theology of evangelism.
1974: 117-118, 256.
Joint Committee on Evangelism of the CRC/RCA prepared many papers in preparation for "An Evangelism Manifesto."
1975: 112-116. To be continued for two years.
Statement presented by the Joint Committee on Evangelism of the CRC/RCA.
1975: 114-116. To be referred to our churches, agencies for study and reflection.
Recommended that a "Unity Day" be designated between neighboring CRC/RCA churches.
1975: 206.
Recommended that the Joint Committee prepare a study guide based on the Evangelism Manifesto for use in the churches.
1976: 58-59. Adopted.
The Evangelism Manifesto recommended for study in the churches.
1976: 132. Adopted.
Several items of CRC-RCA relationship listed including the unity day.
1976: 214, 228-229. Adopted.
Background and history of the Joint Committee for study of the Theology of Evangelism.
1977: 55-56.
Text of Evangelism Manifesto.
1977: 56-58.
Areas of cooperation already underway: Evangelistic program in Detroit Inner City; ministries in Grand Valley Colleges; Bethesda; Pine Rest; Bethany Home. Other possibilities: Hispanic work; Jewish Evangelism and some Overseas Work.
1977: 59-60.
Recommended that the Evangelism Manifesto be used in the RCA efforts in evangelism and church growth.
1977: 252, 268. Adopted.
Recommended that dialogs and relationships between all levels of the RCA/CRC be continued and encouraged, and that new areas of common concern be explored.
1977: 268. Adopted.
Joint Committee on Evangelism has completed assignment. Committee discontinued.
1977: 60.

CHRISTIAN UNITY, COMMITTEE ON
Instituted—membership and responsibilities.

1975: 101.
Report.
1976: 211-216.
1977: 251-271.
Three-fold work: Church-to-church matters, ecumenical agencies, and new developments in the Christian Church.
1977: 251.

CHRISTIAN UNITY, REVIEW COMMITTEE ON
Report.
1976: 228-230.
1977: 268-271.

CHRISTIAN UNITY, WEEK OF PRAYER FOR
Recommended by the IRC that the churches participate each year from Jan. 18-25 in the Week of Prayer for Christian Unity, in whatever ways may be open to them in their local situation, using the prayer guide in the local church and community services.
1966: 249. 1971: 236.
1967: 231. 1972: 231.
1968: 247. 1973: 229.
1969: 275. 1975: 206-207.
1970: 229.

CHRISTIAN WITNESS, RELIGIOUS LIBERTY AND PROSELYTISM
1961: 168.

CHRISTIAN WORLD MISSION, BOARD OF
President's Report.
1959: 82-90.
1960: 79-83.
Standing Committee report.
1958: 81-94.
1959: 91-104.
1960: 76-87.
Overture regarding teaching of Doctrinal Standards on the mission fields.
1958: 92. Statement of policy made. Adopted.
Amendment to the Constitution proposed—that the word BIBLE be mentioned explicitly.
1958: 89. Approved.
Overture regarding pension policy for missionaries.
1958: 93. Approved. Referred to Finance Committee of BCWM.
Overture regarding relations between missionaries and the Board.
1958: 90-91. Approved. Opinions of missionaries should be considered in decision making.
Attempt to improve relationships.
1959: 82-90; 98-100.
Relations improving between missionaries and the Board.
1960: 80-83.
Discussion on name of Committee.
1959: 96, 101.
Overtures regarding possible work in South America.
1958: 93.
1959: 310.
1960: 85. Previously considered (1956). No action, but study will continue.
Annual reports of the Board of Christian World Mission appear in APPENDIX, which see.
Name changed to BOARD OF WORLD MISSIONS.
1960: 331.
See also WORLD MISSIONS, BOARD OF (name after 1960).
After 1970 see GPC reports, as well as individual fields.

CHURCH
Definition of.
1962: 137-138.

CHURCH ADDRESS LIST
Listed by name of church.
1970: App. 2, 94-102.
1971: App. 2, 145-154.
1972: App. 2, 148-157.
1973: App. 2, 131-140.
1974: App. 2, 171-180.
1975: App. 2, 187-196.
1976: App. 1, 179-188.
1977: App. 1, 181-190.

CHURCH ADDRESS LIST
Listed by state.
1970: App. 2, 72-93.
1971: App. 2, 87-144.
1972: App. 2, 86-147.
1973: App. 2, 85-130.
1974: App. 2, 126-170.
1975: App. 2, 126-186.
1976: App. 1, 116-178.
1977: App. 1, 116-180.

CHURCH AND ECONOMIC LIFE
1959: 209-210.
1960: 183-184.
1961: 213-214.
1962: 220-221.

CHURCH AND ITS COLLEGES
First report on the Covenant of Mutual Responsibilities.
1967: 76. Referred to the Division of Higher Education for refinement.
Special Committee named.
1968: 61.
A Preamble to, and the Covenant of Mutual Responsibilities.
1969: 64-70. Endorsed and commended to churches and colleges.

Document to be published and distributed for the next five years in the MGS.
1971: 50-55. 1974: 50-55.
1972: 43-48. 1975: 46-48.
1973: 48-53. 1976: 161-162.

CHURCH AND SOCIETY CONFERENCE
1968: 229-230.

CHURCH AND STATE
Report of committee on "Confiscated Property."
1958: 203.
Relationships.
1961: 211-212.

CHURCH ARCHITECTURE
Commission not to be established.
1962: 351-352, 354. Referred to TC.
Study will be presented at a later date.
1963: 269.
TC report. An article by Richard C. Oudersluys to appear in the Church Herald.
1964: 211, 212. Adopted. Article appeared May 22, 1964.
Publication of *Christ and Architecture; Building Presbyterian/Reformed Churches,* by Donald J. Bruggink and Carl H. Droppers.
1965: 171. A definitive treatment.
The above mentioned book recommended to all congregations planning building programs.
1966: 205.

CHURCH DIRECTORY
List of RCA Churches.
1964: 487-517.
1965: 451-481.
1966: 498-531.
1967: App. 2, 113-146.
1968: App. 2, 114-147.
1969: App. 2, 72-107.
Formerly listed as CHURCHES OF THE RCA, ROLL OF, which see.
After 1969, CHURCH ADDRESS LIST, which see.

CHURCH EMBLEM
Overture requesting new symbol.
1960: 108, 116. Committee to be appointed.
Report of Committee: suggested that old *seal* remain, but a new *emblem* be drawn.
1961: 392-393. Adopted.
Description of proposed emblem.
1962: 408-409. Study to continue.
Questionnaire sent out.
1963: 274. Fifty percent returned with varied responses. The project was dropped and the committee dismissed.
Overture requesting OPC design new symbol for the RCA.
1972: 89. No action.
Overture requesting formation of a committee to determine the need of a design of a new symbol for the RCA, which shall reflect the heritage and ministry of the RCA, which could be understood by the populace and future generations.
1977: 112. No action.

CHURCH EXTENSION
Guidelines
1958: 102-103.
Executive Secretary approved
1958: 100.
Number of new churches organized.
1958: 97.
Other references.
1958: 251.
1961: 105-110, 272-274, 331.
Concerning loans and salaries
1961: 108-110.
New name, REFORMED CHURCH IN AMERICA—CHURCH EXTENSION FOUNDATION, INC., which also see.

CHURCH EXTENSION MINISTRY
President recommended possibility of an Orientation Center be explored in cooperation with sister communions.
1966: 346, 354, 356. Approved. Referred to BNAM.
President suggested that upon approval of Center, the BNAM withhold salary supplement for a mission church unless the mission pastor has been certified by the Center.
1966: 346, 354, 356. Referred to BNAM.

CHURCH FUNDING, CONSULTATION ON
Meetings being held and concerns from all levels of judicatories requested.
1975: 98.

CHURCH FUNDING, SPECIAL COMMITTEE ON
Report.
1976: 67-76.
COCG recommends that GS approve and recommend to classes for approval the following amendment to the BCO: "nor shall the consistory incur any indebtedness on behalf of the church without approval of the classis of which that church is a member."
1977: 318-319. Adopted.

CHURCH GOVERNMENT, COMMITTEE ON
1958: 143. No report.
1959: 150. No report.
1960: 126. No report.
1961: 154. No report.
1962: 144. No report.

Covered by GENERAL SYNOD EXECUTIVE COMMITTEE, which see.

CHURCH GOVERNMENT, PERMANENT COMMITTEE ON

Report.

1969: 210-230. 1973: 179-182.
1970: 195-199. 1974: 189-199.
1971: 198-209. 1975: 159-160.
1972: 186-187. 1977: 314-319.

Name of committee before 1969, PERMANENT COMMITTEE ON THE REVISION OF THE CONSTITUTION, which also see under CONSTITUTION. Change in organization—membership, responsibilities, etc.

1970: 149.

CHURCH GROWTH

1974: 60-61, 70.

The President shows concern about falling off of RCA membership and RCPR wishes to refer this mandate to the PS's and classes to work on evangelism and growth.

1975: 243-246, 250.

GPC instructed to pursue an aggressive and challenging program for Church Growth.

1976: 132. Adopted.

Congregational involvements.

1976: 65-66.

Classis involvements.

1976: 65.

PS involvements.

1976: 63-64.

Report.

1976: 44, 63-66.

In urban ministries.

1976: 122-125.

"Reformed Church Growth: Perspectives and Proposals," a booklet containing a basic position paper and some research findings for a plan of action for the Church Growth Fund.

1977: 122-125, 145-147.

See CHURCH GROWTH FUND, and EVANGELISM AND CHURCH GROWTH.

CHURCH GROWTH FUND

Officially launched March 27, 1977, as a counter part of Church Growth. A goal of $5,000,000 set for Church Growth beyond our congregations, in new communities and around the world.

1977: 27.

President recommends that GS call upon all congregations, and upon the total membership to contribute seriously and sacrificially to the drive in order that God's will for his church may be more fully realized.

1977: 27, 35. Adopted.

Overture requesting GS to order GPC to suspend the fund raising drive for $5,000,000 for church growth, pending a review of its theological implications by the TC.

1977: 109. No action.

The fund is a $5,000,000 challenge to the churches for (1) the establishment of several Reformed Churches in geographical areas where the RCA has never witnessed; (2) that new churches be established in un-churched areas contiguous to other RCA communities; (3) that new congregations using existing facilities such as schools, shopping centers and homes, rather than new churches; (4) training and assistance for congregations signifying their intention to grow by 50% in the next 5 years; (5) a new area of world mission.

1977: 129-131, 148-149. Approved.

Proposals: (1a) New Geographical area—Dallas, Texas, $800,000; (1b) New congregations contiguous to RCA ministries—12 locations, $1,420,900; (2a) New congregations without buildings (minority ministries) using existing facilities, such as schools, shopping centers, drive-ins, homes, etc., $280,000; (2b) New congregations without buildings (mainstream ministries) using existing facilities such as schools, shopping centers, drive-ins, homes, etc., $295,000; (3a) transitional congregations, 14 churches, $364,520; (3b) expanding congregations—30 churches to increase 50% in a five year period, $890,220; (4a) new areas of world mission—two new fields—Venezuela and Indonesia, $450,000; (5) Leadership development for RCA pastors charged with responsibility of church growth, $250,000.

1977: 149-151. Rev. and Mrs. Samuel Solivan to be first missionaries to Venezuela.

Criteria for this over-all denominational plan: Community awareness; Congregational development; Leadership resources; Denomination support.

1976: 125.
1977: 128-129, 147-148.

Solicitations to end by Dec. 31, 1977.

1977: 51.

CHURCH HERALD

Report of Editor.

1958: 116-119. 1964: 109-113.
1959: 110-113. 1965: 97-101.
1960: 96-99. 1966: 110-111.
1961: 116-120. 1967: 102-107.
1962: 105-108. 1968: 87-90.
1963: 93-95.

Report of Editorial Council.
1958: 120. 1968: 90.
1959: 113. 1969: 116-118.
1960: 99. 1970: 75-77.
1961: 120. 1971: 83-88.
1962: 108-109. 1972: 77-79.
1963: 95-97. 1973: 79-81.
1964: 107-109. 1974: 89-90.
1965: 96. 1975: 78-79.
1966: 111-115. 1976: 165-167.
1967: 103. 1977: 183-184.
Overture regarding Church Herald.
1960: 112, 116. No action.
Every Family Plan encouraged.
1960: 96-97.
1962: 105-106 (500 congregations).
1971: 84.
1977: 184.
Overture requesting that "Official Organ of the RCA" be removed from the masthead, or that it (CH) be placed under the GPC.
1969: 130, 145, 152. No action. The paper should be free from ecclesiastical control.
Further definition of relationship between the CH and the new Office of Promotion and Communication.
1969: 171.
Subscribers number 74,485, even with a drop of circulation for the fifth consecutive year.
1975: 78.

CHURCH MEMBERSHIP, TERMINATION OF
See INACTIVE MEMBERS.

CHURCH, MISSION OF
Recommendation that a process be developed by GS under GSEC to bring about correlation of various sites and new functions of the church so that our corporate and individual responsibilities for mission might be strengthened and enlarged. Listed are ways there could be interaction between boards and judicatories and professors of seminaries and colleges.
1973: 189. Adopted.

CHURCH OF THE AIR
1958: 246. 1963: 280.
1959: 236. 1964: 181.
1960: 218. 1965: 147.
1962: 359.

CHURCH OFFICES AND MINISTRIES, COMMITTEE TO STUDY
See OFFICES AND MINISTRIES, COMMITTEE TO STUDY.

CHURCH PROPERTY AN EXPRESSION OF SOCIAL CONCERN
CAC recommends: (1) GS urge RCA congregations to consider making their facilities available for community needs; (2) congregations planning new buildings should make them flexible for use of congregation and community; (3) all committees, classes and PS's should do all in their power to implement their concern.
1968: 214, 220. Adopted.

CHURCH PROPERTY, LOCAL OWNERSHIP OF
Seven overtures requesting GS to appoint a Committee to make a comprehensive study of the implication and responsibility of having the property vested in the congregation of the local church.
1971: 90-94, 106, 110-111, 116. Adopted.
Report of Special Committee.
1972: 188-193.
Recommended that an active congregation be permitted to retain its real and personal property upon disassociation from the denomination.
1972: 193. Adopted, and COCG instructed to form amendment.
COCG will make a recommendation in 1974.
1973: 179-180.
Detailed rewriting of the BCO concerning transfer of property both to and from other denominations.
1974: 189-194. Adopted.
Overture to instruct JC24 to complete and promote Plan of Union.
1967: 122-123, 126, 128. Already adopted. No action.
Overture requesting that the Theology of the United Church be prepared before, instead of after consummation.
1967: 118, 126, 128. No action.
Overture requesting approval of "Proposed form of Government for a Presbyterian Reformed Church in America" and that no further reconstruction of RCA boards take place until action on the Plan of Union.
1967: 116-117, 125, 128. No action.
Overture requesting a 2/3 congregational quorum, and that churches not approving merger retain property rights.
1967: 117-118, 125, 128. No action.
Overture requesting Plan of Union grant fair share of RCA capital assets to churches proposing to continue as RCA.
1967: 118, 125, 128. To be referred back to Classis of Illinois for clarification.
Overture requesting that those congregations not accepting merger may continue under RCA.
1967: 119, 126, 128. No action.
Overture urging withdrawal from merger

conversations with PCUS since they are now active participants in COCU.
1967: 119-120, 126, 128. No action pending action on COCU.
Two overtures requesting each congregation have the opportunity to vote on Church Union.
1968: 108-109, 121, 124. No action.
Overture requesting 2/3 majority of all consistories rather than 2/3 vote of classes.
1968: 115, 121, 124. No action.
Three overtures requesting a 2/3 vote in 2/3 of the classes be required for adoption of Plan of Union in PCUS.
1968: 107-108, 121, 124. No action. Referred to ECRC.
Seven overtures concerning amendments to Plan of Union, some concerning withdrawal from Plan.
1968: 109-113, 117. Referred to the C12.
Overture urging JC24 to proceed with vigor.
1968: 115, 122, 124. Plan already completed. No action.
Three overtures requesting RCA cease Plan of Union with PCUS.
1968: 106, 114-115, 121, 124. GS has already approved Plan. It will now go to the classes for their response. No action.
Suggested changes in proposed Plan of Union.
1968: 285-297. No action.
Procedure for dealing with Plan of Union.
1968: 273-276.
Vote of Synod on proposed union with the PCUS.
1968: 275, 284. PCUS: 406 for, 36 against; RCA: 183 for, 103 against. Referred to classes for approval.
Plan of Union failed to carry 2/3 of classes.
1969: 205. Plan of Union lost.
Overture asking for clarification of pension rights in event of merger.
1969: 130, 145, 152. No longer relevent since classes defeated merger.
Overture asking RCA to call off finalizing negotiations with the PCUS in the interest of peace and harmony in our denomination.
1969: 133, 146, 152. No action. No longer relevant because of defeat of proposed Plan of Union.
Ad Hoc committee regarding defeat of Plan of Union appointed.
1969: 162. See COMMITTEE OF 18.
Continued observing of meetings of other denominations.
1970: 226-228, 241-242.
Overture requesting GS take appropriate steps toward union with the UPUSA.
1970: 101, 112. No action in view of present divisions in the RCA.
For entries prior to 1967 see MERGER; MERGERS PROPOSED; MERGER PROBLEMS; and COMMITTEE OF TWELVE and JOINT COMMITTEE OF TWENTY-FOUR.

CHURCH UNION, CONSULTATION ON
See CONSULTATION ON CHURCH UNION (COCU).

CHURCH UNITY
Overture regarding
1958: 134. Referred to Committee on Approaches to Unity.
President suggests an attempt be made for a closer relationship with those outside the ecumenical movement.
1963: 375-376, 437, 439. A committee on WIDER ECUMENICITY appointed, which see.

CHURCH WORLD SERVICE, RCA COMMITTEE OF
Report.
1958: 195-200, 234.
1959: 202-207.
1960: 175-178.
1961: 203-207.
1962: 199-204, 272.
1963: 211-217.
1964: 287-295
1965: 264-270.
1966: 284-291.
1967: 87 and App. 1.
1968: 70 and App. 1.
1973: 65-66.
1974: 65-66.
1975: 66.
Overture suggesting budget be included in Stewardship Council.
1960: 111, 117. No action.
Overture suggesting CWS be included with other boards and agencies in the receipt of funds from Staff Conference.
1966: 123, 143, 149. Contained in GSEC report, therefore no action.
Transferred from BE to BWM.
1966: 170-171.
From 1973 on, found in GPC report.

CHURCHES
Change in name/status.
1970: App. 2, 138.
1971: App. 2, 234.
1972: App. 2, 238.
1973: App. 2, 215.
1974: App. 2, 256.
1975: App. 2, 271.
1976: App. 2, 274.
1977: App. 1, 282-283.

CHURCHES OF THE RCA, ROLL OF
1958: 422-462. 1961: 457-497.
1959: 425-465. 1962: 475-516.
1960: 398-438. 1963: 472-501.
Listing changed to CHURCH DIRECTORY, from 1964-1969; and CHURCH ADDRESS LIST from 1970-1977, both of which also see.

CHURCHES, SUPERVISION OF
Amendment: "Every church of the RCA is under the jurisdiction of a classis and subject to its supervision."
1961: 152, 153. No action.

CHURCH'S CONSCIENCE
Motion that CAC and GSEC consult and find a method whereby a broader cross section of the church's conscience may be reviewed and incorporated in motions brought before 1972 GS.
1971: 228. Adopted.
Meetings held and report will be given by CAC
1972: 113-114.
Two papers on the right of conscience presented by Donald T. Butler and Raymond J. Pontier.
1972: 221-228.

CIRCULATING THE DENOMINATION
Overture opposing such action by individuals or classes, if issues are already properly before ecclesiastical assemblies.
1962: 125, 127. No action.

CITY WORK
see INNER CITY and URBAN CHURCHES AND MINISTRIES.

CIVIL DEFENSE
1958: 309-310.

CIVIL RIGHTS BILL
Overture requesting support of, and that the action be conveyed to Senators.
1964: 132, 144, 151. Referred to CAC.
Report of CAC.
1964: 227-229. GS and all interested persons to write Senators.

CLASSES, ASSESSMENTS OF
Overture requesting a change in BCO indicating that when a classis votes to assess its churches financially only those elders and minister delegates representing the churches to be assessed shall be entitled to vote on the assessment.
1971: 103-104, 114. No action since it will come in the COCG report.
Recommended that assessments must be paid up in order to have delegates from classis seated.
1975: 133. Adopted.
Unpaid assessments of two classes referred to COR for consideration and report.
1975: 15. Adopted.
Assessment for each classis listed.
1977: 105-106. Total for 1976—$428,516.

CLASSES, CANADIAN GOVERNMENT AND
Overture requesting an amendment to Government regarding disbanding of churches and the Canadian Government. Committee should be appointed to study all aspects of the problem and report to GS.
1969: 123-124, 142, 152. Adopted.

CLASSES, FINANCIAL RESPONSIBILITY OF
Overture requesting clarification of financial obligations to churches under care of classis.
1962: 117. Referred to CJB.
Referred back to committee. Classis responsibility can be arrived at by reading the constitution. CJB was of the opinion that the Constitution did not contemplate financial responsibility of the classes.
1963: 121-122.
Three overtures indicating that the Constitution states that the classis has a legal and moral responsibility of the individual churches under its care.
1964: 131-132, 133-134, 152. No action. Referred to CJB.
Report of CJB: The Constitution of the RCA does not contemplate financial responsibility by classis for the debts and obligations of a church except upon dissolution of the church, and then only to the extent of the value of the assets of the church transferred to classis pursuant to the provisions of the Constitution.
1964: 157-159. Referred to a special committee.
Special committee approves findings of the CJB and recommends adoption, together with two added recommendations.
1965: 162-165. Adopted.

CLASSES, MEETINGS OF
Overture requesting omission of the word "semi" which would result in requiring only one meeting a year.
1972: 88. Adopted.

CLASSES, REALIGNMENT OF
Complaints concerning. A detailed account of meetings and appeals of several churches in the P.S. of New Jersey, resulting in the realigning of some churches, while others remained in their classes.
1961: 144-147, 326, 327.
1962: 131, 133, 134, 340.

CLASSES, REPRESENTATION IN
Overture requesting that the number of el-

ders represented at classis equal the number of ministers.

1968: 96, 118, 123. Referred to CRC for study.

COCG (CRC) recommends: a church with 300 or fewer active communicants shall have one elder delegate, and one elder delegate for each additional 300 members. A church shall not have more than four delegates except a church without an installed minister, which shall have an additional elder delegate in his place. A Collegiate Church shall have at least one elder for each constituant congregation.

1969: 211. Adopted and sent to classes for approval.

Approved by classes.

1970: 141.

Overture regarding minister-elder imbalance.

1969: 124-125, 143, 152. Already being studied by CRC. No action.

Overture asking for an amendment in the BCO to allow an elder to replace a minister as a delegate to classis when a minister cannot attend because of illness or a funeral of a member of the congregation.

1976: 105-106. Referred to COCG for study and report.

COCG reports that since a minister is a member of classis, he is free to exercise his own judgment rather than attempt to represent a congregation. An elder is ordained by the congregation and is a representative of the church. Therefore, an elder cannot truly represent a minister at classis meetings.

1977: 315.

Overture requesting an increase in elder representation with an amendment to read: "a church with two hundred or fewer active communicant members shall have one elder delegate and an elder for each additional 100 active communicants, or fraction thereof. A church shall not have more than three elder delegates. A church without an installed minister shall have an elder delegate not to be counted as one of the above delegates. A Collegiate church shall have at least one elder delegate for each of the constituent congregations.

1977: 112-113. No action. Voted to refer to COCG for study and report in 1978.

CLASSES, REPRESENTATION OF DEACONS IN

Two overtures asking that deacons be delegates to classis with full voting powers equal to elders and ministers. This would make them also delegates to PS and GS.

1971: 101-102, 106-107, 113, 115. Adopted and referred to TC for study.

TC reports that neither the New Testament nor the Doctrinal Standards give theological grounds for opposing this action. It will have to be taken up with COCG and be an action of the GS.

1972: 197-199.

Overture requesting that deacons be allowed full participation as voting delegates to classes and high judicatories of the church.

1973: 109. No action.

Overture requesting deacons be voting members of classis.

1976: 105. No action.

Two overtures requesting an amendment to BCO making it possible for deacons to be official and voting delegates of Classis.

1977: 114-115. No action. Referred to TC for study and report in 1978.

CLASSES REPRESENTATION TO GENERAL SYNOD

Overture requesting a change in method in determining representation: suggest two minister and two elder delegates from each classis having less than 3,000 communicant members and one minister and one elder delegate from each additional 3,000 or fraction thereof, and two delegates from each of the seminaries.

1973: 98-99, 183. Adopted and sent to classes for approval.

Approved by classes.

1974: 119.

CLASSES, SUPERVISION OF CHURCHES

Overture requesting the words "which have jurisdiction over it" for "of which the church is a member."

1960: 111, 117. No action.

President suggests a Classis Committee on Church Supervision, and asks that copies of a booklet on the subject be sent to each classis.

1966: 347, 354, 356. Adopted.

COCG recommendation: Classis has a right to supercede a consistory in administration of a local church if conditions make the church unable to fulfill the functions of the church, and if conditions will include one of the following: (1) before superceding a consistory, the classis shall state such intention and summon the consistory to show cause that it should not be dissolved and the church and its property be administered by classis. If the classis after having heard the consistory continues its intention it shall dissolve the consistory and bring the church, its ministry and its

property under direct administration of classis. The classis shall designate persons not necessarily members of the church who will exercise functions of a consistory. All action of classis will necessitate a 2/3 vote, and it may dissolve the corporate entity of the church.
1973: 181–182. Adopted and sent to classes for approval.
Approved by classes.
1974: 119.

CLASSES, ROLE OF
Overture requesting clarification of "superintendence of the churches" as to whether this is active, continuing superintendence or is limited to an appellate role.
1974: 107–108. Adopted and referred to COCG.
COCG reports no amendment necessary.
1975: 159.
Overture requesting interpretation of BCO in regard to this matter: "The classis shall exercise original and appellate supervisory power over the acts, proceedings, and decision of the board of elders and consistories, both in temporal matters and in those relating to Christian discipline."
1977: 117. No action.

CLASSES, VARIOUS RELATED SUBJECTS
See the following:
CONGREGATIONAL BORROWING POLICIES.
DEACONS, FULL DELEGATES TO JUDICATORIES.
DEACONS, ROLE OF.
LOCAL AND REGIONAL JUDICATORIES.
SAN DIMAS NOTES.
THEOLOGY, STUDENTS OF, CLASSICAL EXAMINATION AND SUPERVISION OF.

CLC
COVENANT LIFE CURRICULUM, which see.

CLERGY, CONTINUED EDUCATION OF
See MINISTERS, CONTINUED EDUCATION OF.

CLERKS OF JUDICATORIES IN THE RCA
Manual for.
1964: 201.
Responsibilities of.
1964: 184–202.

CLINICAL PASTORAL TRAINING (CPT)
Recommended.
1962: 406.

COAT OF ARMS
See CHURCH EMBLEM.

COCU
CONSULTATION ON CHURCH UNION, which see.

COLLEGE COOPERATION
Presidents to meet at least three times a year.
1973: 54, 177, 276, 280. Adopted.

COLLEGE FACULTIES
Recommended that OHR prepare a file of RCA members who serve on faculties of non-RCA colleges in order to lead to a cross fertilization of ideas and ideals.
1973: 54. Adopted.

COLLEGE PASTORS, RCA
Convocation of.
1971: 67–68.

COLLEGES
See CHURCH AND ITS COLLEGES; REFORMED CHURCH COLLEGES; CENTRAL COLLEGE; HOPE COLLEGE; NORTHWESTERN COLLEGE.

COLLEGIATE CHURCH
Definition of.
1961: 152.
Overture questioning method of election of consistory members (by consistory, itself)
1961: 131, 142. To be referred to CJB.
1962: 131, 134, 136. Further study required.
This manner of electing is in conformity with the Collegiate Church Charter, and their consistory members so elected are eligible to represent the Collegiate Church in any judicatory of the RCA.
1963: 118–121.
Rules of Order to be changed to include this situation.
1964: 204–205. Adopted.

COMMITMENT SERVICE
Recommended a Sunday be specified for such a service throughout the RCA.
1973: 280.
President suggests that again each church plan a service of commitment in order to keep before all the continuing need for dedication.
1974: 277, 282–283. Adopted and referred to GSEC.
Funding for task force on.
1974: 118.

COMMITTEE OF 18
Committee of 18 appointed, 3 from each PS, to explore every possibility of understanding and reconciliation within the RCA. If they find relations to be irreconcilable, another Committee of 18 shall be

appointed to draft a plan for the orderly dissolution of the RCA.
1969: 201-204. Adopted.
List of subjects found to be areas of tension in the RCA.
1970: 188-190.
List of solutions which the committee feel can be a part of the process of relieving the tension.
1970: 190-191. Committee believe reconciliation is possible.
Recommended that Committee be dissolved after report is received.
1970: 191. Adopted.
Recommendations referred to GSEC for later report: a) dialogue among delegates before meetings of GS for face to face communication between those having differing opinions. b) other provision for face to face communication, c) provision for pulpit and youth group exchange, d) initiate a crash program for training laity, e) regionalism is imperative to ecumenicity, evangelism, and mission.
1970: 191, 192-193. GSEC to report in 1971.
Progress report from GSEC: a) task force appointed to design the 1971 GS, b) and c) promotion task force was formed to make plans for face to face communication—pulpit and youth exchange, with a pilot project by which an exchange was arranged with members of the Classes of Orange and Dakota, and d) information given on the Lay Witness Mission and other programs.
1971: 132.
See also DAKOTA-ORANGE CLASSIS EXCHANGE and PLAN FOR UNDERSTANDING.

COMMITTEE FOR UNDERSTANDING
see COMMITTEE OF 18.

COMMITTEE OF STAFF EXECUTIVES
Organized in May, 1965 for mutual sharing and coordination of programs.
1966: 163-164.

COMMITTEE OF 12 (RCA)
Purpose of the Committee is to hold discussion with the PCUS. Report.
1963: 209.
1964: 324.
1965: 277.
1966: 300-306. Addendum report states that after the Report of the JC24 was prepared, the PCUS voted to become full participants in the COCU. Voted that CIR study possibility of RCA's participation in COCU.
1967: 272.
1968: 283-285. The proposed Plan of Union is not bound in the Minutes.
1969: 304.
Committee Dismissed.
See also CHURCH UNION (PCUS) and JOINT COMMITTEE OF 24.

COMMITTEES
Rules concerning membership on.
1960: 302.

COMMITTEES COMMISSIONS AND DELEGATIONS
Lists of members.
1958: 380-391.
1959: 385-396.
1960: 356-367.
1961: 415-426.
1962: 431-442.
1963: 460-471.
1964: 476-486.
1965: 439-450.
1966: 397-408.
1967: app. 2, 2-14.
1968: app. 2, 2-16.
1969: app. 2, 3-10, 12
1970: app. 2, 2-11.
1971: app. 2, 9-17.
1972: app. 2, 9-18.
1973: app. 2, 9-18.
1974: app. 2, 10-13.
1975: app. 2, 10-13.
1976: app. 1, 10-13.
1977: app. 1, 10-13.
See also BOARDS AND AGENCIES.

COMMUNICANTS' CLASS
TC recommends that there be retained in the church a program of Christian Education, the purpose of which is to prepare young people for confirmation of their faith (Communicants' Class).
1973: 193. Adopted.

COMMUNION
See LORD's SUPPER.

COMMUNION INQUIRY
See CONSTITUTIONAL INQUIRY #5.

COMMUNISM
Laos, Congo, Cuba, Algeria, China.
1961: 210.
Literature recommended.
1962: 218.
Premises Regarding Communism to be circulated throughout the church.
1963: 316, 319.

COMMUNISM AND WAR
Overture regarding NCC attitude of apathy.
1961: 140, 142. No action.

COMPLAINTS, REGISTRATION OF
Overture requesting provision be made in the BCO for complaint of one judicatory against another if an action has been taken in conflict with the BCO.
1976: 98. No action. To adopt this would subject all judicatories, from consistories through particular synods, to the complaints of all other judicatories.
Overture requesting a study be made to determine if it is possible for one judicatory to make a complaint against another if an action has been taken in conflict with the BCO.
1976: 98-99. Referred to COCG.
COCG reports that in order to lodge a complaint the judicatory (or communicant member) must be subject to the immediate administrative authority of the judicatory against which the complaint is to be lodged.
1977: 314.
See also APPEALS AND COMPLAINTS.

COMPLAINTS
See BERGEN, CLASSIS OF; NEW JERSEY, PS OF; MICHIGAN, PS OF: CHICAGO, PS OF.

COMPREHENSIVE MAJOR MEDICAL INSURANCE PLAN
See MAJOR MEDICAL INSURANCE PLAN.

CONFESSION OF FAITH, CONTEMPORARY
See CONFESSION OF FAITH, NEW; and OUR SONG OF HOPE.

CONFESSION OF FAITH—NEW
The TC was originally suggested for the purpose of producing a document outlining the Christian Faith of the RCA.
1958: 355.
Overture suggesting that the material in the present standards be incorporated into one statement.
1959: 123, 128.
Need for a freshly formed confessional standard.
1962: 377.
TC will continue study.
1963: 269.
TC report
1964: 211, 212. Experimental draft is being prepared by one member.
Draft going into second revision and assuming character of a new and contemporary confession.
1965: 171.
Third revision—a provisional document for distribution to classes.
1966: 207-212. To be sent to classes.
Overture regarding the preparation of a new confession.
1967: 114, 125, 128. Referred to TC.
Confession appeared in Easter issue of Church Herald, with a printing of 12,500 copies exhausted; 2,000 more copies printed.
1967: 187. Classes to give their attention to the confession.
TC believes it unwise to go further with the present document.
1968: 186-190.
TC reports that the 1966 confession was received without enthusiasm; recommends preparation of a confession should continue—one that concerns itself with the Reformed emphasis which we consider necessary and vital for our day.
1969: 235.
TC recommends an Ad Hoc committee (permanent) be appointed to undertake the writing.
1969: 236, 237. Postponed until 1970.
A new confession recommended by the Committee of 18 as one of the ways in which tension can be relieved in the RCA.
1970: 191. Adopted and referred to TC.
TC recommends the preparation of a Contemporary Confession.
1970: 208, 191. Referred to TC.
Rev. Eugene Heideman appointed chairman of a committee to write a contemporary confession.
1971: 130, 268.
Recommended support, cooperation and prayer for Dr. Eugene Heideman in his work on a confession.
1972: 279. Adopted.
TC has been in touch with Dr. Heideman who has written the new confession, "Our Song of Hope." The TC has given him their evaluation and will meet with him soon.
1973: 201.
Overture requesting GS to instruct the TC to formulate a new expression of faith.
1973: 98. No action since this project is in progress.
"Our Song of Hope"
1974: 165-173.
See also OUR SONG OF HOPE.

CONFESSIONAL INTERPRETATION, COMMITTEE ON
Report on importance of a Theological Commission and a handbook of instruction of the Reformed Faith we confess.
1958: 355.
1959: 363-367. Adopted.
See THEOLOGICAL COMMISSION.

CONFLICT OF INTEREST
Policy on; to be scrupulously avoided.
1976: 54.

CONGREGATION, DEFINITION OF
Overture regarding definition of the word as used in the revision of the Constitution.
1960: 108, 116.

CONGREGATIONAL BORROWING POLICIES
Twenty recommendations on the borrowing of funds by congregations, advertising sales of notes in the Church Herald, and the role of classes and PS's in these actions.
1976: 68-76. All approved.
See also CLASSES, SUPERVISION OF CHURCHES.

CONGREGATIONAL TRANSFER
Overture asking GS to provide in the BCO for the transfer of a congregation to another denomination or received from another denomination.
1973: 110-111. Adopted.

CONSCIENCE AND AUTHORITY
The Special Committee to Review Reformed Church Participation in the NCC recommends that the TC be requested to study the related questions of Conscience and Authority, especially in reference to statements of church bodies (whether consistory, classis, synod or council) and the role of these statements in the life of the church and its members.
1974: 134, 135. Adopted.
TC will report in 1976.
1975: 189.
Paper, "Authority and Conscience in the Church," submitted by TC. A detailed study of Scripture and the Standards leads to the conclusion that a Council speaks *to* the member churches and not *for* the member churches whereas GS speaks *for* the church as well as *to* the church.
1976: 233-235. Adopted.

CONSCIENCE, RIGHTS OF
See CHURCH'S CONSCIENCE.

CONSCIENTIOUS OBJECTION
The Right of Dissent and Conscientious Objection—CAC statement.
1967: 207-208, 212, 214. Items a and b adopted; c and d deleted.
CAC recommends support be given CO's and help in finding employment that will satisfy requirements in lieu of military service.
1971: 227-228. Adopted.

CONSCRIPTION
Three recommendations of CAC: (1) call upon RCA to recommend that compulsory military service be limited to periods when survival is threatened; (2) if compulsory service is a means of avoiding the costs of a paid voluntary establishment, it be declared contrary to both moral imperatives of religion and ethical imperatives of a democratic society; (3) call for immediate abolition of draft exemptions for seminary students and clergy.
1969: 205-208, 219. (1) Referred back; (2) Referred to COR; (3) Lost.
Overture asking GS to petition the Congress and the President to remove 4-D exemption for ministers and ministerial students.
1969: 137, 148, 153. Adopted.

CONSERVATION
See ENVIRONMENT.

CONSISTORIAL REPORTS, COMMITTEE ON
Report.
1958: 360-361.
Changes in headings authorized upon instruction of 1957 GS. Suggested: Post Office addresses be eliminated, and that a notation be made in the Classical Summary, of page numbers in the Catalogue of Ministers, for address information; (2) that "Adherants" column be reinstated; (3) that the term "Doctrinal Instruction" be dropped and divided into "Catechetical Classes" and "Communicants' Classes," and "week day Bible classes" be dropped.
1958: 360-361. (1) and (2) adopted; (3) to be worked out with BE.
Overture asking that "Adherants" column be reinstated.
1958: 130. No action, since this is being worked on.

CONSISTORIES, STUDY OF
See LOCAL AND REGIONAL JUDICATORIES.

CONSISTORY MEMBERS—LENGTH OF TERM
Any term up to five years authorized.
1958: 141.

CONSISTORY PRESIDENT, ELECTION OF
Overture requesting that the President of Consistory be elected from the membership of the consistory.
1965: 103-104, 116, 123. No action.
Overture requesting amendment indicating that the consistory may elect an elder to be president of consistory so that the minister might be relieved of administrative duties.
1972: 95-96. No action.

CONSTITUTION AND RULES OF ORDER, REVISION OF, COMMITTEE ON
Report.
1963: 126–137.
1964: 204–207.
1965: 166–168.
1966: 196–202.
1967: 178–186.
1968: 175–178, 179–184.
Name changed to Permanent Committee on Church Government; see CHURCH GOVERNMENT, PERMANENT COMMITTEE ON.
1969: 210.

CONSTITUTION OF THE RCA
Revision title: *The Book of Church Order including The Government, The Disciplinary Procedures, The Bylaws & Rules of Order of the General Synod, The Reformed Church in America,* generally referred to in this Digest, as the *Book of Church Order* (BCO).

CONSTITUTION, REVISION OF
Overtures regarding changes in.
1958: 132. No action.
Overture requesting an enlarged committee.
1958: 132–133. No action.
Overture requests that a 1955 overture be revived, suggesting a new constitution.
1958: 133. Referred to CRC.
Overture in regard to the validity of the procedure of sending the proposed revision of the Constitution to the classes.
1959: 121–122. Procedure already adopted.
Revision of the constitution was assigned by Stated Clerk.
1959: 125. Received for information.
Overture that a new committee be appointed to make a complete revision of the Constitution.
1961: 128–129, 142. No action.
Overture that GS rescind the proposal by the Committee on Revision of the Constitution that they be allowed to "edit" or "proofread" the constitution to make necessary changes and revert back to former procedures.
1962: 117. Approved.
Rules of Order integrated with the Constitution.
1963: 136. Received for information.
Recommended by CRC that all amendments coming up at Synod be referred to the CRC for study and presentation at the next Synod.
1965: 167–168. Adopted. Revision to continue.
Recommended by CRC that GS of 1966 adopt the reorganization of Order under the titles of *The Government of the RCA, Disciplinary Procedures and the Organization and Rules of Order of the General Synod.*
1966: 200–201. Adopted and sent to classes for approval.
Above statement adopted by 1967 Synod.
1967: 183, 185. Adopted.

CONSTITUTION, REVISION OF, COMMITTEE ON
Report.
1958: 138–142.
1959: 143–149.
1960: 119–125.
1961: 149–153.
1962: 137–143.
Changed to CONSTITUTION AND RULES OF ORDER, REVISION OF, COMMITTEE ON, which see.

CONSTITUTIONAL INQUIRIES
Tabulation of answers.
1958: 362–363.
1959: 368–369.
1960: 337–338.
1961: 397–398.
1962: 413–414.
1963: 116–117.
1964: 155–156.
1965: 128–129.
1966: 153–154.
1967: 130–131.
1968: 126–127.
1969: 155–156.
1970: 115.
1971: 119.
1972: 108.
1973: 116.
SCSM suggests that classes and Ps's exercise their shepherding responsibilities over churches that do not submit a Constitutional Report.
1969: 154. Adopted.
Overture requesting the requirement of having the replies reported in tabular form be dropped.
1975: 94. No action, since BCO does not require it.

CONSTITUTIONAL INQUIRY #5 AND OTHER QUESTIONS
Overture regarding: "Do the ministers and elders carefully inquire at least four times a year concerning spiritual condition and needs of the members?"
1962: 121, 127. Referred to TC.
TC sympathetic to the problem and will give further study to a possible rephrasing of the question, and guidance in implementing the inquiry.
1963: 267–268. Approved.
TC offers several recommendations, among them that regular visitation of the members of the church by the elders be encouraged. A handbook provided.
1964: 209–210. Adopted.
"Elders' Manual for Family Visitation" by James C. Eelman.
1965: 174–182.
Overture requesting amendment to the BCO regarding rewording of article on

communion inquiry, removing negative overtones and showing more Christian concern and compassion.
1970: 80, 103, 200. Sent to classes for approval.
Approved by classes.
1971: 151.
Overture requesting amendment to read: "before at least four celebrations of the Lord's Supper each year."
1972: 94-95. No action since this has already been implemented.
Overture asking for an amendment stressing the exercise of Christian discipline.
1975: 84-85. No action since elders' responsibility for discipline is expressed in another place.
Overture requesting an examination of the BCO for possible changes re questions concerning Canons of Dort and Heidelberg Catechism.
1976: 111. Referred to TC.
TC agrees that the present form of self-examination could well be supplemented by other questions which would help evaluate the total mission and effectiveness of a given congregation; but TC affirms its conviction that Standards of Unity are to be tested against the Word of God and that the fundamental doctrines be proclaimed.
1977: 307.

CONSTITUTIONAL (U.S.) AMENDMENT
CAC recommends approval of the amendment to allow eighteen-year-olds to vote.
1970: 218. Adopted.

CONSULTATION OF NATIONAL AND REGIONAL PEOPLE
Recommended that people from the PS's and classis level be included.
1972: 279. Adopted.
President recommends consultation for the purpose of studying financial support for national program.
1972: 274. Adopted.
See also FUNDING, CONVOCATION ON.

CONSULTATION ON CHURCH UNION (COCU)
Overture requesting Committee on "Approaches to Unity" to formally join the discussion of the Committee comprised of the UPCUSA, the Protestant Episcopal Church, the United Church of Christ, and the Methodist Church as proposed by Dr. Eugene Carson Blake. See also BLAKE, DR. EUGENE CARSON.
1961: 137-138, 142. Approved that GSEC hold conversations with COCU.
Sub-Committee of Observers to be named.
1963: 141.
PCUS voted to be a full participant in COCU.
1966: 301-304.
Recommended CIR study the possibility of RCA participation in COCU.
1966: 306. Adopted.
Three overtures requesting RCA not to become participant in COCU.
1967: 120-121, 122, 123. Referred to CIR.
Overture urging RCA to become a full participant in COCU.
1967: 123. Referred to CIR.
Overture requesting RCA rescind 1966 action on "Unity We Seek to Manifest."
1967: 121, 126, 128. No action pending report of CIR.
Study Report on COCU.
1967: 264-267.
CIR recommends that the RCA become a full participant in COCU.
1967: 266. Lost. 128 in favor; 148 opposed.
Resolution suggesting continued study on COCU.
1967: 336. Adopted.
Overture urging full participation in COCU.
1968: 103-104, 120, 124. To be deferred until the matter of merger with PCUS is decided. No action.
CIR recommends that the RCA become full participant in COCU.
1969: 290-291, 293-294. Action postponed indefinitely.
Four overtures, two for and two against participation in COCU.
1969: 137-139, 149-150, 153. Adopted that a Committee be formed with appointments from lower judicatories to work on means of dialogue, understanding, acceptance and reconciliation within the RCA. See COMMITTEE OF EIGHTEEN.
Overture suggesting that the RCA become a full participant in COCU.
1970: 102, 112-113. No action.
Plan of Union to be sent to each RCA church.
1970: 243. Adopted.
Overture urging RCA to become full participant in COCU.
1971: 105-106, 115. No action.
In response to invitation to participate in COCU it is recommended that it is not timely to become involved, but that two observers will continue to represent the RCA.

1972: 257-258. Adopted.
Eleventh Plenary Session of COCU met in April in Memphis.
1973: 231-232.
RCA does not hold membership in COCU but is represented by an observer at all meetings. Vital, significant ecumenical dialogue held at 13th Plenary Session.
1977: 253.

CONSUMER PATRONAGE, WITHHOLDING OF
CAC urges Christians and Christian institutions to withhold patronage in order to secure justice.
1968: 215, 220. Referred to classes for study and consideration.
CAC recommends that lists of manufacturers of widely used brands be annually updated so that RCA members can express their concern about products, packaging, advertising or pollution.
1971: 224. Defeated.
See also BOYCOTTS, ECONOMIC.

CONTEMPORARY CONFESSION
See CONFESSION OF FAITH—NEW and OUR SONG OF HOPE.

CONTRIBUTION CHARTS
Stewardship Council.

1958: 230-231.	1964: 349-352.
1959: 226-227.	1965: 294-295.
1960: 210-211.	1966: 323-324.
1961: 260-261.	1967: 287-288.
1962: 247-268.	1968: 316-317.
1963: 344-366.	

CONTRIBUTORY ANNUITY FUND
1958: 125. Membership of 894 ministers and 249 lay workers.
1966: 106. Membership of 1,078 ministers and 355 lay workers.
1968: 84. About 35% of the churches now paying both Contributory Annuity and Social Security.
Overture suggesting added benefits to widows.
1968: 94, 117, 123. To be referred to BP for study.
Overture requesting optional participation by Canadian ministers because of Canadian government regulations.
1970: 97-98, 109-110. No action. The classis was misinformed.
Overture asking that a special committee be appointed by GSEC to study policies and practices of the fund in the light of the present day problems of ministers.
1971: 104, 114. Adopted and referred to GSEC.
GSEC directed the OHR to develop a network of advisers to be available to RCA personnel in their personal financial planning.
1972: 113.
Overture requesting that all rights and privileges of the CAF belonging to the member, upon his death be transferred to his widow and that these rights not be affected by her remarriage.
1973: 113. Referred to RCBP.
RCBP recommends approval.
1973: 175. Approved.
Overture requesting GS to instruct BP to discontinue the practice of setting a minimum payment to the Annuity Fund and that the practice of a flat 11% payment for every congregation be substituted.
1973: 100-101. Referred to RCBP.
RCBP recommends no action since current practice was passed in 1971.
1973: 174. Adopted.
Overture requesting RCA Annuity Funds be turned over to one or two insurance companies for better dividends.
1973: 100. Referred to RCBP.
RCBP recommends no action since the BP is already considering other proposals.
1973: 174. No action approved.
Overture asking that there be a more equitable return on investments into the CAF by both churches and ministers; and that all funds contributed by pastors or for pastors by their churches become the sole property of the minister.
1974: 98-99. No action.
Overture requesting a study of the feasibility of raising the pension fund payments from 11% to 12%, and that the 1% be put in a separate fund for assisting churches who request salary supplements.
1975: 87-88. No action.
Overture asking for a provision of conscientious objection on the part of a minister who wishes to withdraw from the RCA plan.
1976: 99, 139. Referred to BP for study and recommendation. No action.
For further references to CAF see the annual reports of PENSIONS, BOARD OF, and also RETIREMENT PROGRAM, R.C.A.

CONVERSATIONS WITH OTHER DENOMINATIONS
1970: 226-228, 241-242.
1971: 234-235.
1973: 231-233.
1974: 227.
1976: 214-215.
See also CHURCH UNION, MERGERS, MERGERS PROPOSED, COCU, or specific denominations—PRESBYTERIAN CHURCH IN THE U.S., UNITED PRESBYTERIAN CHURCH, U.S.A., CHRISTIAN REFORMED CHURCH, etc.

CONVERSION
Overture requesting a study guide so that there might be an in depth study of conversion and Christian action.
1973: 93. No action, since there is ample material.

CONVOCATION OF SEMINARY PROFESSORS
See THEOLOGY, PROFESSORS OF, CONVOCATIONS.

COOK, REV. JAMES I.
Elected Professor of Theology, Chair of Biblical Language and Literature, at WTS.
1967: 44, 53, 56.

COORDINATOR, REGIONAL
President suggests the Office of Regional Coordinator of Program, RCA.
1966: 342, 353. Referred to GSEC for study and report.

CORWIN'S MANUAL
Updating of is progressing.
1959: 237.
Need for updating.
1962: 411.
Suggested that new edition will be an historical directory of churches and ministers.
1963: 335-336.
See HISTORICAL DIRECTORY

COUGHENOUR, REV. ROBERT A.
Appointed for a three year term as Professor of Old Testament at WTS.
1975: 30.

COUNSELOR FOR MINISTERS AND THEIR WIVES
Need expressed for such a counselor.
1962: 286, 342. Referred to CAC for study.
CAC will make recommendation in 1964.
1963: 318.
Report of CAC: Recommends (1) the establishment of and the continuation and expansion of ministerial retreats for ministers and their wives; (2) the establishment of a pastoral relations committee on the consistory level. Adopted.
1964: 218-219, 226.

COVENANT OF MUTUAL RESPONSIBILITIES
See THE CHURCH AND ITS COLLEGES.

COVENANT FOR OPEN OCCUPANCY
See OPEN HOUSING (OCCUPANCY)

COVENANT LIFE CURRICULUM (CLC)
Working (Foundation) Papers prepared, setting forth the basic principles of the curriculum: "Towards a Curriculum for the Covenant Community," "Basic Presuppositions," and "Guiding Principles."
1959: 75-76.
1961: 88.
Other references to CLC.
1963: 57, 378.
1964: 57-58.
1965: 52-53, 54, 55, 333.
Overture requesting the CLC material be submitted to the TC for study.
1965: 112, 122, 124. No action.
Overture questioning policy requiring order of full sets when partial sets only are needed.
1966: 125-126. 142. Referred to SCBE.
Recommended the BE promote material on a church to church basis. Sunday School enrollment dropped 24,509 last year.
1967: 57, 60, 61. Adopted.

COVENTRY, WILLIAM W.
Detailed account of the long history of meetings of Classis, PS, and special CJB, concerning licensure of the candidate.
1959: 130-142.
Candidate licensed January 27, 1959.
1959: 137.

CREDO ON RACE RELATIONS
See RACE RELATIONS and OPEN HOUSING.

CRIME AND VIOLENCE—JUSTICE AND PENITENCE
Report of CAC
1969: 241-242. Adopted.

CRIME, PERSON CONVICTED OF
Overture requesting change of word "shall" to "may" be suspended from privilege of church membership and from ecclesiastical office.
1966: 129-130. 145-146, 150. No action.

CRISIS IN NATION
Racial tensions and social injustices brought to the fore by the death of Martin Luther King. Task Force authorized to conduct an "Emergency Fund Campaign."
1968: 151, 167.
See also KING, MARTIN LUTHER, JR.

CRUMLEY, GEORGE W., JR.
Honored by Synod for work on GPC.
1976: 137. Adopted.

CUBAN CRISIS AND THE WCC AND NCC
Overture expressing strong disapproval of the statement of the WCC and NCC on the crisis.
1963: 107-108, 110, 113. No action.

CUBAN REFUGEES
Motion urging the churches in various places to bring about some relief to the

present pressing refugee situation, and to ask the Church World Service Committee to take the question under advisement.
1962: 378. Adopted.

CURRICULUM, SEMINARY, SPECIAL COMMITTEE ON
Report.
1958: 350-351.
1959: 355-356.
1960: 306.
Committee dissolved.
1960: 303.

CUSTOMS AND USAGES
See DEVOTIONAL EXERCISES AT SYNOD.

DAHLBERG, DR. EDWIN, PRESIDENT OF THE NCC
Overture regarding alleged communist connections.
1958: 135-136. No action.

DAKOTA-ORANGE CLASSIS EXCHANGE
Exchange of participants termed "a great success."
1971: 67.
See also COMMITTEE OF 18.

DANCING AT OUR COLLEGES
Overture requesting the whole matter of social dancing at our colleges be studied.
1963: 108, 109, 112. No action. Referred to CAC.
CAC study: "Social dancing can be good or evil. . . ."
1964: 220-223, 226-227, 230.

DAY, RACHEL SMITH, MISSIONARY TO CHINA, 1908-1929.
Obituary.
1966: Annual report of the BWM, App., 13.

DAY OF PRAYER FOR CROPS AND INDUSTRY
Overture requesting RCA consult Christian Reformed Church on the possibility of setting a common day.
1975: 88. Adopted and referred to IRC for implementation.

DAY'S WAGE FOR CHRIST
Discontinued. The program to be used only for an emergency.
1962: 241-242, 274, 277.
Overture requesting voluntary use of.
1963: 104, 111. No action pending SC's report. To be continued for 1963.
1964: 354.
1965: 299.
1966: 326-327.
1968: 318.
1969: 182-183.

DEACON, ROLE OF
Study of the Committee to Study the Nature of Offices and Ministries.
1960: 312-315.
RCPR recommends workshops for all deacons be held in each classis discussing the responsibilities of deacons, and that classes share their findings with COCG.
1974: 282. Adopted.
President suggests a more significant participation of the Office of Deacon in the mission of the church.
1974: 280, 282. Approved. COCG and GPC to consult on it.
See also ELDERS AND DEACONS, ROLE OF.

DEACONESS, OFFICE OF
Overture requesting such office.
1958: 130-131, 136. Referred to Committee on the Ordination of Women.
Overture requesting GS to instruct CRC to provide for this ministry and after approval to include office for their ordination and installation in the Liturgy.
1966: 119, 144-145, 150. To be studied by TC.

DEACONS ELECTION OF
Suggested change in constitution—deacons shall be chosen from the members of the Church in full communion who have reached the age of 21.
1967: 155. Referred to TC.

DEACONS, FULL DELEGATES TO JUDICATORIES
See CLASSES, REPRESENTATION OF DEACONS IN.

DE BOER, MARTINUS C.
Dispensation from professorial certificate granted.
1976: 146, 148.

DE BRUIN, MRS. FRANCES L., MISSIONARY TO INDIA FOR 40 YEARS
Death.
1972: 65.

DE BRUYN, MR. HARRY
Elected Vice President of GS.
1971: 9.
Elected President of GS.
1972: 9.

DEBT, POLICY ON
1974: 110.

DECLARATION, FORM OF
New name for FORMULA, which also see.
1960: 120-121, 122.

Overture suggesting addition to declaration.
1970: 82–83, 103. Referred to TC.
Overture requesting amendment to the BCO concerning the form of declaration for minister, professor of theology, to make it clear that the Standards of the RCA are historical documents which are only valid when they conform with the Word of God.
1970: 83–85, 104. Referred to TC.
Overture requesting TC to reformulate the form of declaration in an endeavor to make known the affirmation of joy and meaning of the Christian Ministry.
1971: 108–109, 115–116. Adopted.
Forms of declaration for (1) licensed candidates; (2) for Ministers of the Word; (3) for Professors of Theology, prepared by TC.
1971: 209, 215–216. Adopted and sent to classes for approval.
TC forms not approved by classes.
1972: 120.
A form indicating the "joy and meaning of the Christian Ministry" submitted by TC.
1972: 199–201. Sent to classes for approval.
Approved by classes.
1973: 128.
Overture submitting forms of declaration for ministers and licensed candidates.
1972: 104–105, 195. No action since TC has already submitted preferred forms.

DECORA, WILBUR
Dispensation from professorial certificate requested.
1958: 57. Granted.

DEGREES CONFERRED BY THE SEMINARIES
See NEW BRUNSWICK THEOLOGICAL SEMINARY and WESTERN THEOLOGICAL SEMINARY.

DE KOK, DONALD
Dispensation from professorial certificate requested.
1973: 33, 36. Granted.

DELEGATES TO SYNOD
Time of election of.
1960: 219.

DELEGATIONS
1974: app. 2, 14.
1975: app. 2, 14.
1976: app. 1, 14.
1977: app. 1, 14.

DE MARINIS, VALERIE MARIE
Dispensation from professorial certificate requested.
1977: 162, 166, 168. Granted.

DEMITTED
Overture asking for a definition of the word, and a determination of whether this is a disciplinary action.
1976: 111–112. Adopted.
COCG reports, "to be demitted" is inappropriate usage, since "to demit" is a voluntary action. Recommended that BCO shall be changed to read: "The ordination of a minister of the Word may be revoked. . . ."
1977: 316. Adopted.

DENOMINATION
Overture regarding definition of.
1960: 109, 116. No action, since CRC has reported on this matter.

DENOMINATIONAL EXECUTIVE COMMITTEE
See GENERAL SYNOD EXECUTIVE COMMITTEE (GSEC).

DENOMINATIONAL HEADQUARTERS, LOCATION OF
See LOCATION OF NATIONAL OFFICE(S) AND SEMINARY(S).

DENOMINATIONAL NAME ON BULLETIN BOARDS
Overture requesting that Reformed Church in America be added to church name on bulletin boards.
1959: 123–124. Approval of intent.

DENOMINATIONAL POLICY OF AUTHORITY
Two overtures regarding the formulating of denominational policy and the problem of the authority to represent the denomination in church to church relationships.
1958: 133. Referred to CRC.

DENOMINATIONAL STRUCTURE, SUBCOMMITTEE ON
Report.
1966: 165–167, 181–182.
Recommends establishing of one corporation for the National Program of the RCA through merger of BE, BNAM, BWM, and SC.
1967: 168–170. To be reported on at Synod of 1968.
Report on decisions.
1968: 140–142.
Coordinator for changes—Mr. Robert Harrison employed for a three year period.
1967: 157.
Previous reports under BOARDS AND AGENCIES, which see.

DENOMINATIONAL THEME
It appears that GENERAL SYNOD THEME and DENOMINATIONAL THEME are used

interchangeably. The themes are listed under GENERAL SYNOD.

DE PREE, MRS. HENRY, MISSIONARY TO CHINA
Death
1970: 67.

DE ROO, REV. HAROLD
Appreciation expressed for 10 years in the Division of Youth Education.
1967: 60, 61.

DESK PLAN CALENDAR
Planned by SC.
1963: 370.

DE VELDER, REV. MARION
Elected President of General Synod
1958: 8.
Elected Stated Clerk of GS.
1961: 345.
Re-elected Stated Clerk for five-year period.
1966: 168-169, 183.
Named General Secretary.
1968: 141.
Tribute in his honor on his retirement from office of General Secretary, August 31, 1977.
1977: 61-63.
Gratitude for his faithful service in the cause of ecumenicity.
1977: 255, 270, 323.

DEVELOPMENT OFFICES
See GENERAL PROGRAM COUNCIL, STAFF.

DEVELOPMENT PROGRAM, R C A.
A Progress Report—Purpose to raise $6,000,000 under direction of Ketchum, Inc.
1966: 330-335. Approved.
Overture requests these contributions be included in Consistorial Reports of benevolences.
1968: 103, 119-120, 124. Adopted.
Report.
1967: 297-299.
1968: 321-323.
1969: 181-182.

DEVOTIONAL EXERCISES AT GENERAL SYNOD

1958: 224-225.	1968: 310-312.
1959: 220-221.	1969: 314-316.
1960: 202-203.	1970: 251-252.
1961: 227-228.	1971: 264-265.
1962: 237-238.	1972: 269-270.
1963: 337-339.	1973: 271-272.
1964: 345-346.	1974: 269-270.
1965: 288-290.	1975: 239-240.
1966: 317-319.	1976: 250-251.
1967: 282-284.	1977: 321-322.

DE YOUNG, REV. DONALD
Elected Vice President of GS.
1972: 9.
Elected President of GS.
1973: 14.

DIETZ, LINWOOD J.
Dispensation requested from professorial certificate.
1972: 29. Denied for lack of educational requirements.

DIGEST OF SYNODICAL LEGISLATION
Four copies being made to be placed in strategic places.
1958: 246.
Need for a compilation of 1906-1968.
1968: 307.
GS urged to have someone work on supplementary volume.
1970: 249.
No publication date for a new edition.
1972: 268.
Office of General Secretary working on this project.
1973: 269-270.
General Secretary's Secretary, Miss Barbara Mahannah, and Miss Mildred Schuppert working on project.
1976: 197.
Miss Mildred Schuppert now taking responsibility for an Index and Digest of Synodical Legislation, 1958-1977. Publication intended for 1978, a further tribute to the celebration of our 350 years of existence in North America.
1977: 238.

DILL, JERRY
Dispensation requested from the biblical languages. Assume request was withdrawn since Mr. Dill left WTS.
1971: 31. No action.

DIRECTION, BOARD OF
Report.

1958: 13-29.	1968: 17-31.
1959: 12-27.	1969: 17-30.
1960: 12-25.	1970: 16-24.
1961: 12-25.	1971: 17-24.
1962: 13-23.	1972: 15-24.
1963: 13-23.	1973: 20-27.
1964: 14-25.	1974: 21-23.
1965: 15-25.	1975: 23-28.
1966: 16-26.	1976: 91-95.
1967: 16-29.	1977: 99-106.

Possibility of change as reorganization of GS progresses.
1969: 169.
Change in organization—membership, responsibilities, etc.
1970: 143-144.
Recommended by GSEC that as terms of

members of BD expire they be replaced by GSEC members, and that when the BD President's term expires he become a member of GSEC for three years.
1970: 183-184. Adopted.

DIRECTION, BOARD OF, STANDING COMMITTEE ON
Report.
1958: 30-34. 1964: 26-29.
1959: 28-31. 1965: 26-30.
1960: 26-29. 1966: 27-30.
1961: 26-30. 1967: 30-34.
1962: 24-28. 1968: 32-37.
1963: 24-29. 1969: 31-35.
Becomes DIRECTION, BOARD OF, REVIEW COMMITTEE ON, which follows.

DIRECTION, BOARD OF, REVIEW COMMITTEE ON
Report.
1970: 25-26.
1971: 25-26.
Recommended by GSEC that the Committee be discontinued and the Bylaws and Rules of Order concerning the Committee be suspended for this Synod.
1972: 112. Adopted.
Recommended the Review Committee be discontinued.
1973: 122. Adopted.

DIRECTORY OF THE RCA
see HISTORICAL DIRECTORY OF THE RCA.

DISARMAMENT
1961: 215.

DISCIPLINARY PROCEDURES
Rewriting of the section on discipline and appeals submitted by COCG.
1974: 194-199. Adopted.

DISCIPLINE OF A MINISTER
See MINISTER, DISCIPLINE OF.

DISCRIMINATORY PRACTICES AND PROJECT EQUALITY
CAC statement on.
1969: 243-245.

DISMISSION CERTIFICATE
Overture requesting revision of the form using more suitable terminology.
1965: 113, 118, 123. Approved and referred to CRC.
See also TRANSFER OF A CHURCH MEMBER, CERTIFICATE FOR.

DISPENSATIONS
Dispensations requested.
1958: 55-60. 1962: 53, 55.
1959: 51-54, 57. 1963: 48-49.
1960: 51-53. 1964: 50-51.
1961: 68-69. 1965: 46.
1966: 46. 1972: 29.
1967: 52-53. 1973: 32-33, 36-38.
1968: 41. 1974: 36-38.
1969: 39-41. 1975: 33, 34.
1970: 31-33. 1976: 148.
1971: 31. 1977: 162, 166, 168.
Requirements for dispensations—report of the CRC.
1962: 138-139, 141-142. Approval of 2/3 classes required.
Approved by classes.
1963: 283.
Procedures: (1) classis makes request of General Secretary; (2) General Secretary refers request to BTE; (3) person referred to seminary for examination; (4) request and result of examination, referred to Executive Committee of the BTE; (5) report to GS and vote.
1969: 40, 44. Adopted.
RCTE recommends that the Coordinator for HR and Director of Professional Development study several issues regarding dispensations, since there are so many. What should be the responsibility of classis for providing employment for those on whose behalf it seeks dispensations.
1971: 31, 36-37.
Motion made that no further dispensations be considered until GS has received and acted upon the above report.
1971: 31, 37. No action; motion out of order.
Recommended amendments in The Government concerning dispensations.
1972: 29-30, 33. Adopted.
BTE requests amendments concerning 7 matters—a,b,c,d,e,f,g.
1972: 29-30. Adopted and sent to classes for approval.
Classes approved a,b,c,d,e,f,g.
1973: 128.
Overture requesting that if the classis is satisfied with the exam it shall petition GS at least 11 months prior to GS meeting and that GS can then make inquiries deemed necessary.
1973: 109-110. No action.
Recommended that GS refer the responsibility for the 7 items they approved to the classes for implementation and that they assist in providing employment.
1973: 127-128. Approved.
Recommended that GS authorize the BTE to charge a fee of $200 for a dispensation from professorial certificate, and that the fee accompany the application.
1976: 146, 148. Adopted.
Time factor in making application for dispensation is 15 months. A document has been sent to classes indicating that the

student must have a continuing relationship with the classis and truly be under its care.
1977: 161.

DISTRIBUTION OF MATERIALS BY COMMITTEES, BOARDS AND AGENCIES
Overture requesting the boards and agencies to use discretion in distributing materials to the churches.
1966: 120, 142, 149. No action.

DIVORCE AND REMARRIAGE
Basic policy on: CAC report.
1962: 205–217, 223–224.
Overture requesting TC to study and present biblical concepts and give guidelines because of present social problems.
1973: 111–112. Adopted.
Overture requesting OHR and seminaries to require a ministerial candidate who has been divorced to submit a statement giving details.
1976: 103. No action, since calling church can always inquire into the marital status.
TC paper on "Biblical Perspectives on Marriage, Divorce and Remarriage."
1975: 162–172. Document approved, and copies are to be distributed to every minister and elder in the church. Congregations to be encouraged to enter into biblical study on the subject. Every effort should be made to provide Christian counseling, including Marriage Communication Labs, Family Clusters, and such.

DOCTRINAL STANDARDS
"The Place of the Standards in the Life of the Church," a paper presented by TC.
1971: 211–215. Statement adopted.

DOCTRINAL STANDARDS IN WORLD MISSION FIELDS
See CHRISTIAN WORLD MISSIONS, DOCTRINAL STANDARDS.

DOMESTIC MISSIONS AND CHURCH BUILDING FUND, STANDING COMMITTEE ON
Report.
1958: 95–105.
1959: 105–109.
1960: 88–95.
Canadian Work—new ministers needed.
1960: 95, 89–90.
National Strategy plan to be developed.
1960: 93.
Jews, Mission to, to be studied.
1960: 93.
Secretaries—promotions and changes.
1960: 88.
Name of Board changed to Board of North American Missions. See NORTH AMERICAN MISSIONS, BOARD OF, and also see APPENDIX for Annual Reports.

DOSSIERS, OF MINISTERS
See entry under MINISTERS, regarding OHR central file.

DRAFT CARDS
Request of 5 NBTS students that the GS take their draft cards into the possession of the RCA.
1969: 249–250, 250–252. Motion lost.
Motion made that GS be the repository for draft cards.
1970: 218. Defeated.

DRAFT EXEMPTIONS
Two overtures suggesting RCA petition Congress to remove the 4-D draft exemption for Ministers and Theological Students.
1968: 100, 118, 123. Referred to CAC.
Motion made that the GS urge the Selective Service System to eliminate the 4-D classification for theological seminarians.
1971: 289. Adopted.

DRAFT RESISTERS
Pastoral counseling available for them and their families.
1971: 66, 76.

DRUGS
CAC recommendations: (1) Congregations should use available community and congregational resources in implementing programs of open information exchange about drug and marijuana usage; (2) Division of Church Life and Mission to make available lists of material for such programs; (3) urge RCA members to support legislation to bring penalties in line with severity of the offense; (4) urge agencies in federal government to research effects and hazards of marijuana use.
1971: 221–222. Adopted.
"The Drug Problem and the Church," a CAC study paper.
1973: 221–226.
Recommended that the seminaries provide resources to acquaint students with alcohol and drug problems; also that ministers be invited to the seminars.
1974: 40. Adopted.
BTE reports a member of the NBTS faculty has special training in this field and is available if students encounter the problem; WTS has recently brought Rev. Herman J. Kregel, an authority on the subject, to the campus for student seminar.
1975: 32.

See also ALCOHOL and MARIJUANA LEGISLATION.

DUNHAM, LLOYD
Dispensation from languages requested—coming from another seminary.
1959: 51-52, 57. Candidate to apply again after additional study and examination.
Dispensation granted.
1960: 51, 53, 57.

DYKEMA, MR. GERRIT
Dispensation requested from academic requirements and professorial certificate. Serving as lay pastor at Dunningville (Michigan) Reformed Church.
1970: 32. Denied at this time. He should contact WTS for an educational program.

EAST ASIA CHRISTIAN CONFERENCE
1960: 135.

EASTERN COLLEGE
Recommended that the BE take up a study of the possibility of an eastern college.
1959: 81. Adopted.

ECOLOGY AND POPULATION CONTROL
TC member is preparing an article for the CH.
1971: 217.

ECUMENICAL CONFESSION OF FAITH
Confession presented by the World Alliance of Reformed Churches.
1965: 228-229, 233, 243. Reaction of the Church and pastors to be sent to chairman of CIR.
TC had no objection to permissive use of the Confession, but some suggestions were made for strengthening the statement.
1967: 187.
The response from the TC was the only response from the 13 member churches.
1967: 226.

ECUMENICAL INSTITUTE IN GENEVA
1958: 305.

ECUMENICAL MOVEMENT
1958: 354.
Change in.
1975: 203.
See also APPROACHES TO UNITY.

ECUMENICAL YOUTH ASSEMBLY
Lausanne.
1961: 166-167.
Ann Arbor.
1961: 167.

EDITORIAL COMMITTEE (OF THE COMMITTEE ON THE REVISION OF THE CONSTITUTION).
To be present at each session in connection with revisions.
1966: 203.
Report.
1968: 179-182.
1969: 230-232.
1970: 199-201, 202.
1971: 209-210.
1972: 194-196.
1973: 183-184.
1974: 200-202.
1975: 161.
1976: 249.
1977: 320.

EDUCATION, ACADEMIES AND COLLEGES
1958: 65-72.
1959: 58-81.
1960: 61-75.
1961: 75-91.
1962: 66-79.
1963: 57-79.
1964: 56-80.
See also new listing, HIGHER EDUCATION.

EDUCATION, BOARD OF
Report.
1958: App., Bound in after MGS.
1959: App., Bound in after MGS.
1960: App., Bound in after MGS.
1961: App., Bound in after MGS.
1962: App., Bound in after MGS.
1963: App. 1.
1964: App. 1.
1965: App. 1.
1966: App. 1.
1967: App. 1.
1968: App. 1. Last report.

EDUCATION, BOARD OF, STANDING COMMITTEE ON
Report.
1958: 73-80.
1959: 72-81.
1960: 68-75.
1961: 85-92.
1962: 75-79.
1963: 57-63.
1964: 56-65.
1965: 49-55.
1966: 51-56.
1967: 57-61.
1968: 44-48.
The report of 1968 is the last report after 137 years of service. Overture requesting aid to men studying for the ministry be increased.
1960: 74. Referred to Synod's Committee on Educational Institutions.

EDUCATION, CHRISTIAN, AND PUBLIC SCHOOLS
1962: 218-219. RCA members should stubbornly resist attempts to deprive our children of Bible reading and prayer in public educational systems.

EDUCATION SERVICES AND DEPARTMENT OF FIELD SERVICES
Sub-Committee report.
1960: 71.

EELMAN, BRENT J.
Dispensation from professorial certificate granted.
1976: 146, 148.

EELMAN, REV. JAMES C.
Elected Professor in Preaching and Practical Theology at NBTS.
1958: 59, 62, 63-64.
Resigned from Professorship at NBTS.
1967: 36.
Resolution for.
1967: 54.

EENDRACHT
A denominational appeal for money. Final Report.
1958: 245. Eendracht Committee discharged.

EENIGENBURG, REV. ELTON M.
Appointed Academic Dean at WTS.
1963: 42.
1969: 43.
Transferred from Chair of Historical Theology to the newly established Chair of Christian Ethics and Philosophy of Religion at WTS.
1963: 50-51.
Resigned as Dean at WTS. Will return to full-time teaching.
1977: 159.

EGYPT
1974: 62.

ELDER, OFFICE OF
Study of the Committee to Study the Nature of Offices and Ministries.
1960: 309-312.
Elders' visitation manual suggested in connection with Constitutional Question #5.
1964: 209-210.
"Elders' Manual for Family Visitation" prepared for TC by James C. Eelman.
1965: 174-182. Adopted.

ELDER REPRESENTATION IN CLASSIS
See CLASSES, ELDER REPRESENTATION IN.

ELDER, TEACHING
"Teaching Elder" is used in some sister denominations. In the RCA the "Teaching Elder" is the "Minister of the Word."
1971: 204.

ELDERS AND DEACONS, AGE OF
Overture requesting amendment to the BCO: The elders and deacons shall be chosen from the male members of the church in full communion, who have attained the age of twenty-one, or at the discretion of the consistory, eighteen years.
1970: 79-80, 102-103. Adopted.
Approved by Classes.
1971: 151.

ELDERS AND DEACONS, ELECTION OF
Overture suggesting rewording, deleting the word "male."
1965: 104, 109, 110, 123-124. Adopted and sent to classes for approval.
Deleting the word "male" not approved by classes (yes 24, no 21).
1966: 189.
TC recommends "and deacons" be deleted and a new section read: "Deacons to be chosen from the members of the church in full communion who have attained the age of 21 years."
1967: 188, 199. Motion to table the recommendation was adopted.
Overture requesting the word "male" be deleted.
1967: 111, 124, 127-128. Adopted and sent to classes for approval.
Not approved by classes.
1968: 169.
Overture requesting elders and deacons be chosen from male members who have attained the age of 21 or at the discretion of the consistory, 18 years.
1969: 123, 141-142, 151. No action.
Discussion on this subject continues under ORDINATION OF WOMEN, which also see.

ELDERS AND DEACONS, ROLE OF
Amendment stating responsibilities of.
1969: 211-213. Adopted and sent to classes for approval.
Responsibilities of, approved by classes.
1970: 141.
Overture requesting a study be made of individual roles of elders and deacons with special attention to office of deacon.
1972: 101. Referred to TC.
TC is engaged in a study of this matter.
1973: 194.
Suggested that the role of elders and deacons be referred to COCG for clarification.
1974: 206-207.
COCG feels this issue should be studied by the TC. Will report in 1976.
1975: 188.
COCG reports no change can be made unless changes are designed for these offices.
1975: 159.
President and committee recommend TC continue study of roles and functions of elders and deacons.
1976: 33. Adopted.
Suggested by President and RCPR rec-

ommends the GPC produce a provisional guide for the training of elders and deacons.
1976: 27, 33-34. Adopted.
The production of a guide for the training of elders and deacons has been assigned to Rev. Harold Brown, Secretary of Parish Life. Guide is in preparation.
1977: 140.
TC studying the distinction in the roles; to be presented in 1977.
1976: 245.
TC study will be presented in 1978.
1977: 307.
COCG recommends amendment to BCO to read: "Does the consistory have and regularly use a procedure by which the performance of its elders, deacons, and minister(s) is annually reviewed?"
1977: 320. Approved and sent to classes for approval.
See also material under DEACONS.

ELLIS, DR. E. EARLE
Appointed Assistant Professor of Biblical Studies at NBTS.
1966: 47.
Elected Professor of Theology (Biblical Studies) at NBTS.
1977: 165, 167-168. Adopted.

EMBLEM OF THE REFORMED CHURCH
See CHURCH EMBLEM.

EMERGENCY FLOOD RELIEF APPROPRIATION
Special request for help in Fulton, Illinois area.
1965: 302. Approved.

EMERITUS MINISTERS
See MINISTERS, EMERITUS.

ENERGY
Constituency of the RCA urged (1) to exercise responsible stewardship with regard to energy by putting conservation methods into practice; (2) urge churches to make buildings which are vacant during the week, available for community projects; (3) that auxiliary sources such as solar energy should be fostered by the government.
1977: 201-204. All adopted.

ENGLEHARDT, REV. DAVID LE ROY
Appointed Librarian at NBTS.
1968: 40.

ENGLISH CHURCH IN THE HAGUE
1958: 308
1959: 31

ENGLUND, REV. HAROLD
Invited to become Acting President of WTS
1960: 47, 70.
Acted until 1962 when he took a call to the Presbyterian Church. (Not indicated in MGS)

ENVIRONMENT
"A Reformed Theology of Nature in a Crowded World"—paper presented by TC.
1970: 206-208, 210.

EQUALIZATION
(Distribution of undesignated monies) A brief history.
1972: 115-116.
Undesignated funds shall be distributed on a percentage of a given budget to the total benevolent budget as established by GS; when a board has received its askings they will cease to share in the undesignated funds. An attempt will be made to assure all boards of full askings.
1958: 233.
Problems with present equalization process: massive reorganizational changes have taken place, therefore can no longer achieve the objective.
1972: 116.
Consultations for discussing new systems have been held. Recommended that beginning Jan. 1, 1973 the present system be discontinued and that GSEC allocate such monies to funds for extraordinary needs.
1972: 117. Adopted.

ESTHER, REV. AND MRS. JOSEPH
Honored by GS for missionary work.
1976: 134-135.

ETHICS, POLITICAL
Overture suggesting Congress establish such a code.
1967: 112, 124, 128. No action.
CAC recommends a series of election reforms concerning contribution limitations, financial reports from candidates, and urges Congress to adopt legislation on campaign expenditures, and disclosures.
1974: 225. Adopted.

ETHIOPIA
1971: 62-63
1974: 64

EUCHARIST
"Eucharist in the Life of the Church: An Ecumenical Consensus." A report of the NCC.
1971: 238-242.
See also LORD'S SUPPER.

EUTHANASIA
See LIFE SUPPORT SYSTEMS

EVANGELICALS, CONSERVATIVE
Suggested that the RCA cultivate friendships with evangelical denominations not members of the NCC.
1966: 244. See also NATIONAL ASSOCIATION OF EVANGELICALS.
EVANGELISM
Report.
1958: 99, 103-104. 1968: 74-75.
1959: 105. 1969: 72.
1960: 91. 1970: 59.
1962: 97-104. 1972: 52-54.
1963: 88. 1973: 58-60.
1964: 93. 1974: 60-62.
1965: 83, 88-90. 1975: 52-54.
1966: 99. 1976: 118-119.
1967: 92.
Overture requesting Department of Evangelism be raised to a separate board.
1959: 122. No action. Referred to the Committee on BDM.
Rev. Herman Ridder appointed Minister of Evangelism to replace Rev. Jacob Prins.
1960: 92.
Overture requesting that courses in Evangelism be taught in the seminaries.
1960: 110, 116. Referred to the Faculties.
Faculties will work with the Minister of Evangelism.
1961: 70.
Overture regarding church's responsibility for Evangelism, requesting emphasis of it in the Constitution. Suggested changes listed.
1966: 121-122, 145, 150. No action. Opening statement in the Constitution deemed sufficient.
Overture suggesting that in the denominational structure there be greater coordination between the Department of Evangelism and Social Ministries.
1969: 129, 144, 152. No action. GPC already exploring this matter.
RCBTE recommends investigating and implementing a program of training in personal evangelism at NBTS and WTS.
1973: 38. Adopted.
BTE will not study problem of courses in evangelism pending a report on the proposed Task Force on Evangelism. Seminaries will study course possibilities.
1974: 31, 38.
Overture requesting formation of a Commission on Evangelism.
1973: 93-94. Adopted and sent to GSEC for study.
GSEC requests GPC to appoint a Task Force on Evangelism and Renewal.
1974: 116-117.
GPC reports appointment of two Secretaries of Evangelism.
1974: 59.
"Good News People," a three-year program emphasis (1976-1978) to make the Good News incarnate and intelligible amidst all the bad news of injustice, alienation and lostness.
1976: 118, 132.
Recommended that GS strongly affirm "Good News People" as a prime means of renewal and growth in the local church.
1976: 132. Adopted.
See also EVANGELISM AND CHURCH GROWTH; EVANGELISM AND RENEWAL; CHURCH GROWTH; SPIRITUAL LIFE COMMISSION; and entries on Joint Committee on Evangelism (RCA/CRC) and Evangelism Manifesto under CHRISTIAN REFORMED CHURCH, also GOOD NEWS PEOPLE.

EVANGELISM AND CHURCH GROWTH
Goals of.
1974: 60-62, 70.
1975: 52-53.
The President shows concern about falling off of RCA membership and RCPR wishes to refer this mandate to the PS's and classes to work on evangelism and growth, and report to GSEC and GS.
1975: 243-246, 250. Adopted.
GPC instructed to pursue an aggressive and challenging program for Church Growth.
1976: 132. Adopted.
President again stresses Evangelism and RCPR recommends continued study.
1976: 25-26, 33.
Overture requesting the formation of a Commission of Evangelism and Church Growth.
1976: 108. No action since there are two Secretaries of Evangelism and Renewal, the Task Force on Evangelism and Church Renewal, and a Task Force on Church Growth.
See also EVANGELISM; EVANGELISM AND RENEWAL; CHURCH GROWTH; SPIRITUAL LIFE COMMISSION; and entries on Joint Committee on Evangelism (RCA/CRC) and Evangelism Manifesto, under CHRISTIAN REFORMED CHURCH, also GOOD NEWS PEOPLE.

EVANGELISM AND RENEWAL
Recommended that a Task Force be formed.
1974: 61.
Task Force appointed.
1974: 116-117.

Deliberations of two meetings in 1974.
1975: 50–51.
Task Force publishes *Theological Reflections,* a series of occasional papers acquainting RCA members with the church's life and mission.
1976: 118–119.
History and objectives. Task Force to be continued through 1981.
1977: 44–47, 140–141.
Seven-fold objectives: (1) to articulate the implications of the biblical message of the Kingdom of God for evangelical programs; (2) to evaluate and resource RCA evangelical programs (GPC programs and PS programs); (3) to review and critique other evangelism programs currently involving the RCA constituency; (4) to evaluate and support seminary instruction in evangelism and church renewal; (5) to stimulate theological reflection on evangelism and church renewal (publication of *Theological Reflections*); (6) to prepare for GS a presentation to highlight evangelism and church renewal; (7) to identify and promote activities which enable evangelism and renewal, e.g. spiritual disciplines for clergy and laity, renewal communities.
1977: 144–145.
President recommends that GS remembering our Lord's command to "go and make disciples" urge every congregation to enlist actively in the task of evangelism to the end that the Church of Jesus Christ may grow among us also.
1977: 26, 35. Adopted.
See also EVANGELISM; EVANGELISM AND CHURCH GROWTH; CHURCH GROWTH; SPIRITUAL LIFE COMMISSION; and entries on Joint Committee on Evangelism (RCA/CRC) and Evangelism Manifesto under CHRISTIAN REFORMED CHURCH.

EVANGELISM, FESTIVAL OF
Statement of Task Force and concerned delegates: that there be a deep awareness of racist tendencies in spite of our acceptance of our CREDO and other statements.
1970: 185–187.
Festival held in Detroit, April 1–4, 1970.
1971: 66–67.

EVANGELISM, JOINT COMMITTEE ON
A committee of the RCA/CRC for the purpose of preparing a theology of evangelism. See listings under CHRISTIAN REFORMED CHURCH.

EVANGELIST AT LARGE
President suggests possibility of one or more denominational evangelists.
1965: 340, 347, 348. Referred to BNAM for study.
BNAM's report to President's suggestion.
1966: 99. PTR Missioners are already effective.

EVERY MEMBER VISITATION PROGRAM (STEWARDSHIP)
1958: 227, 234.
1959: 223, 224, 228.
1960: 205, 207.
1961: 230–231.
1962: 243–244.
1963: 341.
1964: 347–348.
1965: 291.
1967: 285.

EXAMINATION OF SEMINARY STUDENTS
See THEOLOGY, STUDENTS OF, CLASSICAL EXAMINATION OF.

EX-COMMUNICATION
New form requested.
1960: 300–301. Not adopted.
Overture regarding.
1961: 128, 142. Referred to CRC.

EXECUTIVE COMMITTEE OF GENERAL SYNOD
See GENERAL SYNOD EXECUTIVE COMMITTEE (GSEC).

EXECUTIVE COUNCIL OF GENERAL SYNOD
Provision for.
1958: 139, 256.
Concern over power.
1959: 107.
Provided for in Constitution.
1959: 143.
This decision to be deferred until the five-year program of the SC is completed.
1960: 119.
See GENERAL SYNOD EXECUTIVE COMMITTEE.

EXECUTIVE OFFICERS
Overture suggesting a Special Review Committee so that every five years there may be other ways to voice desires besides withholding funds.
1968: 102, 118–119, 123. Already built into reorganization structure. No action.

EXECUTIVE SECRETARIES
One to be appointed for each of the five Boards.
1958: 235.
Salaries of.
1962: 276–277. Special Study committee to be appointed.
Report of Special Committee.
1963: 296–299. Referred to GSEC.
Salary schedule.
1964: 165–166. Special Committee discharged.

Overture requesting publication in MGS of Executive salaries including benefits.
1970: 98, 110. Salary ranges sufficient. No action. See also SALARY ADMINISTRATION.
Motion requesting Executive Secretaries have privilege of the GS floor as the General Secretary does.
1971: 129. Referred to ECCG.
EC submits the following for approval of classes: "The General Secretary shall be a corresponding delegate of the GS with the privilege of the floor. The Chair may call upon other Executive Staff members to inform and assist the GS on matters under discussion."
1971: 209. Adopted.
Approved by classes.
1972: 120.
See also EXECUTIVE STAFF and GENERAL PROGRAM COUNCIL.

EXECUTIVE STAFF
Administrative policies re.
1970: 138-139.
1973: app. 2, 5-7.
See also STAFF—GENERAL SYNOD AND GENERAL PROGRAM COUNCIL

EXTENSION FOUNDATION
See REFORMED CHURCH IN AMERICA—EXTENSION FOUNDATION, INC.

FAIREY, JACK
Overture requesting dispensation from further study
1959: 52, 57. Granted.

FAITH AND ORDER
North American Conference, Oberlin, Ohio
1958: 165.

FAITH IN ACTION
A program for the discovery of human needs in one's own community.
1975: 59.

FAMILY FESTIVAL
At Estes Park, Summer of 1972.
1973: 63-64.

FARM WORKERS
Two recommendations concerning.
1975: 194. Adopted.
See also AGRICULTURAL AND MIGRANT WORKERS, and BOYCOTTS, ECONOMIC.

FAWTHROP, ARTHUR
Dispensation from professorial certificate requested. Examination at NBTS sustained.
1968: 41, 43. Granted.

FEDERAL AID TO PAROCHIAL AND PRIVATE SCHOOLS
Overture in opposition to.
1961: 131, 132-133, 142. Adopted.

FEDERATED CHURCHES
See UNION CHURCHES.

FEMINISM
"Feminism and the Church"—paper of the CAC
1974: 214-221.
BTE reports both seminaries are active in their efforts to avoid discrimination against women.
1975: 32.
Recommendations of CAC: a) to request church to reaffirm equality of men and women in Christ, b) request agencies of RCA to recognize that discrimination remains and there are points at which the church can change, c) request RCA develop immediate plans to correct (1) Christian Education materials with particular reference to biblical role models, sex stereotyping, (2) adequate representation on consistories, classes, synods, and GS, (3) seminary education including recruitment, field service and placement, (4) RCA Liturgy, examine for sexist bias in liturgy, including opportunity for women to actively participate in leadership of worship, (5) encouragement of lay groups and individuals to educate themselves, and encouragement of the clergy to present and interpret issues.
1974: 221. All Adopted.
See also WOMEN IN THE RCA; ORDINATION OF WOMEN: and MALENESS AND FEMALENESS.

FESTIVAL OF EVANGELISM
See EVANGELISM, FESTIVAL OF

FESTIVALS OF THE RCA
Festival of Evangelism—Detroit, April 1-4, 1970.
1970: 59.
1971: 66-67.
Mission Festival—Milwaukee, October 6-9, 1971.
1971: 67.
Family Festival—Estes Park, 1972.
1973: 63-64.
Jubilee/76—Slippery Rock, Pa., Aug. 13-16, 1976.
1975: 65.
1976: 120.

FIELD SECRETARIES
And Staff serving PS's.
1974: app. 2, 7.
1975: app. 2, 7.
1976: app. 1, 7.

Council of Field Secretaries Report; new opportunities available for ministry by clergymen: Market place ministries; Industrial missions; Tent-making or worker-priest ministries; Ministry in recreational setting.
1974: 137-141.

FINANCE, OFFICE OF
Report.
1974: 159-161.
1975: 144-146.
1976: 81-82.
1977: 89-91.
Responsibilities and functions.
1976: 54-56.
See also ADMINISTRATION AND FINANCE, OFFICE OF (earlier listing).

FINANCIAL REPORTS OF BOARDS AND AGENCIES
Overture regarding uniformity and content of.
1962: 117, 127. Referred to GSEC.
Reports. (Prior to 1969 all financial reports are a part of the annual report of the boards or agencies).
1969: app. 1. 1974: app. 1.
1970: app. 1. 1975: app. 1.
1971: app. 1. 1976: app. 1, 291-388.
1972: app. 1. 1977: app. 1, 299-392.
1973: app. 1.

FISCAL YEAR OF GENERAL SYNOD
1961: 16.

FITCHETT, GEORGE
Dispensation from the professorial certificate requested.
1973: 33, 37. Granted.

FLORIDA, CLASSIS OF
Formation of.
1976: 252.

FOREIGN EXCHANGE PREACHING COMMITTEE
Report.
1958: 223.
Committee discontinued; responsibilities referred to Stated Clerk.
1959: 387.

FOREIGN MISSIONS
See CHRISTIAN WORLD MISSION; WORLD MISSIONS, BOARD OF: and GPC.

FOREIGN POLICY, RCA ATTITUDE
Overture regarding.
1961: 131, 142. Referred to CAC.
CAC report on 1961 overture: a political issue, overture unnecessary.
1962: 221.

FORMULA
(Document signed by licensed candidates, ministers, and seminary professors.) Change in wording.
1958: 140.
Term FORMULA changed to DECLARATION, FORM OF, which also see.
1960: 120-121, 122.

FORMULARIES
See DECLARATION, FORM OF.

FOUNDATION PAPERS
See CLC.

FOURTH OFFICE
Item concerning "fourth office" is item "f" of several recommendations of TC concerning nature of the ministry. It is recommended that the term "fourth office" (term used for Professor of Theology) be discontinued and that the Professor of Theology be a special function of The Office of the Minister of the Word.
1969: 236. Referred to CRC. Report to be presented in 1970.
Report of COCG on item "f" concerning "Fourth Office." COCG approves use of "Professor of Theology" in its place.
1971: 204. Adopted and sent to classes for approval
None of the block of 8 recommendations approved by classes.
1972: 120.
Overture suggesting since GS voted there no longer be a "Fourth Office" that Professors of Theology become members of classis.
1972: 97. No action, since classes did not approve elimination of "Fourth Office."
TC submits recommendations identical with those of 1971 in separate amendments.
1973: 198. Item "f" on "Fourth Office" sent back to TC for further study; other items sent to classes for approval. See MINISTRY, NATURE OF.
Upon further study the TC recommends "Fourth Office" be retained.
1974: 201, 208-209. Adopted.

FRATERNAL AND INTERCHURCH RELATIONS
1958: 359. 1963: 143-144.
1959: 187. 1966: 171-172.
1962: 348-351.
Invitation to participate in conversations with the Christian Reformed Church.
1965: 137.
Invitation to participate in the proposed conversations with the UPCUSA, the

PCUS, the two Cumberland Presbyterian Churches and the Associate Reformed Church.
1965: 137. Referred to PCIR.
See also specific denominations.

FRATERNAL DELEGATES TO SYNOD
1958: 247, 308.
1959: 310.
1960: 290.
1961: 347.
1962: 359, 360.
1963: 279
1964: 180, 462.
1965: 423.
1966: 191, 382.
1967: 173–174, 332.
1968: 170, 364.
1969: 207–208.
1970: 131.
1971: 235. No delegates.
1973: 137, 233. No delegates.
1974: 129.
1975: 112.
1976: 16
1977: 16, 54, 371.

FRATERNAL RELATIONS WITH OTHER DENOMINATIONS, COMMITTEE ON
Report.
1958: 177–178. 1961: 192.
1959: 187. 1962: 185–186.
1960: 160–163. 1963: 200.
Committee discontinued.
1963: 200.

FREDERICKS, STEPHEN C.
Dispensation from the professorial certificate requested; Graduate of Princeton Theological Seminary. Constitutional requirements not met.
1967: 52, 55. No action.
Dispensation requested.
1977: 162. (Request withdrawn)

FREEDOM RESIDERS
See OPEN OCCUPANCY, COVENANT ON.

FRIES, REV. PAUL
Called to be Lector in Systematic Theology at NBTS
1968: 40.

FUGATE, LEONARD
Dispensation from professorial certificate requested. He has not taken the examination at an RCA seminary.

FUNDING, CONSULTATION ON
Suggestion of the President that a consultation of national and regional people be held to (1) assure financial support for national programs; (2) to preserve the traditional balance between assessment and benevolence; (3) to provide channels so that national as well as regional programs have equal hearing in the congregations and consistories of the church.
1972: 274, 279. Adopted with the provision that representatives from the Classis and PS level also attend.
See also STAFF CONSULTING GROUP.

FUNDS, DESIGNATED AND UNDESIGNATED
Recommended that GSEC clarify the individual consistories that each unit receives only designated funds and that undesignated funds will be used for national denominational services.
1972: 49.
Discussed at the Consultation on Funding.
1973: 119.

FUNERAL, CHRISTIAN CONCEPT OF
Report of CAC.
1965: 214–217, 220, 221. Adopted.

FURLOUGHING MISSIONARY CONFERENCE
1970: 64. New York City.
1971: 69. Detroit.
1975: 61. Zion, Illinois
1976: 129. Zion, Illinois
1977: 135–136. Slippery Rock, Pa.

GAMBLING
CAC requests that the local churches maintain strict opposition to all forms of gambling.
1966: 233, 236.
See also LOTTERIES.

GARCIA-RUBIO, ANTONIO WILLIAM
BTE recommends that dispensation from certain educational requirements and the professorial certificate be granted.
1975: 33, 34. Adopted.

GAVEL AND BELL
Presented to President of GS by Men's Brotherhood.
1958: 369. 1968: 371.
1959: 374. 1969: 350.
1960: 345. 1970: 271.
1961: 404. 1971: 291.
1962: 421. 1972: 298.
1963: 450. 1973: 293.
1964: 469. 1974: 301.
1965: 432. 1975: 270.
1966: 390. 1976: 258.
1967: 339. 1977: 326.

GENERAL PROGRAM COUNCIL
Establishment of (formerly BE, BWM, and BNAM, which also see)
1968: 141.

Divided into three major program areas: (1) World Ministries Division; (2) Division of Church Planning and Development; (3) Division of Church Life and Mission.
1969: 71-72.
Administrative Chart and names of staff.
1969: 71-75. See also STAFF—GENERAL PROGRAM COUNCIL.
Report.
1969: 71-105. 1975: 49-79.
1970: 57-67. 1976: 117-137.
1971: 58-73. 1977: 122-151.
1972: 50-66.
1973: 56-67.
1974: 57-69.
Overture requesting that the National Department of Women's Work be incorporated into the GPC.
1969: 129-130, 144, 152. A Committee from the NDWW, GPC and others to study and prepare a plan.
Committee reports that since women have no vote in consistories, classes, PS's, and GS, it is necessary for them to remain a separate department.
1969: 171.
Recommended that GS approve the merger of the BE, BNAM, and BWM and that the name be Program of General Synod, RCA, Inc. and that GS shall be the members of the corporation and the GSEC its directors.
1970: 133. Adopted.
At the November 1971 meeting GSEC approved the name "Trustees of the GPC of the RCA" as the legal name.
1972: 118-119. Approved.
Suggested that Youth be represented on GPC by 4 college students and 4 high school youth as additional members.
1972: 118. Not adopted.
One of each of the above suggested.
1972: 118. Approved.
Five years of service—a review.
1973: 56-58.
Proposed by-laws.
1973: 130-132. Adopted.
Additional representation from minority groups to be added to GPC.
1974: 121. Adopted.
Proposed amendment in membership of council.
1975: 49.
Amendment recommended.
1976: 48-49. Adopted.

GENERAL PROGRAM COUNCIL, STANDING COMMITTEE ON
Report.
1969: 93-105.
See GPC, REVIEW COMMITTEE ON.

GENERAL PROGRAM COUNCIL, REVIEW COMMITTEE ON
Report.
1970: 67-72. 1974: 69-75.
1971: 73-78. 1975: 64-68.
1972: 66-71. 1976: 132-137.
1973: 67-71. 1977: 143-151.

GENERAL SECRETARY
Formerly STATED CLERK, which also see.
1968: 168-174.
1969: 204-210.
After 1969 see reports of GSEC.
General Secretary to be a member of GS. Other executive staff members may be called upon for information.
1971: 209. Sent to classes for approval.
Above approved by classes.
1972: 120.
Search Committee formed to seek a successor to Dr. de Velder.
1976: 57-58.
Search Committee recommended that GSEC employ Rev. Arie R. Brouwer as General Secretary.
1977: 52-54. Approved.

GENERAL SYNOD
Budget.
1958: 27-29. 1968: 26-31.
1959: 25-27. 1969: 25-30.
1960: 23-25. 1970: 151-160.
1961: 28-30. 1971: 190-194.
1962: 26-28. 1972: 160-164.
1963: 26-28. 1973: 169-172.
1964: 22-25. 1974: 179-183.
1965: 22-25. 1975: 151-153.
1966: 23-26. 1976: 84-87.
1967: 25-29. 1977: 93-95.
Incorporation of GS. This information appears in each volume of MGS. Since it reads the same each year, page reference is given for only the last volume.
1977: App. 1, 8.
Benevolence Budget.
1970: 150.
1971: 184-189.
1972: 151-159.
Mission Budget.
1973: 162-168.
1974: 174-178.
1975: 148-150.
1976: 88-90.
1977: 96-98.
Places of Meetings.
1958: Buck Hill Falls, Pa.
1959: Buck Hill Falls, Pa.
1960: Buck Hill Falls, Pa.
1961: Buck Hill Falls, Pa.
1962: Buck Hill Falls, Pa.
1963: Central College, Pella, Ia.
1964: Buck Hill Falls, Pa.

1965: Buck Hill Falls, Pa.
1966: Hope College, Holland, Michigan
1967: King College, Bristol, Tennessee.
1968: University of Michigan, Ann Arbor, Mich.
1969: Douglas College, Rutgers University, New Brunswick, N.J.
1970: Hope College, Holland, Michigan.
1971: Northwestern College, Orange City, Ia.
1972: Siena College, Londonville, N.Y.
1973: Central College, Pella, Ia.
1974: Hofstra College, Hempstead, N.Y.
1975: Elmhurst College, Elmhurst, Ill.
1976: Fairleigh Dickinson University, Madison, N.J.
1977: Community Center, Sioux Center, Ia.

Recent Officers of.

1958: 370.	1968: App. 2, 2.
1959: 375.	1969: App. 2, 2.
1960: 346.	1970: App. 2, 2.
1961: 406.	1971: App. 2, 9.
1962: 422.	1972: App. 2, 9.
1963: 451.	1973: App. 2, 9.
1964: 470.	1974: App. 2, 9.
1965: 433.	1975: App. 2, 9.
1966: 391-392.	1976: App. 1, 9.
1967: App. 2, 2.	1977: App. 1, 9.

A complete list of presidents from 1794 can be found in 1956: 308-311.

Roll of (Delegates present).

1958: 2-6.	1969: 2-8.
1959: 2-6.	1970: 2-8.
1960: 2-6.	1971: 2-8.
1961: 2-5.	1972: 2-8.
1962: 2-5.	1973: 2-13.
1963: 2-6.	1974: 2-14.
1964: 2-6.	1975: 2-15.
1965: 2-7.	1976: 2-16.
1966: 2-7.	1977: 2-17.
1967: 2-7.	
1968: 2-8.	

Themes
1958: 255. "Thy Kingdom Come."
1959: 254. "My Heart I offer to Thee, Lord, promptly and sincerely."
1962: 377. "Come, Holy Spirit."
1967: 143.
1968-1969—"The Living God speaks in Judgment."
1969-1970—"The Living God speaks in Reconciliation."
1970-1971—"The Living God speaks in Mission."
1974: 271. "Reveal Christ Anew."
1974: 57, 59. 1975-1978—"A Heritage of Mission . . . A Mission of Hope."

Delegates to be appointed at Fall Classis Meetings.
1959: 242, 255-256, 257.

Overture requesting the 1959 action be rescinded.
1960: 111-112, 117, 1959 action rescinded.

Suggested that annual meeting be extended from 5 days to 6 days.
1959: 242, 255, 257. A committee appointed to study the problem.

Suggested that places of meetings be planned two years in advance.
1961: 339. Referred to CNPM.

Overtures regarding conflict of dates between Pentecost and Synod.
1960: 108-109, 116. Not approved.
1962: 116, 127. No action.
1965: 103, 116, 123. Referred to GSEC.

President suggests biennial meetings be established.
1967: 309, 312. Referred to GSEC for report next year.

The matter of biennial meetings will be considered along with the study of GS itself.
1968: 139.

Administrative Chart.
1969: 168.

Overture requesting meetings be held within the calendar week (Monday-Saturday) rather than over the weekend.
1969: 133-134, 147, 153. Next year's meetings are scheduled from Monday-Saturday. No action.

Motion that GSEC study feasibility of returning to 6-day schedule.
1969: 349. Adopted.

COCG's rearrangement of the Organization of GS in the *Government*.
1969: 216-226, 229-230. Adopted.

GSEC reports that change to biennial or triennial meetings is premature.
1970: 128-129. No action.

President approves biennial meetings.
1972: 276.

Overture suggesting biennial meetings of GS.
1972: 91-92. No action.

Matter to be studied.
1972: 279.

COR studied matter and recommends no action.
1975: 133. No action.

Suggested RCA return to 6-day synods.
1970: 128. No action.

The study made of GS divides work into three parts: (1) corporate structure of GS; (2) functions and structures of permanent committees and commissions and their interrleationships with other agencies of GS; (3) meeting of GS.
1970: 134-135. GSEC invites reactions.

Amendment setting forth the Order of Business.
1973: 179. Adopted.
Overture requesting a three-payment plan for meeting the assessment: 1/3 March 31, 1/3 June 30, and 1/3 September 10.
1975: 82. Adopted.
RCHE recommends that high priority be given to convening GS meetings at the three RCA colleges on a rotational basis whenever the meeting is held in the midwest.
1975: 48. Adopted.
GSEC reports they have received the recommendation of the RCHE for information and will give consideration to it in planning future synods.
1976: 37.
Overture requesting that GS meet on the campuses of our colleges and seminaries.
1976: 100-101. No action.
Voted to refer the matter to meet biennially to GSEC and report back to 1978 synod.
1977: 325.

GENERAL SYNOD EXECUTIVE COMMITTEE
Overture requesting a denominational executive committee.
1958: 130. Being considered by CRC.
Report.
1962: 345-352. 1970: 125-187.
1963: 140-151. 1971: 128-152.
1964: 160-172. 1972: 112-196.
1965: 133-140. 1973: 118-138.
1966: 162-188. 1974: 114-202.
1967: 139-171. 1975: 95-118.
1968: 131-167. 1976: 35-90.
1969: 158-204. 1977: 37-98.
Membership and duties outlined.
1964: 169-172. 175-177.
Overture requesting representation on GSEC from each geographical area.
1964: 116-117, 139, 149. No action.
Overture requesting that membership on GSEC be adjusted so that there is a more reasonable representation from the large geographical areas of Iowa Synod.
1965: 103, 116, 123. No action. Membership on the basis of communicant membership is fair.
President requests that the retiring President of GS become the President of GSEC for the coming year.
1966: 340, 353, 355. Adopted and referred to CRC.
The above suggestion to be added to the Rules of Order.
1967: 183, 185, 186. Approved.
Responsibilities of.
1967: 139-140.
Joint statement on relationship of GSEC to SC.
1966: 165.
Changes in organization—membership, responsibilities, etc.
1970: 142-143.
After a suggestion of "at large" members being included in GSEC membership, it was voted that there be "three lay persons as corresponding delegates, at least one of whom shall be a woman."
1971: 277. Approved. Will be voted on again next year to make it part of the By Laws.
The above motion no longer necessary since women may now be members of consistory, and hence will be eligible for membership on GSEC.
1972: 120-121.
Role and function of GSEC.
1974: 125-127.
BC recommends GSEC continue conversations with BC leading to BC representation on GSEC.
1975: 71.
Organizational developments.
1975: 108-109.
GSEC took action to dissolve present Role and Function Committee and that a new Role and Function Committee be established to make recommendations for changes they may determine.
1976: 50.

GENESIS, HISTORICITY OF
Overture requesting that GS make a positive statement on the Historicity of Genesis.
1959: 122, 128. Referred to TC.
TC report.
1960: 325-327.
Overtures in opposition to report.
1961: 138-140, 142. No action.
See also ADAM, HISTORICITY OF.

GERE, FRED
Dispensation from professorial certificate requested.
1958: 58. Denied. He is not a graduate of one of our seminaries, is working with Campus Crusade, and does not intend to pastor a church.

GNADE, REV. GERARD
Recognition on retirement after 23 years as Secretary of the BP.
1967: 100, 101, 333-334.

GOOD NEWS PEOPLE
A program of evangelism developed by the two Evangelism Secretaries as a prime means of renewal and growth in the local church. Commended.

1976: 118, 132.
A successful program
1977: 124.

GOSPEL AND THE PHYSICAL NEEDS OF MAN
Requested that the TC prepare a statement.
1966: 387.
TC presents paper "The Evangelistic and Social Task of the Church."
1967: 196–199.

GOVERNMENT, THE DISCIPLINARY PROCEDURES AND THE RULES OF ORDER OF THE GENERAL SYNOD.
Overture requesting this document be published in loose leaf notebook form—free of charge to each minister, and that changes be sent out each year.
1969: 129, 144, 152. The loose leaf changes are being considered, but the Committee feels they should not be free of charge. No action.
Overture requesting an index in subsequent issues.
1969: 128, 144, 152. Being worked on. No action.

GRADUATE FELLOWSHIPS
Recommended by President.
1963: 373, 435. Referred to newly created CHE of the BE.
1964: 57. Study to continue.

GRADUATES OF OTHER SEMINARIES
Examination of.
1958: 140.

GRANBERG, LARS I.
Elected President of Northwestern College.
1967: 70.
Resigned as President of Northwestern College after 9 years.
1975: 44.
Commendation.
1975: 48, 266.

GRAPE STRIKE AND BOYCOTT OF GRAPES
See BOYCOTTS, ECONOMIC.

GREEK LANGUAGE, REQUIREMENT OF IN SEMINARY STUDY
See ORIGINAL LANGUAGES.

GREEN, MISS KATHERINE ROGERS, MISSIONARY TO CHINA FOR 40 YEARS
Obituary.
1963: Annual report of the BWM, App., 55.

GREEN, WILLIAM P., JR.
Dispensation from professorial certificate requested.
1958: 56. Granted since he fulfilled the requirements placed upon him last year.

GROWTH, DENOMINATIONAL, JOINT TASK FORCE ON
Findings developed into a plan for RCA growth.
1976: 125.
See also CHURCH GROWTH and CHURCH GROWTH FUND.

GUILD FOR CHRISTIAN SERVICE
1958: 335, 336–337.
1959: 348.
President suggests a standing committee to study work of.
1963: 375, 436–437, 439. To be referred to Dept. of Adult Work.
See also NDWW and RCW.

GUN CONTROL LEGISLATION
CAC recommends that the RCA request Congress to require federal registration or licensing of all fire arms.
1969: 242–243, 248. Adopted.
Overture requesting the CAC to re-open its study on.
1976: 113. Adopted.
CAC recommends (1) action of 1969 be reiterated; (2) that the RCA request Congress to ban manufacture and sale of handguns for civilian ownership; (3) that members of the RCA be urged to render handguns in their homes inoperable; (4) to urge consituency of the RCA to seek refinement and strict enforcement of present laws.
1977: 200–201. Adopted.

HAGEMAN, REV. HOWARD G.
Elected Vice President of GS.
1958: 8.
Elected President of GS.
1959: 6.
Elected President of NBTS.
1974: 28.

HAKKEN, MRS. BERNARD, SR. (ELDA), MISSIONARY TO THE MIDDLE EAST, 1922–1961.
Death.
1971: 72.

HANDICAPPED, RIGHTS OF
CAC recommends ways in which the churches can minister to the handicapped.
1975: 200. Adopted.

HARRISON, J. ROBERT
Elected Treasurer of the BWM.

1961: 98.
Resolution for 11½ years of work with boards and agencies.
1970: 269.

HARRISON, DR. PAUL WILBERFORCE, MEDICAL MISSIONARY IN THE ARABIAN MISSION FOR 45 YEARS
Obituary.
1963: Annual Report of the BWM, App. 55-56.

HART, DR. LOUISA H., MISSIONARY TO INDIA, 1895-1939
Obituary.
1958: Annual Report of the BCWM, App., 33.

HEBREW LANGUAGE, REQUIREMENT OF IN SEMINARY STUDY
See ORIGINAL LANGUAGES.

HEIDELBERG CATECHISM
400th Anniversary Congress suggested for 1963.
1960: 231-232, 236-237. Referred to the Committee on the Alliance of Reformed and Presbyterian Churches.
New translation and new commentary being prepared.
1962: 399.
New Commentary published, *Guilt, Grace, and Gratitude,* edited by Donald J. Bruggink.
1963: 263-264.
1964: 211, 212.
New translation by Allen O. Miller and M. Eugene Osterhaven.
1963: 268. Adopted as official translation for the RCA.
President suggests courses in the Catechism in our colleges and seminaries.
1963: 378, 437, 439. Referred to the presidents of the schools.
NBTS reports that the Standards form the basis foundation for the work in Systematic Theology.
1964: 34.
Overture requesting Q. 98 be made a footnote since it might be construed to mean that visual aids are not permitted.
1972: 99. No action, since the catechism is an historical document speaking to a particular point in time.
Overture requesting a study of Q. 80 concerning the difference between Communion and the Popish Mass.
1972: 87-88. No action. To be referred to TC.
Motion made that the three overtures suggesting deleting of certain questions and articles be turned over to TC.
1972: 100. Adopted.
TC recommends no revision in this historic document. It is desirable to maintain the integrity of these standards as historical witnesses to biblical faith. In light of this, a new confession becomes important.
1973: 194.

HEIDEMAN, REV. EUGENE P.
Working on a new confession—*Our Song of Hope.*
1971: 130, 268.
1972: 279.
Appointed Associate Professor of Theology and Director of Professional Development at WTS.
1976: 143.

HENDERSHOT, RAYMOND
Dispensation from Hebrew Language requested.
1969: 40, 44. Granted.

HENDRICKS, THOMAS
Dispensation from professorial certificate requested.
1976: 146, 148. Granted.

HENKEL, WILLIAM
Dispensation from professorial certificate requested.
1971: 31, 36. Granted.

HERITAGE AND HORIZON
Historical play written by Lois Joyce, presented at Synod 1976, and 18 centers of RCA membership during the year.
1977: 88, 123.

HERITAGE AND HOPE
GPC commends series for use by congregations as an excellent supplement with other Christian Education materials.
1976: 136. Adopted.

HERWALT, FRED
Dispensation from professorial certificate requested.
1973: 33, 36. Granted.

HESSELINK, REV. IRA JOHN, JR.
Elected President of WTS.
1974: 28.

HEUSINKVELD, DR. MAURICE M., MEDICAL MISSIONARY IN THE ARAB WORLD FOR 21 YEARS
Obituary.
1968: Annual Report of the BWM, App., 41.

HIGHER EDUCATION
Report.
1965: 56-66.
1966: 57-80.
1967: 62-73.
1968: 48-59.
1969: 45-61.
1970: 37-56.

1971: 39-55. 1975: 37-45.
1972: 34-48. 1976: 152-160.
1973: 39-53. 1977: 174-181.
1974: 41-55.

HIGHER EDUCATION, PERMANENT COMMITTEE ON
Permanent committee recommended.
1970: 55. Adopted and referred to COCG.
COCG reports that reasons were not given with recommendation, therefore if Synod wishes to establish such a committee, request and reasons (purposes) and scope of responsibility should be submitted to COCG.
1971: 199.

HIGHER EDUCATION, STANDING COMMITTEE ON
Committee to be constituted.
1964: 64.
Report.
1965: 67-71. 1968: 59-63.
1966: 81-85. 1969: 61-64.
1967: 74-78.
Recommended that a Committee of the Division of Higher Education and representatives from the colleges draw up a Covenant of Mutual Responsibilities between the churches and the colleges.
1966: 83.
Committee submitted document.
1967: 76, 78. Returned for refinement.
At the request of the BE, GSEC appointed an Ad Hoc committee to prepare a statement on the RCA philosophy of Higher Education.
1968: 61, 62.
Report of special committee: "The Church and Its Colleges (A Preamble) and the Covenant of Mutual Responsibilities."
1969: 64-70. See also CHURCH AND ITS COLLEGES.
Further reports under HIGHER EDUCATION, REVIEW COMMITTEE ON.

HIGHER EDUCATION, REVIEW COMMITTEE ON
Report.
1970: 51-56. 1974: 55-56.
1971: 55-57. 1975: 46-48.
1972: 48-49. 1976: 161-164.
1973: 53-55. 1977: 182.

HIGHWAY SAFETY
Overture requesting CAC to make a study and devise a program for greater highway safety.
1970: 96, 109. No action. CAC does not have the expertise.

HIRAM STREET PROJECT
Project for off-campus housing for seminary students in the inner city of New Brunswick.
1969: 42.
Tension building at the site. Residents in the area oppose housing for seminary students in the ghetto area. Construction delayed.
1970: 35.
A series of difficult problems have plagued the project, including arson. BTE voted to authorize sale of property.
1971: 28.

HISPANIC COUNCIL
Council organized.
1974: 122.
Report.
1974: 87-88. 1976: 172-174.
1975: 75-77. 1977: 188-190.
Secretary visited Hispanic congregations in Grand Rapids and Denver, and traveled to Artesia, California with the hope of developing an Hispanic Congregation there.
1977: 188.
Three Hispanic students at NBTS and one at WTS.
1977: 189.

HISTORICAL CELEBRATIONS
Recommended that the GPC plan for the 200th anniversary of our nation (1976) and the 350th anniversary of our RCA (1978).
1974: 73. Adopted.
See HERITAGE AND HORIZON.

HISTORICAL DIRECTORY OF THE RCA
Need expressed for a new edition of Corwin's *Manual*.
1958: 411.
1963: 335-336.
1964: 342.
Will be called "Historical Directory of the RCA, 1628-1965."
1965: 284-285.
Edited by Rev. Peter N. Vanden Berge, and published.
1967: 279.
1520 copies sold as of April 1, 1968.
1968: 307.
Cost of directory.
1965: 284-285.
Hope for an updated edition by 1978.
1972: 267.
1973: 269.
To be edited by Rev. Peter N. Vanden Berge.
1976: 197.
Will represent a fitting tribute for the RCA's three and a half century sojourn on this continent.
1977: 238.
See also CORWIN'S MANUAL.

HISTORICAL LIBRARY AND MUSEUM
Motion that GSEC take definite steps for arranging for such a building.
1969: 313. Approved.
GSEC and Commission on History together have decided that because of many financial pressures no action should be taken at this time. A full time archivist is the first need.
1970: 128, 250.

HISTORICAL SERIES OF THE RCA
No. 1, *Ecumenism and the Reformed Church,* by Rev. Herman Harmelink III. (1968)
1969: 311.
No. 2, *The Americanization of a Congregation; A History of the Third Reformed Church of Holland, Michigan,* by Elton J. Bruins. (1970)
1970: 249.
No. 3, *Pioneers in an Arab World,* by Dorothy Van Ess. (1974)
1974: 266.
No. 4, *Piety and Patriotism: Bicentennial Studies of the Reformed Church in America,* ed. by James W. Van Hoeven. (1976)
1975: 237.
Other volumes in preparation are: a book on the events leading up to the secession of 1834 in the Netherlands, by Gerrit ten Zythoff; A book on Reformed Liturgy by Dr. Howard Hageman; and a book on the Reformed Church in the Colonial Era by Dr. Gerald De Young; also, a new edition of *The Historical Directory,* and An Index to Synodical Legislation, 1958–1977.
1975: 237–238.
1976: 197.
1977: 237–238.
(Note: Due to circumstances beyond the control of the Commission on History, the volumes in the series were not published in the order indicated in MGS. The volume numbers and the dates listed above are correct. M.S.)

HISTORY AND RESEARCH COMMITTEE
Report.
1958: 222.
The Committee was discontinued and an Advisory Committee appointed to work with the Stated Clerk.
1959: 387.
See next listing.

HISTORY AND RESEARCH, ADVISORY COMMITTEE ON
Report.
1960: 335–336. 1962: 410–412.
1961: 394–396.
See next listing.

HISTORY AND RESEARCH, PERMANENT COMMITTEE ON
Report.
1963: 334–336. 1965: 284–287.
1964: 341–344. 1966: 313–316.
Recommendation that the present Committee on History and Research be reorganized into a permanent Commission on History.
1966: 315, 316. Adopted.
Commission on History to be constituted immediately.
1966: 204. Adopted.
Responsibilities and membership.
1966: 315, 204.
See next listing.

HISTORY, COMMISSION ON
Report.
1967: 279–281. 1973: 269–270.
1968: 306–309. 1974: 266–268.
1969: 310–313. 1975: 237–238.
1970: 248–250. 1976: 196–198.
1971: 262–263. 1977: 237–242.
1972: 267–268.
Change in organization—membership, responsibilities, etc.
1970: 145.
Previously known as HISTORY AND RESEARCH COMMITTEE: HISTORY AND RESEARCH, ADVISORY COMMITTEE ON: and HISTORY AND RESEARCH, PERMANENT COMMITTEE ON, which also see.

HOEKSTRA, REV. HARVEY T.
Elected Vice President of GS.
1977: 18.

HOFFMAN, REV. JAMES E.
Retirement from the position of Stated Clerk after 19 years.
1960: 220.
1961: 341.
Resolution for.
1961: 401.

HOLKEBOER, TENA, MISSIONARY TO CHINA AND THE PHILIPPINES, 1920–1961.
Obituary.
1966: Annual Report BWM, App., 13–14.

HOLLEMAN, RUTH VANDEN BERG, MISSIONARY TO CHINA, 1919–1950.
Obituary.
1966: Annual Report BWM, App., 14.

HOLOCAUST DAY
Voted to instruct the CAC to report back to 1978 GS on the meaning and possible participation of our churches in that day.
1977: 204. Adopted.

HOLY SPIRIT, FULLNESS OF
See BAPTISM (HOLY SPIRIT).

HOME FOR RETIRED MINISTERS AND OTHERS
Overture requesting a study be made on the possibility of such a home in the west Michigan area.
1968: 103, 119, 124. Referred back to the judicatories making overtures. (Classis of Holland and PS of Michigan.)

HOMOSEXULAITY, THE CHURCH AND
CAC makes two recommendations: a) that we affirm the biblical teaching against the practice of homosexuality and the study of homosexuality as it relates to the life of the church; and b) to provide the compassionate acceptance of such persons within the life and mission of the church.
1974: 221-222. a, adopted; b, deleted.
CAC recommends that the RCA go on record to uphold the right of all persons including homosexuals to full civil rights and equality under the law; that no person shall be discriminated against in jobs, schools, housing or any other employment or opportunity because of sexual orientation.
1976: 192-195. Tabled. Voted to instruct the CAC to suggest guidelines on methods for the church—local and corporate—to make a responsive attack on the devastating effect of pornography on our present culture.
Motion made and supported that the 1977 GS go on record affirming the human and civil rights of homosexuals and lesbians.
1977: 204-205. In response it was voted to refer the above motion to the TC for study and recommendation.

HONDELINK, MRS. GRACE HOEKJE, MISSIONARY TO JAPAN, 1903-1908.
Obituary.
1962: Annual Report of the BWM, App., 49.

HONEGGER, LA VINA DE MOND, MISSIONARY TO INDIA, 1910-1951.
Obituary.
1966: Annual Report of the BWM, App., 15.

HOPE COLLEGE
Report
1958: 65-67.
1959: 58-60.
1960: 61-62.
1961: 75-78.
1962: 66-67.
1963: 67-69.
1964: 69-72.
1965: 58-60.
1966: 71-74.
1967: 66-69.
1968: 52-57.
1969: 52-57.
1970: 42-46.
1971: 42-45.
1972: 37-39.
1973: 43-45.
1974: 45-47.
1975: 41-43.
1976: 155-157.
1977: 177-178.
Balance of property owned by GS turned over by deed to the Board of Trustees of Hope College.
1967: 22.
Reorganization of the Board of Trustees; reduction of size from 56 to 25 members, 16 of whom must be RCA members.
1968: 144.
Articles of Incorporation.
1968: 157-158.
Amendments in Articles of Incorporation
1972: 166-167.

HOSTETTER, MRS. WINIFRED JEAN, MISSIONARY TO THE SUDAN, 1955-1958; PAKISTAN, 1960-1965.
Obituary.
1968: Annual Report of the BWM, App. 1, 42-43.

HOTLINE
Bi-weekly newsletter began publication Jan. 12, 1972 with a mailing list of 3,000.
1972: 134.
Mailing list 12,000, and distribution commended.
1973: 70, 160.
News received from across the denomination.
1974: 155-156.
Printing and mailing operations moved to Grand Rapids.
1976: 80.
New look and larger readership.
1977: 88.

HOTLINE OF THE AIR
A 15 minute radio program in the Mid-West and East.
1975: 141.
1976: 80.
1977: 89.

HOUSE UN-AMERICAN ACTIVITIES COMMITTEE
Overture regarding.
1961: 132, 142. Referred to CAC.

HOUSING, DISCRIMINATION IN
Overture regarding opposition to discrimination.
1960: 110-111, 117. Adopted.

HUGGINS, DR. GEORGE A.
Recognized for work with the Contributory Annuity Fund.
1960: 104.

HUMAN RESOURCES, OFFICE OF
Office established.
1969: 183-185.
Report.
1970: 162-163.
1971: 154-156.
1972: 122-123.
1973: 155-157.

1974: 161-162. 1976: 82-83.
1975: 146-147. 1977: 91-92.
Coordinator named.
1970: 162.
Functions of Missionary Personnel Office transferred to OHR.
1970: 162.
Profile system for ministers, and churches seeking ministers.
1971: 154.
Review Committee proposed.
1972: 129, 195. Adopted.

HUMAN RIGHTS
CAC recommends ratification of the following: abolition of forced labor, abolition of slavery, and political rights of women; that this be communicated to appropriate bodies and officials of government.
1968: 217, 220. Adopted.

HUNGARIAN REFORMED CHURCH RELIEF
Overture requesting efforts be made through the State Department and WCC to give aid to the earthquake ravaged Hungarian churches in Rumania.
1977: 120. Adopted and sent to GSEC for implementation.

HUNGER
See WORLD HUNGER; BREAD FOR THE WORLD; and CHURCH WORLD SERVICE.

HUNT, MIRIAM
Recognition of retirement as a secretary after 28 years of service.
1974: 130-131.

HURKS, ELDRIDGE
Request for dispensation from professorial certificate. Elder Hurks has been a lay minister of his congregation for 16 years.
1977: 169. Referred to BTE for study and action.

HYMNBOOK, THE
Commended to all RCA churches.
1962: 75, 78. In 5th printing.
Over 1,000,000 copies now in use.
1963: 58.

HYMNAL, SUPPLEMENTAL
Overture requesting a new (loose leaf) hymnbook for usage in the RCA; a book needs contemporary songs, arrangements for many instruments, etc.
1973: 96-97. No action, since such hymnbooks are available such as *Worshipbook and Hymns* (Presbyterian).
Overture requesting Committee on Worship to prepare a supplementary loose-leaf hymn booklet and to collect liturgical aids to worship.
1976: 110. Referred to Worship Committee for study and possible implementation.

INACTIVE MEMBERS
Overture requesting that the Constitution read "a person who ceased to use the means of grace . . . for a period of two years shall be placed on the inactive list" and "if after an additional two years such a person shows no willingness, after further admonition . . . his name should then be removed from the roll of membership. . . ."
1961: 128, 142. Referred to CRC.
Similar overture, making mention of those unable to attend services.
1962: 116, 127. Referred to CRC.
Report of CRC presents amendment similar to above, and urges Elders to work diligently with such members.
1963: 126-127, 135. Approved.
Overture suggesting that inactive members be omitted from total number of communicants.
1963: 106, 111. No action.
Overture presenting amendment to change wording of statement. CRC provided a statement which was adopted.
1966 115, 116, 138-139, 149. Sent to classes for approval.
Classes approved above amendment.
1965: 141.
Overture requesting amendment using the words "may be removed" instead of "shall be removed"—action taken in place of the overture which requested no one be dropped from membership.
1967: 110-111, 124, 127. Adopted and sent to classes for approval.
Above amendment approved by classes.
1968: 169.
Overture asking that the word "one" replace "two" in each case.
1968: 95, 117, 123. No action.
Overture by a classis that did not approve "may," suggesting the word "shall" remain, and words "except under extenuating circumstances" be added.
1968: 95, 117, 123. Referred to CRC.
Overture requesting GS amend the BCO to substitute the word "one" for "two" regarding inactive membership.
1973: 108-109, 183-184. Adopted and referred to classes for approval.
Approved by classes.
1974: 119.
Overture requesting amendment in BCO adding words "non-communicant member" after the words "communicant member."
1973: 106-107. No action.
Overture requesting a clarification of the

terms "communicant" and "non communicant" regarding removal of names from membership rolls.
1975: 85-86. No action.

INDEX OF SYNODICAL LEGISLATION
See DIGEST OF SYNODICAL LEGISLATION.

INDIA
Recommended Arcot Seminary Fund be transferred to Church of South India for an endowment fund for theological education.
1972: 20-21. Adopted.
1974: 64.
Gratitude expressed to the Church of South India for sending Bishop Sundar Clarke to GS.
1977: 144.

INDIAN CAUCUS
1971: 65.
See also AMERICAN INDIAN COUNCIL.

INDIAN (AMERICAN) COUNCIL
See AMERICAN INDIAN COUNCIL.

INFANT BAPTISM
See BAPTISM, INFANT.

INNER CITY WORK
1958: 96. 1962: 91.
1959: 105-106. 1964: 95-96.
1960: 90. 1965: 82.
Church Planning and Development grants to PS's for distribution.
1970: 61.
See also URBAN MINISTRIES.

INSPIRATION OF SCRIPTURE
See SCRIPTURE, INSPIRATION OF.

INSTALLATION
Overture requesting clarification of word "install" in BCO.
1976: 111-112. Adopted.
COCG reports that to be "installed" requires a formal liturgical service.
1977: 316. Adopted.

INSTITUTIONAL CHAPLAINS
See CHAPLAINS, INSTITUTIONAL.

INSURANCE
President suggests Office of Administration and Finance study feasibility of a denominational program of insurance for our churches.
1969: 330, 331. Adopted.
GSEC reports that an insurance plan will be postponed for the present time.
1971: 140.
Overture requesting an annual policy of competitive bidding by various insurance companies.
1976: 106. No action.

INTENTION TO APPEAL
See APPEALS AND COMPLAINTS.

INTERCHURCH CENTER—475 RIVERSIDE DR., NEW YORK.
Investment in.
1959: 19-20. Denominational headquarters moved to the 18th floor at a rate of $7,435.75 per month, or $4.46 per sq. ft. per year.
1960: 17.
1961: 18-19 (Rent $89,299 for 1960).
Symbol of cooperation.
1960: 142-143.

INTERCHURCH RELATIONS
Each classis and PS to establish a committee on.
1965: 232-233.

INTERCHURCH RELATIONS, PERMANENT COMMITTEE ON
Duties.
1964: 174-175.
Report.
1965: 226-234. 1971: 231-251.
1966: 237-306. 1972: 229-259.
1967: 216-272. 1973: 256-263.
1968: 222-268. 1974: 227-257.
1969: 254-289. 1975: 203-209.
1970: 223-239.
Recommended that the by laws and Rules of Order be amended to provide for the Committee to become a Commission.
1974: 201-202.
Amendment on membership and responsibilities.
1974: 201-202. Adopted.
The Committee to become a Commission with following changes: ABS, WHBL, LSA, RIAL be placed in the portfolio of GPC, and that IRC assume a more interpretive role in relaying to the churches the importance of NCC & WCC.
1975: 203-206. Referred to GSEC for report.
GSEC reports approval of IRC's recommendation. After much study they suggest the name of the Committee (Commission) be changed to the Committee on Christian Unity.
1975: 100-101. Adopted.
See CHRISTIAN UNITY, COMMITTEE ON.

INTERCHURCH RELATIONS, STANDING COMMITTEE ON
New Committee constituted.
1963: 139.
Duties.
1964: 175.
Revision of the 1963 Rules of Order.
1965: 143-144.

Report.
1964: 233-240. 1967: 258-263.
1965: 235-264. 1968: 268-272.
1966: 291-297. 1969: 289-295.
Changed to REVIEW COMMITTEE—next listing.

INTERCHURCH RELATIONS, REVIEW COMMITTEE ON
Report.
1970: 240-243. 1973: 256-263.
1971: 252-255. 1974: 252-255.
1972: 255-259. 1975: 230-232.
Recommendation that the Committee make a self-study re-evaluating the functions and purpose of the Committee and its relations to GPC and GSEC.
1974: 253. Adopted.
Recommended that the ABS, WHBL, LDA, and RIAL be taken from the aegis of the IRC and be placed in the portfolio of the GPC.
1974: 254. Adopted.
Becomes, CHRISTIAN UNITY, COMMITTEE ON, REVIEW COMMITTEE ON, which see.

INTERN PROGRAM IN THE SEMINARIES
See INTERNSHIP, A PART OF SEMINARY TRAINING.

INTERNATIONAL AFFAIRS COMMITTEE
Report.
1958: 157-162.
1959: 165-168.
Merged with CAC
1959: 29, 168.
See also CHRISTIAN ACTION COMMISSION

INTERNATIONAL MISSIONARY CONFERENCE
Integrated with WORLD COUNCIL OF CHURCHES
1961: 167.

INTERNSHIP A PART OF SEMINARY TRAINING
Faculties to continue study on.
1958: 351.
To be established on a trial basis.
1959: 356.
Progressing well in both seminaries.
1962: 54.

INTERSEMINARY CONFERENCE—TRIENNIAL
Oberlin, Ohio.
1958: 166.

IOWA, PARTICULAR SYNOD OF
Overture requesting name be changed to PS of the West.
1965: 115, 119, 123. Approved.

JAMES, REV. M. STEPHEN
Retirement from the Presidency of NBTS, resolution for.
1959: 34-35, 38, 54, 371.

JAMISON, REV. WALLACE N.
Appointed Dean of NBTS.
1961: 34.
Elected President of NBTS.
1963: 35, 52.
Resignation from Office of Professor of Theology and President of NBTS. Resolution for.
1970: 34.

JEWS, SUPPRESSION OF IN SOVIET UNION
Overture to petition WCC to speak out on the subject.
1964: 133, 140-141, 151. No action.

JOINT COMMITTEE OF TWENTY-FOUR
(12 representatives each, from the RCA and the PCUS) Report.
1963: 201-209.
1964: 310-323.
1965: 275-277, and 19 page insert.
1966: 297-300.
1967: 267-271.
1968: 273-276, 277-282.
1969: 302-303.
Document approved by the JC24 titled *The Witness of the Reformed Churches,* covering: (1) The Soverignty of God; (2) The Authority of Scripture; (3) Obedience to the Will of God.
1964: 311-316.
(1) Comparison of government and organization in RCA and PCUS; (2) comparison of the permanent agencies; (3) Examination of certain practices. *Plan of Union* in preparation.
1965: 277 and 19 p. insert preceding.
Plan of Union will be prepared after maximum consultation with members of both churches.
1966: 297.
Suggested changes in *Plan of Union.*
1968: 279-280.
Committee dismissed by both denominations.
1969: 303.
See also COMMITTEE OF TWELVE.

JOINT EDUCATIONAL DEVELOPMENT
To provide a cooperative program in joint educational ministries and to make a more creative use of total resources of participating churches; ways of doing things together rather than new organizational structures.
1971: 63. 1976: 120.
1974: 63, 71. 1977: 253.

JOLDERSMA, RUTH
Elected Executive Secretary of the BCWM.
1959: 84, 95, 101, 103.
Resigned.
1968: 71.

JONES, LESTER
Dispensation requested from professorial certificate. Seminary examination not satisfactory.
1971: 31. Denied.

JONES, WALTER
Recommended that he be granted a dispensation from the professorial certificate.
1974: 37, 38. Adopted.

JONGEWAARD, CORNELIA, MISSIONARY TO INDIA, 1925-1965.
Death.
1977: 137.

JUBILEE/'76
Scheduled for Aug. 13-16, 1976 in Slippery Rock, Pa.
Enthusiastic support recommended by RCGPC.
1975: 65. Adopted.
1976: 120.

JUDICATORIES, REGIONAL
See LOCAL AND REGIONAL JUDICATORIES.

JUDICIAL BUSINESS COMMITTEE OF PARTICULAR SYNOD
Overture requesting each PS constitute its Judicial Committee according to its needs.
1965: 111, 117-118, 123. No action.

JUDICIAL BUSINESS, PERMANENT COMMITTEE ON
Report.
1958: 138. 1968: 128-130.
1959: 130-142. 1969: 157.
1960: 118. 1970: 116-120.
1961: 144-148. 1971: 120-127.
1962: 131-136. 1972: 109-111.
1963: 118-125. 1973: 117 (no report).
1964: 157-159. 1974: 112-113.
1965: 130-132. 1975: 94 (no report).
1966: 155-161. 1976: No report.
1967: 132-138. 1977: No report.
Change in organization and membership, responsibilities, etc.
1970: 146.

KAISER, DR. CHRISTOPHER
Appointed Assistant Professor of Theology at WTS.
1977: 165.
Dispensation from professorial certificate requested.
1977: 168-169. Not granted. (Request prepared May 27, 1977.)

KAMPHUIS, ANDREW
Dispensation from academic requirements and professorial certificate requested.
1970: 33. No reason given for candidate not meeting requirements. Successful ministry being carried on without ordination. Denied.
Subsequent recommendation was adopted, granting dispensation.
1970: 31.

KANSFIELD, REV. NORMAN
Becomes Assistant Librarian at WTS.
1970: 29.
Named Librarian at WTS.
1974: 29.

KAO, REV. AND MRS. C. M.
Honored by Synod for their work with the Presbyterian Church of Taiwan.
1976: 135.

KARSTEN, ESTELLA
Retired after 17 years as accountant at WTS.
1977: 159.

KELLIEN, MISS CHARLOTTE, MISSIONARY TO THE MIDDLE EAST
Death.
1975: 64.

KEMPTON, KENNETH
Dispensation from professorial certificate requested again after study.
1958: 56-57. Granted.

KENTUCKY
GPC to study and evaluate the work of the RCA in Jackson County.
1969: 95-96. Adopted.

KENNEDY, SENATOR ROBERT
Resolution on the death of.
1968: 369.

KESSLER, MARTIN
Requests final year of study at Union Theological Seminary.
1958: 58-59. No action.

KEY '73
A nation-wide, denomination-wide program of evangelism.
1972: 53.
RCA participation is wide-spread.
1973: 60.
1974: 61-62.

KINDERHOOK (N.Y.) CHURCH
Entrusting endowment funds in care of GS.
1958: 18.

KING, MARTIN LUTHER, JR.
Motion: "Join hands and hearts with all concerned people of God who continue to

work and pray that righteousness and justice may truly exalt our nation (and that the GS further urge the Congress and President of these U.S. to proclaim the birthday of Dr. Martin Luther King, Jr., January 15th of each year, a national holiday in order to better commemorate the work of justice and equality for which Dr. King was martyred)."
1970: 221-222. Defeated.
CAC again recommends the above motion.
1971: 225-226. Portion in parenthesis deleted; first part approved.

KIRKSIDE, INC
A denominational home for aging ministers, their wives, missionaries and other leaders and lay people of our Church.
1958: Annual Report, App., bound in with GSM.
Report.
1958-1962: App. bound in with MGS.
1963-1968: App. 1.
1969: 114-115.
1970: 73-74.
1971: 81-82.
1972: 124-125, 130-131.
1973: 176-177.
1974: 187-188.
1975: 157-158.
1976: 141.
1977: 155-157.
Other references.
1958: 124, 126, 234. 1964: 102.
1959: 118. 1965: 94.
1960: 103. 1966: 108.
1961: 125, 127. 1967: 98-101.
1962: 114. 1968: 83.
1963: 102. 1969: 111.
Future being studied.
1969: 170.
Recommended .621 acres of land be granted to the Jay Gould Memorial Church.
1972: 21. Adopted.
RCBP recommends the appropriate body make a feasibility study of maintaining Kirkside as a denominational project.
1974: 184. Adopted.
Final report of feasibility to be given by GSEC in Feb., 1976.
1975: 97.
Report will be given in 1977.
1976: 52.
Report of the Kirkside Study Committee outlines the difficulties: Only one retired minister is in residence; all other residents fall outside of the group for which the home was originally intended. The solution seems to be to sell the property and assist present residents with added expenses at replacement homes.
1977: 65-67. Recommended that (1) GS instruct GSEC to terminate financial support of the operation of Kirkside; (2) that the Kirkside Board be invited to present to GSEC prior to October 15, 1977, alternative proposals to continue the home; (3) that if an acceptable alternative is not presented GSEC proceed with implementation of the termination of Kirkside according to the guidelines of the Study Committee.

KLEINHEKSEL, HENRY
Appointed Business Manager at WTS.
1961: 62.
Retired as Assistant to the President of WTS after 17 years of service.
1977: 159.

KNOW YOUR COLLEGE NIGHT
Report.
1963: 79. 1965: 71.
1964: 80. 1966: 85.

KOOPS, REV. HUGH
Appointed Assistant Professor of Christian Education at WTS.
1966: 47.
Leaves faculty of WTS to join faculty of NBTS in the field of Ethics.
1970: 29.
Nominated Professor of Theology, Chair of Church and Community at NBTS.
1974: 29.

KRELLWITZ, GERARD
Dispensation from professorial certificate requested.
1976: 147, 148. Not granted.

KUWAIT
1971: 60.
Letter of intercession from the National Evangelical Church.
1976: 133-134.

KUYPER, REV. LESTER J.
Elected Vice President of GS.
1969: 9.
Elected President of GS.
1970: 9.
Serving as interim president of the seminaries.
1972: 25.
Gratitude to Dr. Kuyper for taking the heavy duties of president of the seminaries for a two year interim; resolutions.
1973: 29, 31, 33, 35.
Resolution upon his retirement as Professor of Old Testament at WTS for 35 years.

1974: 34, 37.
Declared Professor Emeritus.
1974: 130.

KUYPER, MAY DEMAREST, MISSIONARY TO JAPAN, 1912-1946.
Obituary.
1958: Annual Report of BCWM, App., 32-33.

LABOR
Convention on Abolition of Forced Labor. CAC recommends ratification of.
1968: 216-217. Motion to refer this back to CAC adopted.
See also CHURCH AND ECONOMIC LIFE.

LABORATORY SCHOOL
Held at Hope College.
1958: 75.
1959: 73.
1960: 74.
Various locations.
1961: 88.
Hope College named official permanent home.
1961: 91.

LAKE, CHARLES
Dispensation from professorial certificate requested.
1971: 31, 36. Approved.

LANDON, ARTHUR W.
Dispensation from requirements of the Hebrew Language requested.
1958: 57. Granted.

LATIN AMERICA
Overture requesting the BWM to survey opportunities for mission work in Latin America.
1964: 117, 138. Referred to SCBWM.
Overture regarding possibility of work in Latin America.
1964: 85. To be studied.
Study continuing.
1965: 74-76, 78. To be referred to GSEC.
President suggests that there be no more requests for advance in Mission in new areas until long range planning can go into effect.
1966: 341, 353, 355. Referred to GSEC.
Consideration of.
1967: 151. 145.
Rev. and Mrs. Samuel Solivan have been appointed the first RCA missionaries to Venezuela. (A part of the Church Growth Program)
1977: 150.

LAW, OBEDIENCE TO
CAC statement on obedience to law and respect for law enforcement officers.
1966: 218-220, 234. Adopted.

LAY DELEGATES TO CHURCH JUDICATORIES
President suggests a two-session term.
1963: 373, 435, 439. Report to next Synod.
No clear direction from questionnaire.
1964: 164. No action.

LAY DELEGATES TO GENERAL SYNOD
Overture regarding preparation of.
1963: 104, 111. Adequate information is being sent out before Synod. No action.

LAY PERSONS ADDRESS LIST
Lay persons on RCA committees, commissions, boards and agencies.
1971: App. 2, 218-225.
1972: App. 2, 221-229.
1973: App. 2, 198-205.
1974: App. 2, 239-249.
1975: App. 2, 254-264.
1976: App. 1, 251-265.
1977: App. 1, 259-272.

LAY WITNESS MISSION
Success of.
1972: 52, 68, 271.
1973: 56.
1975: 53.

LAYING ON OF HANDS
Overture requesting meaning of
1967: 112, 124, 128. Referred to TC.

LAYMEN FOR CHRISTIAN SERVICE
Place and position of lay people.
1959: 249.
Overture requesting a study of what others are doing to train a lay ministry.
1959: 126, 128. Referred to a Committee to Study Nature of Offices and Ministries.
Report.
1960: 317-320. Many things laymen can do in the church.
An Order of Lay Ministry suggested.
1962: 55, 56, 59. Gifted lay workers encouraged, but "order" not approved.
Lay ordination for specific purposes suggested.
1960: 60. To be studied.
Overtures requesting study of training program for lay workers.
1964: 118-119, 139-140, 150. No action on one; the other approved.
Report of PCTE.
1965: 43, 47. Awaiting study of TC on the Nature of the Ministry.

Recommended that lay leadership training courses be developed.
1969: 330, 331. Adopted and referred to GPC, Division of Church Life and Mission.
Overture requesting training program for lay leadership in order to utilize lay people in a wider use of ministry.
1970: 98-99, 110. Adopted. Referred to OHR.
Recommended that BTE engage in study to determine feasibility of short term program to equip laity for para-professional ministry in local churches.
1972: 32-33. Adopted.
Overture requesting an Office of Commissioned Lay Minister.
1974: 105-106. No action.
Overture requesting TC to make a provision and develop procedures for a lay ministry within the RCA, together with a planned program of study.
1977: 111. No action.
See also PARA-PROFESSIONAL MINISTRY.

LAYMEN ON CHURCH BOARDS
Overture requesting equality of clergy and laymen.
1963: 104, 111. No action. Some committees already have more laymen than clergy.

LEAVE OF ABSENCE (FROM SYNOD), COMMITTEE ON
Report.
1958: 364-365. 1966: 385.
1959: 370. 1967: 335.
1960: 339-340. 1968: 367-368.
1961: 399-400. 1969: 332.
1962: 415-416. 1970: 254-255.
1963: 444-445. 1971: 274-275.
1964: 465-466. 1972: 280-281.
1965: 428-429.
Recommended committee be disbanded.
1972: 281. Adopted.

LENINGTON, REV. GEORGE CHAMBERLAIN
Work as Executive Secretary of Ministers' Fund recognized.
1960: 104.

LETTUCE BOYCOTT
See BOYCOTTS, ECONOMIC.

LIAISON COMMITTEE
Duties: (1) forseeing areas of possible misunderstanding between GSEC and GPC; (2) oversight of General Secretary to assume that the policies of GSEC and GPC are carried out; (3) review of the salary administration.
1969: 163-164.
Report on salaries and/or salary ranges.
1969: 192-193.
Report.
1970: 179. 1974: 128.
1971: 150-151. 1975: 111.
1972: 119. 1976: 78-79.
1973: 136-137.
Restating of duties.
1974: 128.
1977: 52-54.
Upon recommendation of this committee, GSEC has adopted a "Salary Administration Handbook."
1977: 52.

LIBRARIAN OF SEMINARIES
Request from NBTS that the Librarian be nominated as Professor of Theology.
1958: 62-63. Denied, if sole task is to serve as seminary librarian.

LIFE SUPPORT SYSTEMS
CAC gives several suggestions regarding the decisions necessary to withdrawing life support systems and suggests "a living will" be made out by individuals while still in control of their faculties.
1976: 191-192. Adopted.

LIVING WILL
See LIFE SUPPORT SYSTEMS.

LINK OF LOVE
1975: 141.
Used by some churches in connection with DAY'S WAGE FOR CHRIST, which see.
1975: 141.
1976: 80.

LIQUOR TRAFFIC
See ALCOHOLIC BEVERAGES.

LIT-LIT
See WORLD LITERACY AND CHRISTIAN LITERATURE

LITURGY
Recommendation of the SCO that GS instruct the CRC and CRL to ascertain the wisdom of continuing liturgy as a part of the Constitution.
1966: 148-149. Adopted.
CRC and CRL concur that it would be unwise to remove the liturgy from the Constitution.
1967: 181. Received for information.

LITURGY AND PSALMS
Handbook in preparation, several chapters completed.
1970: 211.
Handbook, a book to enhance the use of

the *Liturgy and Psalms;* promotion of sales needed.
1972: 201-202.
First edition exhausted. A second edition in preparation.
1972: 202.
Overture asking GS to order the formitive process for the issuance of a new liturgy.
1973: 97. No action. Experimental liturgies are invited by the committee so that a new or additional liturgy can be formed.
New printing instead of new edition. Captions for particular orders will be printed at the top of the page.
1973: 202.
Overture requesting the wording be changed so that elders, deacons, and ministers of the Word may be those persons who are members of the RCA without regard to race or sex. That attention be given to other words, "brothers," etc.
1974: 98. No action.
Recommended by CRL that consideration be given to modernizing of language.
1974: 210. Adopted.
Printing of second edition approved.
1974: 210.
In reply to overture concerning the "meaning of the sacrament" WC recommends no action since they are beginning work on an entire liturgy.
1976: 247. No action.
Recommended by WC that WC and TC conduct a thorough study of the theology and liturgy of Christian Initiation as a prelude to revision of our forms of Baptism, Admission to the Lord's Table, etc.
1976: 247. Adopted.
See also LITURGY, REVISION OF; and LORD'S SUPPER AND BAPTIZED CHILDREN.

LITURGY, PROVISIONAL
Overture requesting study of Orders of Worship for the Lord's Day and Sacrament of The Lord's Supper.
1959: 126. No action.
Orders of service submitted for evaluation.
1959: 323-345.
1961: 369-377.
1963: 221-262.
Overture requesting permission to continue use of present form and suggesting that printing of the present form be continued.
1963: 106, 111. No action.
Overture requesting that the revision of the liturgy return to the original purpose—to revise, not re-write.
1963: 105-106, 111. No action.
Overture requesting another year for study.
1963: 105, 111. Adopted.
Provisional Liturgy printed in 1963 and sent to classes for their action.
1964: 216.
Changes proposed.
1964: 214-216.
Overture requesting another year for study.
1964: 119-120, 121, 127-128, 141, 151. Forms for Lord's Supper and Baptism to be referred back to CRL.
Overture requesting a study of the Doctrine of Infant Baptism.
1964: 121, 141, 151. Referred to TC. See BAPTISM, INFANT.
Overture requesting changes in wording.
1964: 119, 141, 151. Referred to CRL.
Overture requesting interpretation of the statement: "The Order of Worship of the Lord's Day shall be *in accordance* with the Liturgy."
1964: 121, 141-142, 151. Referred to CJB for report.
CJB interprets the above statement mandatory as to the order of worship in Reformed Churches.
1965: 131, 132.
Overture requesting the report of the CJB be reconsidered.
1966: 137, 147, 150. Voted that the words "in accordance with" be interpreted "in general conformity to." Referred to CRC.
CRC deems it unwise to alter wording for several reasons.
1967: 180-181. Received for information.
Overture rejecting the Provisional Liturgy.
1964: 120, 134-135, 151. No action.
Overture requesting permission to continue use of present form and that printing of the present edition be continued.
1964: 120, 142, 151. No action.
Overture requesting permission to use the present liturgy even if the new liturgy is approved.
1965: 112, 118, 124. No action.
Classes approved 12 orders of the Revised Liturgy.
1966: 189.
Overture requesting GS to resubmit orders for Infant and Adult Baptism to classes for their action—"declaration" a problem.
1966: 138-139, 148, 151. Referred to CRC for a statement.
CRC reports on the above overture.
1967: 181. Awaiting TC's study on Baptism.
Overtures requesting that the present

liturgy be made available for permissive use even if revised liturgy is adopted.
1966: 136-137, 139-140, 149. Motion that the CRL include in the new liturgy, the abridged and unabridged forms of the 1906 for Baptism and the Lord's Supper. Adopted.
Overture requesting permissive use of any form from any previously authorized liturgy.
1966: 137, 143, 149. No action.
Overture requesting inclusion of interrogation and response of congregation in the Office for Elders and Deacons.
1966: 138, 148, 151. Approved and referred to the CRL.
Interrogation and response included.
1967: 200.
Overture requesting an order for the second table of the Lord's Supper be included.
1966: 138, 148, 151. Adopted and referred to CRL.
Order for second table included.
1967: 200.
Liturgy and Psalms to be published by the end of the year.
1967: 201.
The Liturgy and Psalms was published on April 30, 1968.
1968: 199.
Handbook to accompany *The Liturgy and Psalms* in preparation.
1969: 238.
See LITURGY AND PSALMS.

LITURGY, REVISION OF, COMMITTEE ON
Report
1958: 319-320. 1960: 299-301.
1959: 323-324. 1961: 367-377.
See next listing.

LITURGY, REVISION OF, PERMANENT COMMITTEE ON.
Report.
1962: 391-392. 1969: 237-239.
1963: 218-262. 1970: 211-212.
1964: 213-217. 1971: 218.
1965: 183-205. 1972: 201-202.
1966: 212-214. 1973: 202.
1967: 200-203. 1974: 210-211.
1968: 199-201.
Changes in organization—membership, responsibilities, etc.
1970: 149.
Name of committee changed to WORSHIP COMMITTEE, which see.
1974: 202, 211. Adopted.
Approved by GS.
1975: 103.

LIVING MEMORIALS PROGRAM
A means by which people can make a contribution to the benevolence program in lieu of other modes of condolences.
1962: 242-243. 1965: 297.
1963: 341. 1969: 181.
1964: 348. 1972: 132.

LIVINGSTON, REV. JOHN HENRY, 1746-1825, FIRST PROFESSOR AT NBTS.
Memorial—John Livingston Chair of Theology.
1959: 38, 54.

LOCAL AND REGIONAL JUDICATORIES
A part of the study of the Sub-Committee on Denominational Structure.
1968: 146-147.
A study of the need for re-structuring to be done through PS's.
1969: 173-174. To be undertaken if four of the six PS's approve.
Four of the six PS's voted not to make the study at this time.
1970: 133. Still a matter of importance.

LONG RANGE PLANNING
GSEC and Staff Conference asked to study a plan.
1961: 185.
Committee feels this should have priority.
1963: 148-151.
Sub-Committee appointed.
1964: 161.
The President recommends a Council be established for a two-year period for the purpose of long range planning and program evaluation.
1966: 340, 353, 355. No action. Already a high priority on the GSEC agenda.
President suggests planning committee for the space age.
1967: 308, 311-312. Referred to GSEC for report in 1968.
Long range planning will be considered in the change of denominational structure.
1968: 139.
RCPR recommends GPC, GSEC, representatives of colleges, seminaries, RCW, etc. be assigned with the responsibility of developing a long range plan for our RCA life and mission to be presented to 1978 GS.
1976: 33. Adopted.
Committee work begun, and timeline for process presented.
1977: 38-41.

LORD'S DAY ALLIANCE
Report.
1958: 192-194. 1960: 174.
1959: 197-201. 1961: 202.

1962: 196–198. 1970: No report.
1963: 311. 1971: 247–249.
1964: 304. 1972: 251–253.
1965: 262. 1973: 252–255.
1966: 281–282. 1974: 250–251.
1967: 255–256. 1975: 226–227.
1968: 262–263. 1976: 128.
1969: 287. 1977: 138–139.

The year 1976 is the 88th year.
1977: 139.

LORD'S DAY, OBSERVANCE OF

Report of CAC.
1963: 313–316, 318–319.

President requests a letter be sent to Senator Everett M. Dirksen who originated the proposal of making Sunday a national voting day.
1965: 336, 345–346, 348. Adopted.

Overture requesting TC to formulate a statement on the Christian observance of the Lord's Day.
1971: 102, 103, 113–114. Adopted.

RC's Statement to appear later.
1972: 200.

TC is engaged in an extensive study and will have a complete study in the near future.
1973: 191.

TC's paper on the Lord's Day.
1974: 202–206.

Overture requesting dates of Synod be set to eliminate travel on the Lord's Day.
1974: 106. Adopted and referred to GSEC.

GSEC reports that they "will use the overture as a guide in planning GS sessions."
1975: 97.

LORD'S PRAYER

Overture suggesting study be given change in wording.
1960: 109, 116. Adopted.

It would be necessary for all denominations to work together on this wording.
1961: 339.

LORD'S SUPPER

Recommended that NCC's report, "The Eucharist in the Life of the Church: An Ecumenical Consensus" be referred to TC for a report to 1972 GS.
1971: 253. Adopted.

TC has studied the above document and concludes that it is a sign of Christian Unity being wrought by the Holy Spirit in our day; an adequate consensus.
1972: 197.

CRL invites GS to consider the following: that the full formulary be used at least four times a year; that those having a more frequent celebration have the option of a briefer liturgy including the "sursum corda," the words of institution, the congregational response, and the proclamation of the Gospel.
1972: 202.

CRL recommends the above to GS.
1973: 202. Adopted.

TC recommends that in the celebration of the Lord's Supper under RCA auspices, one of the orders which appear in the *Liturgy and Psalms,* or an order theologically and liturgically in agreement with these orders be used.
1973: 192. Adopted.

The Liturgy Committee recommends that the action on the two recommendations adopted in 1973 were hastily taken and can lead to confusion; therefore it is recommended that they be referred back to the LC for further study. (1973: 192 and 1973: 202)
1974: 210. Adopted.

Overture requesting TC to formulate a statement on the RCA's position on serving Holy Communion at informal gatherings (extra-congregational gatherings)
1972: 86–87. Adopted.

Overture requesting pastors abide by all liturgical procedures of administering Holy Communion as outlines in the BCO. (Evidently concerning celebrating Communion in the marriage service)
1972: 87. No action.

TC recommends that in the celebration of the Lord's Supper in a wedding service, no Christians are to be treated as spectators to the sacrament (as is sometimes done at weddings). Where the supper is served all Christians present are to be invited to participate.
1973: 193. Adopted.

COCG's statement: "Whenever the supper is served, all communicant members of the church present are to be invited to participate."
1974: 189. Adopted.

Recommended that TC study the administration of the sacrament by ordained elders.
1973: 38. Adopted.

TC recommends that the Lord's Supper may be served by a Minister of the Word or at the designation of the Board of Elders, by an elder with at least another elder in attendance.
1973: 193. Adopted and referred to EC. See also SACRAMENTS, ADMINISTERING OF BY ELDERS.

Overture requesting that in the event elders are to administer the sacrament the

BCO state that at least another elder be present.

1974: 104–105. No action.

Overture requesting that in addition to saying the Lord's Supper shall be administered at least once every three months in every church, the following be added: "the ideal and scriptural norm is at least once a week. The Office of the Administration of the Lord's Supper shall be read."

1974. 103, 106. No action. Referred to WC.

Overture requesting reinstatement of "sursum corda" in the liturgy.

1975: 89–91. Adopted and referred to WC for consideration.

Examination before the Lord's Supper, see CONSTITUTIONAL QUESTION #5.

LORD'S SUPPER AND BAPTIZED CHILDREN

Overture recommending that the TC study the possibility of allowing baptized members to partake of communion before making public confession of faith.

1972: 86. No action since TC is already making a study.

Overture asking GS to request TC to study the possibility of admitting children to communion prior to confirmation.

1973: 108. No action. This is already dealt with in TC's report to this GS.

TC recommends that all persons may participate in the supper who understand they belong to Jesus Christ. This means covenant children who have this understanding may participate in the sacrament.

1973: 193. Not adopted.

TC working on additional papers in order to better study the subject of The Lord's Supper and baptized children.

1974: 206.

Report will be made in 1976.

1975: 188.

To be presented at the next GS.

1976: 245.

TC's paper, "Baptized Non-Communicants and the Celebration of the Lord's Supper," with several chapters: (1) Baptism in the Life of the Church; (2) The Meaning of Baptized Non-Communicant Members; (3) The Lord's Supper in the Life of the Church; (4) The Place of Children at the Lord's Table; (5) Affirmation of the Baptismal Covenant and Commissioning; (6) Suggested Procedures for the Local Church; The Lord's Supper; (7) Implementation Required; (8) Conclusions and Recommendations: That the proposal to admit baptized children to the Lord's Table is fully consonant with the Reformed doctrine of baptism and that no serious impediments to the proposal emerge either from biblical or theological considerations, but that the proposed change will lay heavier than usual demands on the church to provide continuing instruction, nurture, and pastoral care that will open to the baptized more plainly the way of faith . . . Recommended that this paper be approved for distribution to the churches; that each classis be instructed to submit to the chairman of the TC its evaluation of the theological basis for and suggested implementation of the proposals contained in the proposal; responses to be received no later than May 1, 1978.

1977: 293–306. All approved.

LOTTERIES

Overture, (1) urging a public stand against and (2) take steps through CAC to approach other Reformed and Presbyterian bodies to secure an interdenominational position against.

1966: 119, 142, 149. No action. CAC has already made a "Statement on Gambling."

CAC recommends that RCA members not participate in state lotteries, which are a "costly free lunch."

1976: 185–187. Adopted.

See also GAMBLING.

LOVE, FRANK

Dispensation from the study of Hebrew requested.

1963: 48–49. To be proposed again in 1964.

1964: 46, 47, 50, 53. Granted.

LUBBERS, AREND D.

Elected President of Central College.

1960: 70.

Resigned from Presidency of Central College.

1969: 45.

LUBBERS, ELAINE

Appointed Assistant Professor of Christian Education at WTS.

1963: 39.

Resigned her position.

1966: 36.

LUBBERS, IRWIN J.

Resolution regarding his service, especially as president of two colleges—Central and Hope.

1962: 377.

Retired from the Presidency of Hope College.

1963: 67.

LUBEN, REV. BARNARD M.
Resolution regarding work as missionary and field secretary.
1961: 97-98.

MC LEAN, REV. HUGH BAILLIE
Resolution upon his death.
1960: 55-56.

MC LEAN, STANLEY
Dispensation from professorial certificate requested.
1976: 147, 148. Not granted at this time. Candidate will continue to pursue requirements.

MADER, DONALD
Dispensation from professorial certificate requested.
1976: 146, 148. Granted.

MADSEN, NORMAN
Dispensation requested, but incomplete.
1971: 31. No action.

MAJOR MEDICAL INSURANCE PLAN
1962: 112.
1963: 100.
1964: 103.
1965: 93 (792 members).
1967: 98.
1968: 83.
1969: 110-111 (945 members).
Lay workers eligible.
1960: 103.
Constitution amended re application for benefits.
1960: 104-105.

MAJORITY AND MINORITY REPORTS
Recommendations regarding.
1963: 134. There is no "majority report"—that is the report of the committee.

MALENESS AND FEMALENESS
Motion made to instruct TC to prepare a biblical study of the creation gifts of "male" and "female" and their significance in the totality of life, that will be helpful to our young people as they seek to develop a Christian lifestyle.
1974: 299. Adopted.
TC will report in 1976.
1975: 189.
A comprehensive statement by TC considering several disciplines: biology; sociology; psychology; theology; and biblical view of creation; the fall; Jesus on Maleness and Femaleness; New Testament Churches; with a conclusion that the church should be the place of greatest freedom for all God's people, male and female, to be and to become a part of a royal priesthood that we may declare the mighty deeds of God.
1976: 235-245. Adopted.
See also FEMINISM; WOMEN IN THE RCA; ORDINATION OF WOMEN.

MANAGEMENT AND LABOR
See CHURCH AND ECONOMIC LIFE.

MANAGERS, BOARD OF
See NATIONAL DEPARTMENT OF WOMEN'S WORK.

MANE, EBENEZER
Dispensation from original languages requested.
1968: 41, 43. Granted.

MANN, MRS. KRIS
Retired as Administrative Assistant at NBTS.
1977: 159.

MARIJUANA LEGISLATION
CAC recommends (1) GS urge the Federal Government to appropriate adequate funding for research on the use and effects, and (2) GS urge government to provide more equitable enforcement of the use of marijuana.
1970: 220. (1) adopted; (2) referred back for rephrasing.
CAC reports that smoking marijuana is to be distinguished from the use of other hard drugs, taken orally or injected. See first statement under DRUGS.
1971: 221-222.
A paragraph on marijuana, again separating it from other drug abuse, but not being sure how to handle it.
1973: 224.

MARRIAGE AND FAMILY LIFE
Sub-Committee appointed.
1960: 180-182.

MARRIAGE CEREMONY
Overture regarding mixed marriages (Catholic and Reformed).
1958: 131. Referred to CAC.
Overture requesting a brochure on prenuptial agreements.
1963: 108-109, 112. No brochure. Article will appear in the Church Herald.
Overture seeking guidance in the use of the RCA liturgy in marriage of people not members of the Christian Church. Also whether ministers are permitted to officiate with a Priest of the Roman Catholic Church.
1969: 134, 147, 153. Referred to TC and CRC.
TC recommends the CRL prepare a ceremony with Scripture and prayers for use of

RCA ministers in marrying those who are not members of the Christian Church.
1970: 210. Adopted.
TC report on marriage of those not members of the Christian Church: after counseling and consulting with elders, the marriage service can be a Christian witness and a part of the church's ministry and mission to the world.
1970: 205.
For those not members of the Christian Church: CRL not convinced of the liturgical necessity or theological propriety of such a form. The church should clarify its mind as to the role and function of the church. Is a separate liturgy required?
1971: 218.
TC report on officiating simultaneously with Roman Catholic priests: permissable if consultation with priest and elders is satisfactory.
1970: 205-206.

MARRIAGE, DIVORCE, AND REMARRIAGE
TC studying 1962 action and preparing a new paper.
1974: 209.
TC paper on biblical perspectives. Recommended document be distributed to every minister and elder and congregation for study.
1975: 162-172. Adopted.

MARSILJE, LOIS
Honored by GS for missionary work.
1976: 134-135.

MAULDIN, SIDNEY M., JR.
Requested that he be granted a dispensation from the professorial certificate.
1974: 38. Adopted.

MEDENDORP, JAMES
Recommended that he not be granted a dispensation from the academic requirements and the professorial certificate.
1974: 36, 38. Adopted.

MEDIA
See AUDIO VISUAL AIDS and TRAVARCA.

MEDICAL-MISSIONARY GUILD
President recommends
1963: 373-374, 435, 439. A Committee appointed to report in 1964.
1964: 83. In operation.

MEMBERSHIP OF PARENTS PRESENTING INFANTS FOR BAPTISM
See references under BAPTISM, INFANT.

MEMBERSHIP REFERRAL SYSTEM
Overture requesting an addition be made to the BCO providing for a list of families and their addresses who have moved out of the bounds of the parish during the year and that this list be given to clerks of classes and PS's for referral.
1976: 113. Adopted.
EC's statement same as above.
1976: 249. Adopted, and sent to classes.
Approved by classes.
1977: 42.

MENNENGA, REV. GEORGE H.
Retirement from Office of Dean at WTS.
1961: 61.
Resolution.
1961: 72.
Named Emeritus Professor of Theology.
1962: 58.

MEN'S BROTHERHOOD
1958: 76.
Tenth anniversary under Rev. Bert Brower.
1959: 76.
1960: 69.
1961: 86.
1962: 75-76.
President suggests a standing committee to study work of.
1963: 375, 436-437, 439. To be referred to DAW.
To be continued under ADULT EDUCATION, which also see.
1964: 56.
Name changed to REFORMED CHURCH MEN.

MENTAL HEALTH
Report.
1958: 202.
1959: 209.
1960: 186.

MERGER
Overture opposed to proposed union with the PCUS.
1964: 127, 144, 152. Referred to the C12.
Overture requesting cessation of all merger conversations.
1964: 126-127, 129-130, 135, 152. No action.
Overtures requesting GS to discontinue consideration of merger.
1965: 108-109, 120, 121, 124. No action.
Overtures concerning voting procedure.
1964: 122-123, 130, 152. No action.
Overtures requesting 3/4 vote of congregations, consistories, classes and GS for passing merger vote.
1964: 123-124, 128, 135, 145, 152. No action.
Overture regarding an amendment to the Constitution, already accepted by the UPCUSA and PCUS which provides for federated churches.

1966: 133-136, 146, 150. Referred to CRC. See UNION CHURCHES.

Overture requesting a 3/4 vote of all classes and GS.

1966: 132, 147, 150. No action. The 2/3 vote already set is deemed fair to all.

Overture requesting a 2/3 vote of approval by the congregations of the RCA.

1966: 132, 147, 150. No action. Congregations not deemed necessary.

Beginning with 1967 entries pertaining to merger with PCUS will be listed under CHURCH UNION (PCUS), which see.

MERGER PROBLEMS

Overture requesting the privilege of a congregation to refrain from merger by a 2/3 vote.

1963: 104, 105. Referred to JC24.

Overture regarding pension rights of ministers who might choose to serve congregations voting against merger.

1963: 105, 111. Referred to BP.

Overture regarding property rights of congregations not voting for merger.

1963: 105, 111. Referred to JC24.

Overture regarding disposition of pension funds if minister is unhappy about plans for merger.

1964: 124-126, 128, 152. Referred to C12 and BP.

Overture asking for a statement as to where property rights are to be adjudicated in the event of merger.

1965: 109, 121-122, 124. Referred to CJB.

CJB reports on the above overture: a complex matter which should be presented to C12 for inclusion in the Plan of Union.

1966: 155-157, 160. Adopted.

Overture regarding property and annuity rights requesting that the Plan of Union safeguard this problem by allowing congregations to remain apart from merger without forfeiting rights.

1966: 131, 141, 146. Approved.

Overture asking GS to delineate whether property rights of a local church rest solely in the hands of classis.

1966: 130, 146, 150. No action.

Overture requesting that the desire for the assurance of autonomy in case of merger be communicated to those working on the Plan of Union.

1966: 130-131, 146, 150. Communicated to C12.

Overture requesting assurance of pension rights of ministers serving congregations that wish to retain their identity apart from merger.

1966: 131, 146, 150. Adopted. BP to study matter of reciprosity between RCA and other denominations.

Overture requesting that if merger be consummated or defeated, a congregation by a 2/3 ballot be allowed to transfer to another denominational fellowship.

1966: 132-133, 147, 150. No action.

Beginning with 1967 all entries pertaining to merger with PCUS will be listed under CHURCH UNION (PCUS), which see.

MERGER TALKS WITH PRESBYTERIAN CHURCH, U.S.

See also JOINT COMMITTEE OF TWENTY-FOUR and COMMITTEE OF TWELVE.

MERGERS PROPOSED

Overtures regarding merger with PCUS

1961: 133-138, 142. Conversations to be held with PCUS and UPCUSA.

Overtures regarding mergers with other Presybterian churches.

1962: 122-124, 125, 127. Steps to be taken to merge with the PCUS. Other attempts to be held in abeyance.

Overture requesting enlarging conversations to include not only PCUS, but also UPCUSA.

1964: 135-136, 145, 152. Efforts to be limited to merger with PCUS.

Overture requesting a plan of merger be worked out with the PCUS and presented in 1965.

1964: 122, 146-148, 152. Adopted.

Overtures requesting the C12 to proceed toward union with PCUS.

1965: 107-108, 112, 120-121, 124. No action.

MEXICO

Cooperative work with Presbyterian Church.

1961: 110.

Other references.

1971: 62.

1974: 64.

MICHIGAN, PARTICULAR SYNOD OF

Two members of the PS enter a complaint against the action of the PS in transferring two churches from Classis of Muskegon to Classis of North Grand Rapids. Recommended that actual transfer be held in abeyance until after a hearing.

1971: 121. Approved.

History of the above complaint: in 1970 a study committee of the PS recommended no realignment. Request was repeated at the 1971 meeting of PS, whereupon oppo-

site action was taken and the churches given permission. The CJB upheld the complaint and declared the transfer invalid.
1972: 109-111. Adopted.

MICROFILMING OF DENOMINATIONAL ARCHIVES
See ARCHIVES, DENOMINATIONAL.

MIDDLE EAST
Declaration on presented by Lewis Scudder, Jr.
1976: 255-256. Adopted.
Two study papers in response to the above, on the Middle East Crisis between the Moslems, Jews and Eastern Christians, and a series of many recommendations presented because of our desire to see justice equally distributed in the Middle East.
1977: 198-200, 204, 208-236. All except one recommendation adopted.
A church growth proposal is under consideration for special ministries to Arab students and expatriots in the U.S.
1977: 141-142.

MILITARY-INDUSTRIAL COMPLEX
Several recommendations and motions (CAC) concerning (1) urging abolition of selective service system; (2) commending federal government on successful negotiations concerning nuclear testing and banning chemical and biological weapons; (3) urge the government to move with greater determination toward the conclusion of the SALT talks; (4) urge the president to withdraw all conscientious objectors and try to provide employment that will satisfy requirements in lieu of military service, etc.
1971: 226-228. (1) lost; (2,3,4,5) adopted.

MINISTER
"Minister of the Word" to be used in Church Government for "Minister."
1971: 206, 208.

MINISTER, ASSISTANT
Defined.
1958: 140.
Overture regarding definition of.
1960: 109, 116. Referred to CRC.
Definition appears in revised Constitution.
1961: 150.

MINISTER, ASSOCIATE
Defined.
1958: 140.
Overture regarding definition of.
1960: 109, 116. Referred to CRC.
Definition appears in the revised Constitution.
1961: 150.
Overture regarding relationship with congregation when Senior Minister leaves.
1962: 124, 127. Referred to CRC.
Report of CRC—Classis shall appoint another minister as moderator.
1964: 205-206.

MINISTER, SENIOR
Overture regarding relationship with Associate Minister.
1962: 124, 127. Referred to CRC.

MINISTERS, CALLING OF
Overture regarding ethical code for.
1959: 124, 128. Referred back to committee for study.
Manual proposed.
1960: 321-322. Referred back for study.
Committee suggests manual be drafted.
1961: 382. Adopted.
"Manual for the Calling of a Minister" prepared by Rev. Alvin J. Neevel.
1962: 368-374.
Overture regarding publishing of calls suggests that only accepted calls be listed in the Church Herald.
1960: 109, 116. Not adopted.
Overture regarding publishing of calls suggests that only those calls be published which are officially released by either party.
1962: 117, 127. No action.
President suggests that since negotiations are being carried on with the PCUS, that churches needing ministers consider calling Presbyterian ministers.
1967: 307, 311. No action.
Overture requesting amendment to the BCO to clarify contractual agreement between an active ordained person, the contracting church body, and classis involved.
1976: 115. No action.
Overture requesting the following words be inserted in the call between the words "annually" and "for": "for a study program mutually agreed upon between you and us."
1976: 109, Adopted.
Amendment approved by classes.
1977: 42.
Recognizing the President's concern regarding "professionalization," RCPR recommends that the TC study implications of "call contracts" in relation to a) the call to the ministry, b) call to a particular church, in discussion with the OHR and that they report to GS of 1978.
1977: 31-32, 36. Adopted.

MINISTERS, CENTRAL FILE FOR

Resolution requesting the establishment of a central file on ministers to which churches can turn for information on a candidate.

1967: 336. Referred to GSEC.

GSEC reports that the Office of Human Resources will give early attention to such a file.

1968: 140.

Central file service for ministers now administered by OHR.

1970: 162.

Overture requesting the OHR to get permission of minister before sending out dossier.

1971: 109, 116. No action. Already the practice of OHR.

Effort to update the profile system after 4 years.

1974: 161.

MINISTERS' CHILDREN, EDUCATION OF

Sub-Committee on Studying the Education of Ministers' Children appointed.

1966: 164. Will report to GSEC.

GSEC took action to drop the matter.

1967: 144.

MINISTERS, CHURCH MEMBERSHIP OF

A minister may be a member only of classis—not of an individual church.

1958: 139.

To implement this new provision, it is recommended that GS direct every ordained minister in the RCA to present to his classis at its next regular meeting a formal certificate of dismission from the church of which he is now a member.

1959: 148.

A missionary while serving in a foreign field, may, with the consent of the judicatory of which he is a member, hold membership also in a indigenous church with all the privileges pertaining thereto.

1959: 146, 148. Adopted and sent to classes for approval.

Approved by classes.

1960: 219.

Overture requesting amendment in the Government to provide for provisional membership in a classis of a non-RCA minister who is serving a Reformed congregation in an approved cooperative parish.

1975: 86, 161. Adopted and sent to classes for approval.

Classes approved.

1976: 46.

Overture requesting amendment in the BCO allowing a minister who accepts a call to another denomination in another country, to be responsible to the RCA as well as to the indigenous church in which he serves.

1976: 101. Referred to COCG for consideration and report.

COCG recommends addition to BCO: If a minister of the RCA accepts a call from a church of another denomination in another country he may remain a member of the classis in which he last served. A minister of the Word remains solely amenable to classis.

1977: 314–315. Adopted.

MINISTERS, CONTINUING EDUCATION OF

GSEC recommends consistories consider arrangement whereby pastors may take refresher courses and attend workshops.

1964: 163–164.

A scholarship fund of $8,000 available for continuing education of ministers beyond BD degree.

1970: 33.

Recommended that consistories give 1 week and $100 for professional development for each year of service with the present congregation, for ministers and directors of Christian Education.

1971: 37–38, 210. Adopted and sent to classes for approval.

Approved by classes.

1972: 120.

Overture requesting this statement be added to the call: "We promise to provide for professional development by mutual agreement between consistory and minister" (no amount stipulated).

1972: 88. No action.

Recommended by President that competence through continuing education should be encouraged and that the statement in BCO needs more interpretation.

1974: 279, 281–282. Adopted and referred to COCG and OHR.

Committee to work on plans for continuing education of ministers.

1974: 29–30.

The President suggests and RCPR recommends that continuing education for clergy be referred to the Coordinator for HR for further recommendations to classes and consistories, and a progress report be made to GS 1976 through GSEC.

1975: 251. Adopted.

President suggests and RCPR recommends that each church consider desirable goal be the granting of 2 weeks' study leave in addition to vacation, financed by a $250 grant.

1975: 251. Adopted.

Continuing education representatives in 45 classes.

1977: 92.
WTS studying plans for the proposal of offering a Doctor of Ministry degree.
1977: 160.

MINISTERS, DISCIPLINE OF
Overture requesting an added sentence concerning discipline of a minister, to make a stronger statement.
1974: 105. No action.

MINISTERS ENTERING SECULAR FIELDS
Overture regarding a means to prevent this practice.
1960: 110, 117. Referred to Committee to Study the Nature of Offices and Ministries.
Suggested such ministers demit the ministry, but such demission would not be considered dishonorable.
1961: 347. Referred to Convocation of Seminary Professors.
Report of the Committee on Professorate.
1962: 55-63. Adopted. Referred to CRC.
CRC report: Minister shall not relinquish the work of his office except after application to and consent of classis.
1963: 130-131, 136. Adopted.
Overture requesting clarification in the BCO regarding ministers of the Word who do not receive their primary means of support from the practice of ministry.
1976: 100, 112. Voted that TC review their study of 1968 on the Nature of the Ministry with particular interest to the functions of ministry which require ordination, e.g. "tent-maker" and "worker priest."

MINISTERS, PASTORAL CARE OF
Ministerial relations and church supervision. President recommends such a committee in each PS.
1967: 307, 310-311, 312. Approved.
Overture requesting BCO be amended to include a new section which directs the classis to determine annually whether each enrolled minister has entered into an agreement with another minister for pastoral care for himself and family.
1977: 108-109. Referred to OHR to be reported through GSEC.
See also COUNSELING OF MINISTERS AND THEIR WIVES.

MINISTERS, PERFORMANCE OF
Recommended that a new sentence be added to the *Government:* "Does the consistory have and regularly use a procedure by which the performance of its minister(s) is reviewed?"
1975: 160. Adopted and referred to classes.
Classes approved.
1976: 46.
Self evaluation sheets sent out to ministers. Replies reveal ministers are pursuing studies. Performance review being voted on by classes to determine if it should be a constitutional question.
1976: 44-45.
Overture requesting clarification of the procedure of "goal setting and growth" of both pastor(s) and consistory on a regular basis.
1976: 103. No action.
Overture requesting an amendment in the BCO reading: "Does the consistory (elders, deacons and pastors) have a procedure by which the performance of each of its perspective areas of responsibility and methods are annually reviewed?"
1977: 110, 320. Adopted and sent to classes for approval.
The inclusion of the performance review in the list of "constitutional questions" has resulted in many requests for assistance.
1977: 92.

MINISTERS, RELOCATION OF
Overture requesting study of a plan whereby pastors can be assigned to other congregations when either the pastor or congregation seeks a change.
1975: 87. GSEC to appoint a study committee.
PCPR recommends that a plan for a pastoral placement committee be formed by the OHR, the field secretaries, and one representative from each seminary to devise an optional relocation for a three year period, and bring in a final recommendation at the end of three years.
1975: 251. Adopted.
GSEC reports information sheets have been prepared and provision made for consulting service. Considerable interest shown.
1976: 37-38.
See also PASTOR-CONGREGATION RELATIONSHIPS.

MINISTERS, RETIRED
Early retirement option.
1959: 119.
Retirement age of ministers.
1960: 120.
~~Overture suggesting that all ministers of a~~ church be listed with the church instead of "other ministers" of classis.
1963: 107, 111. No action.
Overture regarding role of retired ministers

and ministers not in parish ministry in church judicatories.
1966: 123-124, 145, 150. Referred to TC.
An amendment recommended concerning Emritus Ministers, their rights and privileges.
1974: 201, 208. Adopted and sent to classes for approval.
Classes approved.
1975: 99.

MINISTERS, SABBATICALS FOR
Sabbaticals for ministers suggested by BE.
1962: 78. Referred to GSEC.
GSEC recommends consistories consider arrangement whereby pastors may take refresher courses and attend workshops.
1964: 163-164.
The President suggests that the call to a minister include consistory's willingness to release the pastor for a maximum of 3 months for study once each 7 years.
1966: 344-345, 354. Adopted and referred to GSEC.
Three other recommendations of the President on sabbaticals.
1966: 345, 354-356. No action pending GSEC report.
Study committee on sabbatical leaves for ministers and ministerial mobility.
1967: 152-153. Work referred to PCTE for further study.
Sabbaticals referred to the Program Design Committee of the BTE.
1968: 42.
GS commends to classes for action, that time and funding for continuing education and sabbaticals be provided.
1969: 41, 44. Adopted.

MINISTERS, SALARIES
A permanent committee on salaries of ministers suggested for annual review.
1960: 92, 94. Adopted.
Overture regarding minimum salaries.
1960: 109. To be set by classis.
President recommends BNAM study possibilities of adequate salary supplement for experienced ministers serving Mission churches.
1966: 346, 354, 356. Referred to BNAM.
Overture suggesting change in wording in the Call letter to make it mandatory that each church annually review salary arrangements.
1966: 120-121, 142, 149. Adopted and referred to CRC.
CRC reports the following will be added, "yearly and every year," hence salary will be considered annually.
1967: 180. Approved.
Overture requesting amendment to read: "Do the salary, housing and all other benefits received by the minister(s) meet the terms of the original call, subsequent revisions thereof, and the minimum standards of the classis?"
1972: 95. Adopted.
Approved by classes.
1973: 128.
Overture seeking interpretation of the right of a PS to legislate for a local congregation concerning minimum salary schedule.
1973: 102. Referred to CJB.
CJB recommends "that the PS of Chicago may not legislate a minimum salary schedule for pastors within its bounds nor make it binding on the congregation."
1974: 112. Adopted. According to BCO, classis only has the right.
President suggests a consultation on salaries and RCPR recommends the COCG and OHR study the problem and report to the next GS.
1974: 275-276, 282. Adopted.
COCG reports an amendment to the section concerning salary, housing arrangements for professional development in connection with a call.
1975: 159-160. Adopted and referred to classes.
Classes approved.
1976: 46.
Overture requesting GS to study the merits of ministerial remuneration being set and distributed by the denomination.
1977: 110-111. Approved and referred to GSEC.

MINISTERS, GENDER OF
Overture requesting that the Government be amended to include the word "male" in the qualifications.
1973: 110. No action.
EC seeks to amend the definition by deleting the word "persons" and substituting the words "members of the RCA."
1973: 184. Adopted and sent to classes for approval.
Not approved by classes.
1974: 119.

MINISTERS WITHOUT CHARGE, STATUS OF
Overture requesting that ministers who take calls to Boards, etc., of the RCA and those taking calls to other agencies not related to the RCA be considered as ministers with charge in the RCA.
1965: 104-106, 120, 124. Adopted. Referred to TC and CRC.

Overture requests BCO amendment to clarify status of a minister without charge. Suggests they be associate members of a classis with full privilege of the floor, but without right to vote.
1970: 81, 103. No action. Parity should be responsibility of classis.
Overture requesting guidelines concerning "voting rights shall be limited to . . . those ministers of the Word who are actively serving under the jurisdiction, or with the approval of the classes," indicating retired ministers are allowed to vote in some classes and not in others.
1977: 113–114. Adopted and referred to COCG.

MINISTERS, WORKLOAD OF
President suggests each congregation should periodically make a study of the minister's workload.
1965: 338–339, 346–347. Recommended CRC make a study of the feasibility of an added constitutional inquiry.
CRC reports this matter is already handled in the Constitution.
1966: 199. No action.

MINISTERS' ADDRESS LIST
Formerly MINISTERS AND CANDIDATES, CATALOGUE OF, which also see.
1965: 482–504.
1966: 532–557.
1967: App. 2, 147–182.
1968: App. 2, 148–179.
1969: App. 2, 108–140.
1970: App. 2, 103–128.
1971: App. 2, 155–217.
1972: App. 2, 158–220.
1973: App. 2, 141–197.
1974: App. 2, 181–238.
1975: App. 2, 197–253.
1976: App. 1, 189–250.
1977: App. 1, 191–256.

MINISTERS AND CANDIDATES, CATALOGUE OF
1958: 396–419.
1959: 397–422.
1960: 368–395.
1961: 427–454.
1962: 443–473.
1963: 502–519.
1964: 518–535.
New listing, MINISTERS' ADDRESS LIST, which also see.

MINISTERS DISMISSED TO OTHER DENOMINATIONS
1958: 257.
1959: 259.
1960: 239.
1961: 276.
1962: 474.
1963: 520.
1964: 536.
1965: 513.
1966: 565.
1967: App. 2, 181.
1968: App. 2, 188.
1969: App. 2, 155.
1970: App. 2, 149.
1971: App. 2, 244.
1972: App. 2, 248.
1973: App. 2, 226.
1974: App. 2, 272.
1975: App. 2, 287.
1976: App. 1, 289.
1977: App. 1, 298.
(Misnumbered 288 in MGS.)

MINISTERS' FUND
See PENSIONS, BOARD OF.

MINISTERS OF OTHER DENOMINATIONS SERVING REFORMED CHURCHES
1958: 420.
1959: 423.
1960: 396.
1961: 455.
1962: 474.
1963: 520.
1964: 536.
1965: 512.
1966: 564.
1967: App. 2, 180.
1968: App. 2, 183–184.
1969: App. 2, 153–154.
1970: App. 2, 147–148.
1971: App. 2, 242–243.
1972: App. 2, 246–248.
1973: App. 2, 223–225.
1974: App. 2, 269–271.
1975: App. 2, 283–286.
1976: App. 1, 286–288.
1977: App. 1, 295–297.

MINISTERS RECEIVED FROM OTHER DENOMINATIONS
1958: 257.
1959: 259.
1960: 239.
1961: 276.
1962: 474.
1963: 520.
1964: 536.
1965: 513.
1966: 565.
1967: App. 2, 181.
1968: App. 2, 188.
1969: App. 2, 155.
1970: App. 2, 149.
1971: App. 2, 244.
1973: App. 2, 226–227.
1974: App. 2, 272.
1975: App. 2, 287.
1976: App. 1, 289.
1977: App. 1, 298.
(Misnumbered 288 in MGS.)

MINISTERS SERVING OUTSIDE THE RCA.
1970: App. 2, 139–141.
Changed to MINISTRIES, SPECIALIZED, which see.

MINISTRIES, SPECIALIZED
1971: App. 2, 236–238.
1972: App. 2, 240–242.
1973: App. 2, 217–219.
1974: App. 2, 258–264.
1975: App. 2, 272–279.
1976: App. 1, 275–281.
1977: App. 1, 284–291.
See also previous listing.

MINISTRY
New opportunities for.
1974: 137–141.

MINISTRY, CANDIDATES FOR FROM OTHER DENOMINATIONS
Candidates for licensure and ordination

from other denominations to be studied.
1960: 58-59, 60.
Examination required.
1961: 152.
To be examined by professors of one of the RCA seminaries.
1962: 138.
Academic attainments should be considered when ministers transfer from other denominations.
1962: 56.
Overture requesting that those coming into the RCA from other seminaries take at least one year of training in one of the RCA seminaries.
1974: 100. No action.
Faculty convocation outlines procedure for conducting examinations for licensure and ordination.
1966: 47-49. Adopted and referred to CRC.

MINISTRY, DOCTRINE OF
To be studied by TC in 1963.
1962: 285-286, 342.
Will present study at future GS.
1963: 269.
TC report.
1964: 208-209, 212. Adopted.

MINISTRY, NATURE OF
TC making a study; will report later.
1966: 206.
TC report.
1968: 185-186, 190-198.
TC recommends 8 changes in *Government* concerning ministry; a) require installation by a judicatory each time a person enters an ecclesiastical function appropriate to a minister of the Word; b) require judicatories to declare demitted from the office of minister of the Word those who have relinquished the function into which they were installed and have not been installed in a new ministerial function; c) require judicatories to limit the office of minister of the Word to those whose function is 1) a full-time occupation which requires a theological education for its effective performance; 2) and performed under the supervision of a judicatory; and 3) aimed at the edification and equipment of the church for her mission in the world; d) the restriction of voting rights in any judicatory by ministers of the Word to those ministers who are actively serving in ministries under the jurisdiction of a judicatory; e) require classes to declare all retired ministers Emeritus ministers of the Word with all the privileges of the office *except* the right to vote in any judicatory; f) change the present "fourth office" of Professor of Theology to include it as a special function of the office of minister of the Word with membership and voting rights in the General Synod; g) specify that proper ecclesiastical designation of ministers of the Word accord with their function (e.g. pastor, teacher, professor, president, executive secretary, director, chaplain, etc.); h) specify that the nature of the task of the minister of the Word is to serve as pastor, teacher, and enabler of the Christians among whom he works, to build up and equip the whole Church for her ministry in the world.
1969: 235-236. Referred to CRC.
Liaison committee (3 members from the TC and 3 from CRC) to be appointed to study proposed changes.
1970: 198, 209.
Above principles presented by TC.
1971: 203-205. Adopted and sent to classes for approval.
Not approved by classes.
1972: 120.
Overture suggesting a revision of preamble to office of Minister of the Word.
1972: 98. No action.
TC again proposes the 8 principles formulated in 1969 and presented to classes in 1971, but this time each section will be voted on separately.
1973: 195-201. Amendments a,b,c,d, e,g,h were approved; f was referred back to TC for further study.
Items a,b,c,d,e,g,h approved by classes.
1974: 119.
See also FOURTH OFFICE.

MINISTRY, OLDER MEN FOR
President's suggestion for training.
1961: 269, 329, 331. Referred to PCP.
Shortened course recommended for men over 35.
1962: 59-60. Referred to CRC.
CRC report.
1963: 132-133, 136. Referred to PCTE and the seminaries.

MINISTRY TO RCA COMMUNICANTS AT NON-REFORMED CHURCH COLLEGES AND UNIVERSITIES.
Overture regarding.
1960: 74, 75. Special committee to be appointed.
See also CAMPUS MINISTRY.

MINKE, WERNER
Dispensation from AB degree granted and permission to be tested for seminary entrance approved.
1961: 66, 69, 74.

MINORITY COUNCILS

Joint Committee on Responsibilities and Relationships of Minority Councils and Denominational Policy Bodies to be appointed.

1975: 110. Appointments being made.

Report.

1976: 51.

1977: 47–48.

Two overtures requesting an examination of the value and validity of perpetuating the proliferating of minority councils within our denomination.

1976: 104–105. Referred to TC for consideration and report.

The TC can appropriately speak only to the question of the theological validity of such councils. The Commission finds no biblical or theological impediments to the existence of minority councils in the RCA.

1977: 307.

History of the formation of the joint committee; statement of purpose of minority councils; and theological basis for statement and recommendations.

1977: 76–84.

Revision of the report relating to an Affirmative Action Plan. A series of recommendations concerning minority representation, deleting sex bias language, including appointment of an Affirmative Action Coordinator.

1977: 85–87.

Recommended (1) all boards and agencies, committees and commissions change their constitutions to allow representation of at least one member from each council; (2) that CPC establish a full-time or part time director for the American Indian Council; (3) study advisibility of an annual report of the minority councils.

1977: 76–84. To be presented to 1978 GS.

See also BLACK COUNCIL; AMERICAN INDIAN COUNCIL; and HISPANIC COUNCIL.

MINORITY EDUCATION FUND

Set up in connection with the Black Studies Program.

1971: 66.

To be continued.

1972: 48. Adopted.

1973: 63.

CAC recommends that GS appoint a committee to study the situation of minority enrollment in the RCA colleges and seminaries to be implemented by GSEC.

1975: 200. Adopted.

GSEC gives a full report of findings from questionnaires regarding minority enrollment and efforts being made on each campus.

1976: 38–44.

MINORITY REPRESENTATION ON GSEC

Overture requesting GS to provide for minority representation on the GSEC.

1975: 92–93. Adopted. To be encouraged through PS's.

MISSION

TC statement on: an article will appear in the Church Herald and work has begun on a new confession which will also be concerned with mission.

1971: 217.

MISSION BUDGET OF GENERAL SYNOD

1974: 174–178.

1975: 148–150.

1976: 88–90.

1977: 96–98.

For earlier listings see BENEVOLENCE BUDGET OF GS.

MISSION BOARDS

Overture regarding the unifying of the two mission boards.

1960: 114–115, 119. To be studied and reported on.

Possibility of merger of the BWM and BNAM suggested.

1965: 74, 78, 84–85. Study to continue.

Joint committee report.

1966: 103–105. Single board concept met with approval of the Joint Committee; study to continue.

Possibility of including SC and BE.

1967: 157–158. SCDS to continue study.

Became part of CPC in 1968. See also GENERAL PROGRAM COUNCIL.

MISSION CHURCH

Overture suggesting a church be declared a "mission church" if it has fewer than 75 members.

1964: 132–133, 140, 151. Referred to CRC.

CRC statement: "Insufficiency of communicant membership to fulfill the purposes and responsibilities of an organized church."

1965: 166–167. Sent to classes for approval.

Classes approved.

1966: 189.

Overture requesting that a) the real or essential work of the church be included in reasons why a church be called a mission church; b) that a new term be found for "mission church" and c) that "give reason" be substituted for "give cause."

1966: 127-129, 145-146, 150. a) adopted; b) and c) no action.

MISSION FESTIVAL '71 (MILWAUKEE)
1971: 67.
1974: 59.

MISSION INVESTMENT POLICY
Report.
1970: 180-181.

MISSION OF THE CHURCH
1959: 246-247.

MISSION OF THE MONTH
Learning more about each RCA Mission; and giving something extra.
1974: 156. One-third of RCA churches participating.
Used by 300 churches.
1975: 141.
1976: 80.
1977: 88.

MISSION PROGRAM IN COOPERATION WITH PCUS
Suggested that JC24 study and make report.
1964: 85-86. Postponed until report of JC24 is discussed.

MISSION PROGRAM
RCGPC recommends that GS instruct GPC to evaluate and continue to improve methods of relating the denomination's mission program to the local church, increasing support of the churches and their members.
1977: 144. Adopted.

MISSIONARIES, CHURCH MEMBERSHIP OF
May be members of the indigenous church as well as the RCA. (See letter to the Presbyterian Church of Taiwan regarding Ruth Broekema and Jeanne Walvoord.)
1958: 87-88.
1959: 146.

MISSIONARIES, DIRECTORY OF
1958: App., Report of BCWM, 74-82; report of BDM, 37-41.
1959: App., Report of BCWM, 75-82; Report of BDM, 42-46.
1960: App., Report of BCWM, 74-81, Report of BDM, 34-38.
1961: App., Report of BWM, 71-80; Report of BNAM, 35-39.
1962: App., Report of BWM, 69-80; Report of BNAM, 41-46.
1963: App., Report of BWM, 73-84; Report of BNAM, 39-43.
1964: App., Report of BWM, 90-96; Report of BNAM, 41-46.
1965: App., Report of BWM, 49-59; Report of BNAM, 46-50.
1966: App., Report of BWM, 1-12; Report of BNAM, 39-43.
1967: App. 2, 15-21.
1968: App. 2, 17-23.
1969: App. 2, 141-146.
1970: App. 2, 129-137.
1971: App. 2, 226-233.
1972: App. 2, 230-237.
1973: App. 2, 206-214.
1974: App. 2, 250-255.
1975: App. 2, 265-270.
1976: App. 1, 266-273.
1977: App. 1, 273-281.

MISSIONARIES, PENSIONS AND SOCIAL SECURITY
Overture regarding.
1960: 84. No action.
1969: 79. GPC working on the problem.

MISSIONARY CONFERENCES
President suggests material be produced on "How to conduct a missionary conference."
1965: 338, 346, 348. BNAM and BWM to prepare packets.

MISSIONARY PERSONNEL, CHANGES IN
1970: 64-66.
1971: 69-73.
1972: 61-66.
1975: 61-64.
1976: 129-131, 119.
1977: 135-137.

MISSIONS
Recommendation that GPC and OPC consider development of overseas programs as a part of the program administrator's responsibilities.
1972: 67. Adopted.
President urges GS to reverse our decline in overseas missionary witness and to encourage the GPC to begin a transcultural evangelistic witness, in addition to the proposed new fields in the Growth Fund Drive, in at least two other unevangelized or inadequately evangelized areas overseas or in Mexico.
1977: 28-29, 35. Adopted.
See ADVANCE IN MISSIONS; CHURCH GROWTH; GENERAL PROGRAM COUNCIL reports; and also DOMESTIC MISSIONS; CHRISTIAN WORLD MISSIONS; NORTH AMERICAN MISSIONS; and WORLD MISSIONS.

MIXED MARRIAGES (CATHOLIC AND REFORMED)
See MARRIAGE CEREMONY.

MOL, NORMAN
Dispensation from professorial certificate requested.
1973: 33, 36. Not granted.

MONEY RAISING
Asked that GS be authorized to employ Ketchum, Inc.
1964: 355.
Overture opposing commercial money raising organization.
1965: 113, 116. Referred to SCSC.
SCSC confident that a fund raising organization is consonant with the biblical principles of Christian stewardship.
1965: 300. No action.

MOON, SUN MYUNG
Bibliography on.
1977: 282-284.
The Divine Principle: A critique of the thought of Sun Myung Moon, presented by TC. The NCC of Korea states unequivocally that his (Moon's) Unification chruch is not Christian. Recommended that the critique be made available in print to the church at large.
1977: 272-284. Adopted.

MOORE, REV. BOUDE C. AND MRS. ANNA C., MISSIONARIES TO JAPAN FOR 38 YEARS
Honored at Synod.
1962: 87.

MULDER, REV. BERNARD J.
Retiring after 19 years as Executive Secretary of the BE.
1964: 60.
Resolution.
1964: 60-61, 63.

MULDER, REV. EDWIN G.
Appointed Minister of Evangelism.
1964: 93.

MULDER, REV. JOHN R.
Retirement from the Presidency of WTS.
1960: 47, 70.
Resolution and declared President Emeritus.
1960: 56.

MULTIPLE PARISH
Definition of: a group of local churches sharing services of one or more installed ministers.
1972: 195. Adopted and sent to classes for approval.
Classes approved.
1973: 128.
Overture requesting additional elder representation at classis when there are fewer ministers than churches.
1972: 97-98, 195. Adopted and sent to classes for approval.
Classes approved.
1973: 128.
Overture requesting that each congregation in a multiple parish have the same number of delegates to classis as it would, were it not a member of a multiple parish.
1973: 108. No action.

MULTIPLE STAFF MINISTRY
Recommended that the BTE investigate possibility of the seminaries providing resources in this area.
1974: 39-40. Adopted.
Recommended by RCBTE that seminaries equip students for multiple staff positions and specialized ministries with the same diligence in which individuals are prepared for preaching pastorates.
1975: 35. Adopted.
BTE reports that WTS and the WRC are preparing a day with the ministers who are in churches that have more than one ministry. Study to continue.
1975: 31.

MY FATHER'S BUSINESS
Children's magazine—10th year.
1960: 68-69.

NAIROBI, 1975
See WCC, 5TH ASSEMBLY.
1977: 256, 257.

NATIONAL ASSOCIATION OF EVANGELICALS
Recommended the IRC explore possibility of RCA membership in the NAE.
1973: 258-259.
Chairman to attend the annual conference of.
1975: 206, 231. Approved.
Report.
1976: 213-214.

NATIONAL COUNCIL OF CHURCHES
Report.

1958: 163-172.	1968: 224-230.
1959: 169-182.	1969: 256-257.
1960: 142-153.	1970: 231-235.
1961: 172-185.	1971: 238-242.
1962: 161-178.	1972: 237-240.
1963: 175-184.	1973: 237-241.
1964: 241-258.	1974: 232-235.
1965: 247-253.	1975: 212-214.
1966: 239-242.	1976: 218-221.
1967: 218-225.	1977: 258-263.

Overture requesting the RCA reconsider affiliation with.
1961: 129, 142. No action.
Overture regarding Broadcasting and Film Division.
1961: 130, 142. Adopted.
Overture regarding communist infiltration.
1961: 140-141, 142. No action.
Overture regarding membership in.
1963: 110, 112. No action.

Overture requesting a study of the RCA's position in relation to NCC (Communism).
1965: 106, 116. Referred to SCIR.
SCIR reply to overture.
1965: 235-236. Referred to PCIR for study, particularly the NCC's alleged Communistic tendencies and unscriptural teachings.
Report of PCIR regarding financial support.
1965: 233, 239, 243. Adopted.
Overture urging withdrawal from.
1965: 113-114, 116. Referred to SCIR.
SCIR reply to above overture.
1965: 113, 236-238, 243. Church Herald and PCIR will inform the RCA about the work and witness of the NCC.
Overture requesting withdrawal of membership.
1967: 114-115, 123. Referred to CIR.
Motion that NCC and WCC be removed from GS assessments to benevolence askings.
1967: 296-297. Referred to GSEC.
Overture urging RCA to withdraw membership because of alleged radical positions.
1968: 104, 120, 124. No action.
Overture to a) request NCC to withhold making pronouncements that generate disunity; b) to allow the churches to support the council on a voluntary basis.
1968: 105, 120, 124. a) adopted; b) referred to GPC.
Overture requesting a new committee be appointed to investigate the programs, goals, and declarations of groups under the control of the NCC, and if the patterns of action should be in contradiction of RCA standards we take steps to withdraw.
1968: 105-106, 120, 124. Adopted. Referred to GSEC.
Above action referred to a Sub-Committee on Miscellaneous Business. A special Committee to Evaluate RCA Relationships to the NCC will report later.
1969: 160, 162.
Report of Special Committee.
1969: 295-302. Voted to retain membership.
Recommended nominations from all parts of the RCA for membership on RCA-NCC Committee.
1969: 301, 302. Adopted.
Involvement of RCA in several divisions of NCC: 1) Area Departments (Africa, Southern Asia, East Asia, Latin America, Middle East, Europe); 2) overseas ministries; 3) RAVEMCO, Lit-Lit; 4) Church World Service, and many others—work a denomination could not do alone.
1969: 86-90.
Overture suggesting membership be on a voluntary basis.
1970: 95, 108. Recommended that funds now given NCC from GS be solicited on a voluntary basis. Adopted.
Seven overtures requesting withdrawal of membership in the NCC.
1970: 90-95, 107-108. No action.
Radical Conciliar Theory: an Ecumenical Movement of Mission by the whole church to the whole society.
1970: 231-235.
Document, "The Eucharist in the Life of the Church: An Ecumenical Consensus."
1971: 238-242.
Overture urging withdrawal of membership from both NCC and WCC.
1971: 101, 113. No action.
Two overtures requesting retaining the present practice of non-assessment to NCC and WCC.
1971: 100-101, 113. No action.
Two overtures requesting restoring assessment amount in the GS budget for the NCC and WCC.
1971: 99-100, 109, 113, 116.
Recommended that GS place in its budget $9100 or RCA's share in administrative expenses.
1972: 259. Adopted.
Recommended that RCA continue participation in.
1973: 257. Adopted.
GSEC recommends that as a responsible member denomination the RCA must find ways to contribute our RCA proportionate share of administrative expenses.
1973: 133-136.
Two overtures requesting withdrawal of membership.
1973: 88-89. No action.
Overture requesting that the CIR review our participation in NCC in view of their restructuring.
1973: 87-88. Adopted. Special committee appointed.
Report of special committee: recommended RCA reaffirm membership in.
1974: 132-135. Adopted.
Special Committee's minority report.
1974: 135-137.
Four overtures suggesting the contributions to NCC and WCC be on a voluntary basis.
1973: 85. No action.
Overture asking that 1972 action be re-

scinded so that the assessment will not be included in GS budget.
1973: 84. No action. As a responsible member we must pay our fair share.
Overture requesting the NCC assessment be made an "asking."
1973: 84–85. No action.
IRC recommends importance of affiliation with the NCC and WCC be relayed to the churches; that feedback be sent to the churches about the conferences and assemblies to which we send delegates.
1974: 253. Adopted.
Recommended that the TC study the related question of conscience and authority, especially with reference to statements of church bodies (whether consistory, classis, synod, or council) and the role of these statements in the life of the church and its members.
1974: 135. Adopted. See also AUTHORITY AND CONSCIENCE.
Since ways must be found to pay participating share for interchurch bodies, outside of assessments to classes, the matter of funding was referred to the CIR, a special committee of which will make proposals to GS.
1974: 115, 117.
Overture requesting GS to maintain support of the NCC only by voluntary contributions of an individual member or church.
1975: 92. No action; declared out of order because of previous action.
Recommended the GS re-affirm RCA membership in NCC.
1976: 135. Adopted (yes, 186; no, 52).
Attitude toward Cuban Crisis—see CUBAN CRISIS.

NATIONAL DEPARTMENT OF WOMEN'S WORK.
Report.
1960: 304–306. 1967: 322–323.
1961: 379–380. 1968: 348–352.
1962: 396–398. 1969: 341–347.
1963: 275–277. 1970: 363–368.
1964: 450–453. 1971: 283–287.
1965: 411–414. 1972: 289–290.
1966: 369–372.
Formerly WOMEN'S WORK, which see.
In 1972 name was changed to REFORMED CHURCH WOMEN, which also see.
Women's Day at Synod.
1958: 333. 1961: 380.
1959: 347. 1962: 396.
1960: 304. 1963: 275.
1964: 451–453. 1966: 371–372.
1965: 413–414. 1968: 351–352.
Triennial (First) at Holland, Michigan.
1962: 396.
Triennial (Second) at Chicago, Illinois.
1965: 412
Triennial (Third) at Philadelphia, Pa.
1968: 349–350.
Other triennials listed under REFORMED CHURCH WOMEN.
Relationships between NDWW, GS and GPC stated. The fact that women have no vote in consistories, classes, PS's and GS make it necessary to remain a separate department.
1969: 171.
Committee met and suggests a recommendation be made next year.
1970: 127–128.
Recommendations: (1) that women be appointed to serve on future meetings on regionalization; (2) more women be appointed to other committees especially to CAC; (3) women be appointed to PS committees; (4) more women appointed to classis committees.
1971: 286–287. All adopted.
Two members to be appointed as corresponding delegates to GS.
1971: 210. Adopted and sent to classes for approval.
Classes approved corresponding delegates.
1972: 120.
Purpose and relationships of the NDWW.
1971: 141–142.
Study book 1972: "To Live with Joy" by Ruth Dickson.
1972: 293.
See REFORMED CHURCH WOMEN.

NATIONAL GUARD.
Overture opposing Sunday drills.
1960: 110, 117. Adopted.

NATIONAL PARKS, CHRISTIAN MINISTRY IN
1958: 167.
1959: 173.

NATIONAL OFFICES (DENOMINATIONAL), LOCATION OF
Six overtures suggesting a committee study the possibility of relocating boards and agencies in a more central area of the church. One or two include the seminaries in this move.
1971: 97–99, 106, 112–113, 115. No action since GSEC is already recommending a committee.
GSEC and COR recommend a special

committee for study of location of national offices.
1971: 140, 195-196. Adopted.
GSEC's outline of study on.
1971: 138-140.
GSEC recommendations: (1) relocation should take place within two or three years; (2) must have the following characteristics: a) a geographic location not further west than Chicago, nor further south than Cincinnati, nor further north than Cleveland, b) within approximately 20 miles of a major airport, c) as close as feasible to, but not further than 20 miles from two or three theological colleges of national stature, d) building would include a united seminary, a national conference center, and education facilities.
1971: 137.
Detailed report of the Special Committee on the location of national offices and seminaries, and their conclusions: Recommended (1) that the two present seminary locations, in Holland and New Brunswick, and the national headquarters in New York be retained for the present time for expanded ministries and relationships; and (2) that the present committee continue for another year.
1972: 185. Adopted.
Committee recommends that the RCA retain its national offices at 475 Riverside Dr., N.Y. for functions distinctly national in concept of developing "centers."
1973: 188-189. Adopted.
Complete report.
1973: 185-190.
Committee discharged.
1973: 189.

NATIONAL YOUTH ORGANIZATION
Overture regarding relationship with Christian Endeavor.
1959: 78, 127, 128.
Organization proposed.
1959: 66-71, 78-79.
Proposed Constitution.
1959: 66.
Directives.
1960: 69.
See also APPENDIX, Annual report of BE.

NATURE OF OFFICES AND MINISTRIES AND THEIR RESPECTIVE FUNCTIONS, COMMITTEE TO STUDY, see OFFICES AND MINISTRIES OF THE CHURCH, NATURE OF, STUDY COMMITTEE ON.

NECROLOGY, PERMANENT COMMITTEE ON
Report.
1958: 206-221. 1960: 188-201.
1959: 212-219. 1961: 218-226.
1962: 225-236. 1970: 244-248.
1963: 324-333. 1971: 256-262.
1964: 330-340. 1972: 260-266.
1965: 278-283. 1973: 264-268.
1966: 307-312. 1974: 258-265.
1967: 273-278. 1975: 233-236.
1968: 298-306. 1976: 199-210.
1969: 305-310. 1977: 243-250.
Changes in organization—membership, responsibilities, etc.
1970: 146.
Recommended that the work of the Committee on Necrology be taken over by COH.
1974: 267-268. Adopted.
1975: 102. Adopted.

NEDERDUITSE GEREFORMERDE KERK (SOUTH AFRICA)
See SOUTH AFRICA.

NEPOTISM
Committee of Nominations shall be guided by this rule: No person shall be employed as a member of the executive or administrative staff who is more closely related by blood or marriage to any other such staff or board/council/committee member than by the degree of first counsinship for the following: GSEC, BD, GPC, RCA Extension Foundation, BTE, ECCH, NDWW, KIRKSIDE, BP, CAF, OHR, OPC.
1970: 148. Adopted.
GSEC recommends amendment: "That no one shall be employed in Classifications I-IV who is more closely related than by the degree of first cousinship to anyone else employed in Classification I-IV; that no one shall be employed in Classification V-VI who is more closely related than by the degree of first cousinship to anyone employed in Classification I-IV—also applies to relations by marriage. No member of a committee, board, or council shall vote on a matter affecting the employment of anyone who is more closely related than by the degree of first cousinship, nor speak to the matter in regularly convened meeting.
1973: 132-133. Adopted.
Amendment must also be approved by 1974 GS.
1974: 120. Adopted.

NEW BRUNSWICK THEOLOGICAL SEMINARY
Report.
1958: 35-44. 1963: 30-37.
1959: 32-44. 1964: 30-35.
1960: 30-43. 1965: 31-36.
1961: 31-57. 1966: 31-35.
1962: 29-40. 1967: 35-42.
Subsequent reports under THEOLOGICAL EDUCATION, BOARD OF.

Board of Superintendents, list of.
1958: 374-376. 1963: 455-456.
1959: 379-381. 1964: 473-474.
1960: 350-352. 1965: 436-437.
1961: 409-411. 1966: 394-395.
1962: 426-427.
1967: See SEMINARIES, BOARD OF.
After 1967, see THEOLOGICAL EDUCATION, BOARD OF.
Degrees conferred.
1958: 36. 1967: 36-37.
1959: 34. 1970: App. 2, 142-144.
1960: 32. 1971: App. 2, 239-240.
1961: 217. 1972: App. 2, 243-244.
1962: 29-30. 1973: App. 2, 220-221.
1963: 30. 1974: App. 2, 265-267.
1964: 30-31. 1975: App. 2, 280-282.
1965: 31-32. 1976: App. 1, 282-285.
1966: 32. 1977: App. 1, 292-294.
Professors and Lectors, list of.
1958: 372. 1967: App. 2, 11.
1959: 377. 1968: App. 2, 13.
1960: 348. 1969: App. 2, 11.
1961: 407. 1970: App. 2, 12.
1962: 424. 1971: App. 2, 19-20.
1963: 453. 1972: App. 2, 19-20.
1964: 471. 1973: App. 2, 19-20.
1965: 434. 1974: App. 2, 20-21.
1966: 392. 1975: App. 2, 21.
1976: App. 1, 21.
1977: App. 1, 21.
Students, List of.
1958: 36-37. 1966: Names not listed.
1959: 33-34. 1967: Names not listed.
1960: 31-32. 1968: App. 2, 176.
1961: 32. 1969: App. 2, 152.
1962: 29-31. 1970: App. 2, 145-146.
1963: 30-31. 1971: App. 2, 241.
1964: 30-31. 1972: App. 2, 245.
1965: 31-32. 1973: App. 2, 222.
1974: App. 2, 268.
One hundred seventy-fifth anniversary (First Theological Seminary in America).
1958: 346-349.
1959: 349-354.
Plan of Organization.
1961: 52-57.
Questions considered by Planning and Development Committee: (1) relocation of seminary; (2) joining with WTS and seeking a new location.
1961: 38-39.
See also.
1923: 96-97.
1948: 90.
Request for $1,500,000 Building Program.
1961: 42, 73. Approved.
Hertzog Hall removed; Samuel M. Zwemer Hall nearing completion.
1967: 35.
Dr. Howard Hageman appointed President of NBTS.
1973: 28.
See also THEOLOGICAL EDUCATION, BOARD OF.

NEW BRUNSWICK AND WESTERN THEOLOGICAL SEMINARIES, BOARD OF SUPERINTENDENTS OF.
Report.
1968: 38-40.
By Laws of the two seminaries.
1968: 158-164.
For ensuing reports see THEOLOGICAL EDUCATION, BOARD OF.

NEW IDEAS COMMITTEE
Overture requesting such a committee to receive each classis President's report. The committee in turn to refer suggestions to classes.
1965: 106, 117, 123. No action.

NEW JERSEY BENEFICIARY FUNDS
1959: 18-19. 1969: 19-20.
1960: 16-17. 1970: 18-19, 20.
1961: 14-15. 1971: 19.
1962: 15-16. 1972: 19.
1963: 16. 1973: 24.
1964: 17. 1974: 21, 25.
1965: 17-18. 1975: 23, 26.
1966: 19. 1976: 94.
1967: 19. 1977: 102.
1968: 20.
Scholarships for ministerial students amounted to $21,162 in 1976.

NEW JERSEY, PARTICULAR SYNOD OF,
Overture regarding realignment of classes.
1961: 133, 142. No action.
Report of Committee on Judicial Business.
1961: 145-147.
Realignment of classes.
1962: 131, 133-135. Action taken on Feb. 21, 1961 not valid since the meeting of PS had not been called in accordance with the Constitution.
Question of the constitutional powers of the PS.
1963: 122.
Realignment as voted on Sept. 12 and 13, 1962 retained.
1963: 122-125.
Text of complaint and addendum concerning a united synod.
1970: 118-120.
Complaint by four members that forming a united synod with the UPCUSA was unconstitutional.
1970: 166-117. committee recommended dismissal of complaint—lost.

It was voted to form a plan for a united PS and present it to GS. Adopted.
A Plan for the United Synod of New Jersey
1971: 122–124, 269. Approved.
Four members of PS enter a complaint against the PS in adopting a "Plan of Operation for the United Synod of New Jersey." Committee determined that the plan does not entail merger or union, but simply establishes a structure for engaging in cooperative programs.
1971: 120–121. Complaint dismissed.

NEW MORALITY, THE
President recommends that CAC study the problem and present a substantial statement.
1965: 335, 345, 348. Referred to CAC.
CAC requests another year for study.
1966: 223–224, 235.

NEW YORK FUNDS
1958: 16. 1968: 18–20.
1959: 12–13. 1969: 18–19.
1960: 12–13. 1970: 19–20.
1961: 12–13. 1971: 18–19.
1962: 14–15. 1972: 15–16.
1963: 14–15. 1973: 20–21.
1964: 15–17. 1974: 21, 22, 24.
1965: 16–17. 1975: 23.
1966: 17–19. 1976: 91–92.
1967: 17–19. 1977: 99.

NEW YORK, PARTICULAR SYNOD OF
Overture regarding realignment of.
1961: 132, 142. Adopted.
Complaint of consistories to.
1976: 62. Complaint dismissed because it should have been made to the next higher judicatory.

NEW YORK WORLD'S FAIR
RCA to have display in Protestant Center.
1963: 147.
Exhibit in cooperation with UPCUSA.
1964: 101, 167.

NEXT PLACE OF MEETING (GENERAL SYNOD) COMMITTEE ON
1958: 368. 1962: 419–420.
1959: 373. 1963: 449.
1960: 343–344. 1964: 467.
1961: 403.
Committee discontinued.
1964: 175.

NIENHUIS, MISS JEAN, MISSIONARY TO CHINA FOR 33 YEARS, 1920–1953.
Death at 88, April 3, 1975.
1976: 131.

NOMINATIONS, STANDING COMMITTEE ON
Report.
1958: 332. 1959: 346.
1960: 302–303. 1963: 443.
1961: 378. 1964: 443–444.
1962: 393–395. 1965: 401–404.
Suggested this committee become a Permanent Committee.
1962: 393.
See next listing.

NOMINATIONS, PERMANENT COMMITTEE ON
Report.
1966: 359–362. 1972: 283.
1967: 314–315. 1973: 281.
1968: 338–341. 1974: 285.
1969: 334. 1975: 253.
1970: 256–257. 1976: 248.
1971: 276–277. 1977: 313.
Changes in organization—membership, responsibilities, etc. Committee became Review and Permanent Committee.
1970: 146–148.

NON-DISCRIMINATORY EMPLOYMENT PRACTICES
Urged by CAC in all church related institutions.
1971: 225–226. Approved.

NON-VIOLENCE (PEACE)
GSEC reports that CAC is to study the meaning of non-violence in all of life.
1975: 99.
See also PEACE.

NOORDHOFF, MISS JEANNE, MISSIONARY TO JAPAN, 1911–1952.
Death.
1971: 73.

NOORDYK, WILHELMINA, MISSIONARY NURSE IN INDIA FOR 38 YEARS
Obituary.
1964: App., Report of the BWM, 71–72.

NORTH AMERICAN MISSIONS, BOARD OF, STANDING COMMITTEE ON
Report.
1961: 102–115. 1965: 80–88.
1962: 89–96. 1966: 92–103.
1963: 85–92. 1967: 88–97.
1964: 91–101. 1968: 73–82.
See also Appendix, or Appendix 1 for annual reports of the Board. After 1968, see GENERAL PROGRAM COUNCIL.

NORTH GRAND RAPIDS, CLASSIS OF
Since the non-payment of classical assessments in full is in the judicial process in the PS of Michigan, delegates will remain seated as full voting delegates at this session. They must pursue the judicial process and report to GSEC before their April meeting.
1973: 177. Adopted.

NORTHWESTERN COLLEGE AND ACADEMY
Report.
1958: 71-72. 1960: 65-67.
1959: 61-63. 1961: 81-84.
Academy discontinued. The report for 1962 marks a total four year program without the secondary program of the Academy.

NORTHWESTERN COLLEGE
Report.
1962: 71-74. 1970: 47-51.
1963: 70-72. 1971: 46-49.
1964: 73-76. 1972: 40-42.
1965: 60-66. 1973: 45-47.
1966: 75-80. 1974: 48-49.
1967: 69-73. 1975: 44-45.
1968: 57-59. 1976: 158-160.
1969: 57-61. 1977: 179-181.
Amendment to By Laws.
1973: 129-130. Adopted.
1977: 43. Adopted.

NUCLEAR TESTING
Limiting of recommended.
1958: 160, 162. Lost.
1963: 319, 322. Adopted.
CAC recommends commending the government for the negotiation of a treaty banning nuclear testing from the ocean floor.
1971: 227. Adopted.

NYKAMP, REV. ROBERT A.
Nominated to Office of Professor of Theology at WTS.
1976: 146, 148. Elected.
Accepted a call to a pastorate in Florida prior to being installed.
1977: 158.

NYKERK, DR. GERALD HERBERT, MEDICAL MISSIONARY IN THE ARABIAN FIELD, 1940-1964.
Memorial for.
1964: 84-85.

NYKERK, ROSE (MRS. GERALD)
see BATTLESON, ROSE NYKERK

OBITUARIES
See NECROLOGY.

OBSENITY
See PORNOGRAPHY.

OFFICE OF FINANCE
See FINANCE, OFFICE OF.

OFFICE OF HUMAN RESOURCES
See HUMAN RESOURCES, OFFICE OF.

OFFICE OF PROMOTION AND COMMUNICATION
See PROMOTION AND COMMUNICATION, OFFICE OF.

OFFICES AND MINISTRIES AND THEIR RESPECTIVE FUNCTIONS, COMMITTEE ON
Report.
1959: 357-360. Committee continued.
1960: 307-324.
1961: 381-382.
Committee dissolved.
1961: 382.

OGGEL, REV. M. VERNE
Elected Vice President of GS.
1962: 6.
Elected President of GS.
1963: 7.

OLDER MEN FOR THE MINISTRY
See MINISTRY, OLDER MEN FOR.

OMAN
1971: 59-60.
1974: 64-65.

ONE GREAT HOUR OF SHARING
Part of CHURCH WORLD SERVICE, R.C.A., which see.

ONTARIO CLASSIS
See CANADA.

OPEN HOUSING (OCCUPANCY)
1960: 179-180.
1961: 209, 215, 216.
1962: 222-223, 287-289, 343.
CAC report.
1965: 206-208, 218-219. Adopted.

OPPENEER, MR. ALFRED
Resolution upon 39 years of service in Kentucky.
1959: 108, 109.

ORANGE-DAKOTA CLASSIS EXCHANGE
1971: 67.
See also COMMITTEE OF 18.

ORDINATION OF WOMEN
Overture requests postponement of action, and wider study of.
1958: 131. No action.
Three classes report on their actions on women's ordination.
1958: 131. Received for information.
Report of the Committee on Ordaining of Women.
1958: 321-331. Some of the subjects covered, follow.
Sociological aspects of.
1958: 321-328.
Theological and biblical aspects.
1958: 328-330. Committee discharged.
Committee recommends classes vote on "the offices in the RCA will be open to women and men alike beginning in 1962."
1958: 330. Adopted.
Ordination of women defeated by classes.
1959: 236.

Overture requesting Constitution be amended to permit ordination of women.
1964: 117, 139, 142–143, 149–150. Not approved.

Recommendation to delete the word "male" from the election of elders and deacons.
1967: 188, 199. Adopted and referred to classes.

Overture requesting the word "male" be deleted from the election of elders and deacons, permitting the ordination of all members for the office of elder and deacon.
1969: 121, 140, 151. Adopted. Referred to CRC for wording.

Overture requesting that elders and deacons be chosen from the membership above age twenty; and the ordination of women to the offices of elder, deacon, and minister of the Word be placed in the jurisdiction of each classis.
1969: 122–123, 141, 151. Adopted and referred to CRC for wording. GSEC to appoint a committee of men and women to involve the church in an educational program regarding the right of women to the offices of the church.

ECRC presents the following amendment of the Government: "Elders and deacons shall be chosen from the members of the church in full communion who are at least 21 years of age."
1969: 230, 232. Adopted and referred to classes.

Not adopted by classes.
1970: 141.

ECRC recommends the following amendment of the Government: "The ministers of the Word are those *men and women* who have been inducted into that office by ordination in accordance with the Word of God and the order established by the church."
1969: 231, 232. Adopted and referred to classes.

Not adopted by classes.
1970: 141.

Overture requesting the classes be allowed to permit the churches within their bounds to choose elders and deacons from the members of the church.
1969: 121, 141, 151. No action. This should be a decision of the denomination—not of a classis.

"Equality for Women in the Reformed Church"—paper presented by the CAC.
1970: 218–220. NCC statement to be sent to classes for study.

Report of committee providing an educational program on the subject.
1970: 127. Three articles to appear in CH.

Overture requesting BCO be amended to empower any classis to ordain and install to the Office of minister of the Word and any church to ordain and install elders and deacons such persons most fitted without distinction as to sex.
1970: 101, 112, 201. Adopted and referred to EC. Amendment in four parts sent to classes, each to be voted on separately.

All four parts defeated by classes.
1971: 151–152.

Overture requesting biblical cause why three congregations should not have elected women elders and deacons.
1970: 99, 110–111. No biblical cause for not doing so, but admitted violation of the BCO. No action.

Overture requesting the word "male" be omitted from the article.
1970: 99, 111. No action.

Recommended that wording in the Government be "Elders and deacons shall be chosen from the members of the church in full communion who are at least twenty-one years of age."
1971: 289. Adopted and sent to classes for approval.

Above action approved by classes.
1972: 119, 120 (yes, 30; no, 14). See also ELDERS AND DEACONS, ELECTION OF.

Overture urging ordination of women to the office of minister of the Word.
1972: 96. Adopted and sent to classes for approval.

Not approved by classes.
1973: 128–129.

Overture requesting that individual churches be permitted to limit consistory membership to male members of the congregation 21 years of age and above, or at the discretion of the consistory, 18 years.
1973: 111, No action.

Overture requesting an addition to the approval of women being elders and deacons; "no one who by reason of conscience, cannot participate in the election, ordination, and installation of women to church office, shall be expected to do so."
1973: 112. No action.

Overture requesting GS to declare that no woman shall be ordained into the office of minister of the Word in the RCA until such time as the classes approve this and change "persons" to "men and women."
1974: 108–109, 200. No action.

Overture requesting amendment concerning ministers of the Word, to change the word "persons" to "male members of the church."
1974: 97. No action.
GSEC recommends amendment concerning ministers of the Word, to change "persons" to "men and women."
1974: 93-94, 124-125, 200. Adopted and referred to classes for approval.
Not approved by classes.
1975: 99.
RCBTE recommends that the word "persons" be changed to "men and women" in the BCO.
1975: 35. Adopted and sent to classes for approval.
Not approved by classes (yes, 29; no, 16, 1 tie).
1976: 46.
Recommend amendment to BCO substituting words "men and women" for "persons."
1976: 249. Adopted.
CAC recommends that GS support the right of choice for women to respond to the call of God to be ministers of the Gospel in the RCA.
1976: 190-191. Adopted.
President strongly suggests and committee recommends that "persons" be replaced by "men and women."
1976: 28-29, 34. Approved and sent to classes for approval.
Not approved by classes.
1977: 42 (Yes, 29; No 16).
Overture recommending GS substitute the words "men and women" for the word "persons."
1977: 117-118. Approved and referred to EC.
COCG recommends the amendment in the BCO substituting the words "men and women" for the word "persons."
1977: 320. Sent to classes for approval.
Recommended that GS request all classes to refrain from ordaining women to the office of ministry of the Word until such time as the BCO is amended.
1977: 64. Adopted.
President expresses the hope for an orderly solution of differences without compromising convictions—to "keep the unity of the spirit in the bond of peace."
1977: 29-30.
See also STEDGE, JOYCE.

ORGAN TRANSPLANTS
See BIOLOGICAL ENGINEERING.

ORIGINAL LANGUAGES, REQUIREMENT OF IN SEMINARY STUDY
Report of Special Curriculum Committee on Greek requirements.
1958: 350.
Report of Special Curriculum Committee on Hebrew requirements.
1958: 350.
Overture urging the following: (1) eliminate Greek and Hebrew as required subjects, but provide them as electives; (2) seminaries to provide suitable background courses to acquaint students with the flavor of the languages; (3) that these changes be made by fall of 1971.
1969: 135, 148, 153. BTE has this under study. No action.
Two overtures requesting Greek and Hebrew be made electives in the seminaries, rather than required.
1968: 101, 118, 123. Referred to Program Design Committee of BTE.
BTE recommends no action until adoption of new curriculum or program design.
1969: 42, 44. No action.
Overture requesting that Hebrew and Greek be made electives.
1972: 92-93. Referred to BTE for study.
BTE requests that GS defer this matter to 1974.
1973: 32, 36. Adopted.
BTE committee recommends the amendment should read: "The interpretation of the Scriptures, including a basic working knowledge of the original languages," be referred to the GS and that they adopt the wording and refer it to classes.
1974: 30.
RCTE recommends the above not be approved and that the wording be retained as presently stated in the BCO.
1974: 38-39. Recommendation of RCTE adopted.

OTHER MATTERS
1964: 468.
1965: 430.
1966: 386-389.
1967: 336-338.
1968: 369-370.
1969: 349.
1970: 270.
1971: 289-290.
1972: 297.
1973: 292.
1974: 299-300.
1975: 267-269.
1976: 254-257.
1977: 325.

OUDERSLUYS, REV. RICHARD C.
Retiring after 35 years as Professor of New Testament Studies at WTS.
1977: 159.
Tribute and resolution.
1977: 169-170.
Declared Emeritus.
1977: 63.

OUR FATHER'S BUSINESS
(Brochure of Stewardship Council)
1960: 207. 1965: 299.
1961: 235-236. 1966: 328.
1964: 354. 1967: 291.

"OUR SONG OF HOPE"
The new Confession of Faith by Prof. E. Heideman. First draft completed.
1973: 201.
Its center is to proclaim the good news of hope for the world.
1974: 167-169.
Recommended that GS encourage a wide use of the Confession.
1974: 169. Adopted.
GSEC recommends that GS reaffirm the use of "Our Song of Hope" and the study guide as a provisional standard for a period of three years, ending in 1978.
1975: 97. Adopted.
Designated as a Provisional Standard with recommendation for approval to be made in 1978.
1976: 257.
The Confession and study guide have been distributed throughout the RCA. A report with recommendation of its approval will be made in 1978.
1977: 325.
See also CONFESSION OF FAITH—NEW.

OVERSEAS PERSONNEL RECRUITMENT OFFICE
RCA Personnel Office to use the services of a cooperative recruitment program together with eight denominations.
1969: 79.
Assists in testing, screening of applicants, etc.
1970: 63.
Decision to withdraw membership and handle recruitment through OHR.
1971: 63.

OVERTURES TO GENERAL SYNOD
Received.
1958: 10-12 (19).
1959: 10-11 (24).
1960: 10-11 (53).
1961: 9-10 (30).
1962: 10-11 (50).
1963: 11-12 (26).
1964: 11-13, 115-137 (50).
1965: 12-13, 103-115 (28).
1966: 13-14, 117-141 (44).
1967: 13-14, 109-123 (29).
1968: 14-15, 92-116 (47).
1969: 14-16, 119-140 (40).
1970: 78-102 (44).
1971: 89-111 (39).
1972: 80-81 (45).
1973: 82-83 (49).
1974: 91-92 (30).
1975:.80-81 (22).
1976: 96-97 (34).
1977: 107 (17).

OVERTURES, STANDING COMMITTEE ON
Report.
1958: 130-136. 1964: 138-153.
1959: 121-128. 1965: 116-124.
1960: 107-117. 1966: 142-151.
1961: 128-142. 1967: 123-128.
1962: 116-128. 1968: 117-124.
1963: 104-113. 1969: 140-153.
Overture suggesting that if an item has been considered, it should not be reconsidered for a period of three years.
1968: 102, 119, 123. Each year presents a new deliberative body. No action.
Overture requesting all overtures be presented through the SCO.
1968: 103, 119, 124. Adopted.
Overture requests that the SCO be called into session 24 hours prior to the time other standing committees are called.
1969: 151, 153. Referred to GSEC.
See next listing.

OVERTURES, REVIEW COMMITTEE ON
Report.
1970: 102-113. 1974: 93-111.
1971: 111-117. 1975: 82-94.
1972: 82-106. 1976: 98-116.
1973: 84-114. 1977: 108-121.
Recommended that all overtures making charges be accompanied with supportive materials and that all possible facts be discovered.
1974: 123. Adopted.
Voted that overtures from classes to GS be sent to the General Secretary postmarked no later than April 30, and that this revision be made in the Manual for Stated Clerks.
1977: 121. Adopted.

PAARLBERG, JOHN
Dispensation from professorial certificate granted.
1976: 146, 148.

PAIGE, EDWINA
Resolution for work with the BWM.
1961: 97.

PAN-PRESBYTERIAN CONFERENCE
Six denominations.
1966: 244-245.
1967: 228.
1968: 233-234.

PARAMEDICAL PERSONNEL
CAC recommends para-professionals augment health care service to the Ameri-

can public and that this approval be sent to the AMA and state licensing boards.
1971: 224-225. Adopted.

PARA-PROFESSIONAL MINISTRY (LAITY)
Study recommended.
1972:32-33. Adopted.
After study the BTE looks with favor upon such a program.
1973: 32.
Rev. Richard Detrich engaged for this project; will report at the May meeting.
1974: 29.
Motion made to instruct classes to urge their consistories to publicize the program of the Reformed Bible College in Grand Rapids, which specializes in this training.
1974: 299. Adopted.
Rev. Richard Detrich's paper—"Rediscovering the Diaconate." Recommended by BTE that GS request appropriate committee to study the office of deacon in the RCA.
1975: 31, 34. No action.
In the study it became evident that minority groups were asking for ministers with training equal to that normally required of RCA ministers.
1975: 30.
Motion that the study be referred back to BTE for another year and that it prepare a report with a plan for implementation.
1975: 35-36. Adopted.
BTE suggests a committee study "Rediscovering the Diaconate" and meet with the chairman of the BTE Committee on Continuing Education, and report recom mendations to GS.
1976: 144, 147. Adopted.
See also LAY MINISTERS, TRAINING OF.

PARLIAMENTARIAN AT SYNOD
Discussion of need of a professional parliamentarian.
1966: 185-186. Motion made to refer the matter to GSEC.
Rev. Elton Eenigenburg designated as parliamentarian.
1967: 155-156. 1970: 269.
1968: 370. 1971: 287.
1969: 347.

PARSONAGE ALLOWANCE FOR RCA PASTORS
Raised from 15% to 20%
1970: 140. Adopted.
Overture requesting the BP to adjust the percentage currently added to base salary of a pastor for the parsonage for the RCA Annuity Fund from 20% to 40%.
1976: 99, 139-140. Referred to BPRC. No action. Needs further study.
Recommended that basis for the value of a parsonage be raised from 20% to 30%.
1977: 154. Adopted.

PARTICULAR SYNODS
Overture regarding functions and areas.
1961: 130-131, 142. Referred to Committee on President's Report.
Suggested changes.
1961: 270, 329. Referred to PS's.
Overture requesting the word "particular" be deleted wherever it occurs in the Constitution.
1965: 112, 118, 123. No action.
Overture regarding representation to, asking that the Constitution be amended to provide that representation to PS be determined in the same manner as for GS.
1965: 115, 118-119, 123. Approved and referred to CRC
Overture asking for official representation of PS at GS.
1966: 140-141, 144, 149. Approved one member from each PS.
CRC requests another year of study, since the above was once a part of the Constitution and the Committee wants to discover why it was deleted.
1967: 183. Adopted.
Request that GSEC resume study on "The Role and Purpose of PS's" in the denomination.
1970: 197. Adopted.
GSEC reports on "The Role and Purpose of PS's": (1) PS has supervision over classis; (2) has only one function over a church—the transfer of a church to another classis; (3) may devise ways of advancement of the Kingdom of God which classes cannot do alone.
1971: 130-131. Adopted.
Overture suggesting amendment in the BCO giving the PS's the right to determine method of selection and the number of delegates from each classis. PS also defined.
1972: 90, 194. Adopted and sent to classes for approval.
Definition approved by classes.
1973: 128.
Two overtures requesting name be changed to "Regional Synod."
1972: 102, 105. No action, since PS relates to GS in a special way.

PARTICULARIA
1958: 308-310. 1961: 347-348.
1959: 310-311. 1962: 376-378.
1960: 290-292. 1963: 441-442.

PARTNERSHIP IN MISSION
Recommended as a way for churches to be involved in mission.
1973: 69. Adopted.

PASTOR-CONGREGATION RELATIONSHIPS
Overture requesting clarification on the constitutional grounds and required procedures for termination of a relationship requested by a consistory and not concurred in by the pastor, or vice versa.
1974: 107. Adopted and referred to COCG.
COCG reports no amendment necessary to achieve intent of overture.
1975: 159.
Overture suggesting four recommendations concerning relationships, and asking for clarification in BCO.
1975: 84. No action. Amendment not deemed necessary.

PASTOR RELOCATION COMMITTEE
See MINISTERS, RELOCATION OF.

PASTORAL CARE OF RETIRED CONTRIBUTORY ANNUITY RECIPIENTS
1973: 157.

PASTORAL LETTERS
From President L. J. Kuyper and Vice President C. H. Walvoord on Christian love and reconciliation.
1970: 193–195.

PEACE
CAC's suggestions for withdrawing troops from SE Asia, etc.
1973: 218–219.
CAC paper—"The Church and a Witness for Peace."
1974: 222–225.
CAC recommends that GS appoint a study committee to explore the meaning of nonviolence in all of life, which is rooted in the Gospel of Jesus Christ particularly in its relation to war, as a viable option to be pursued by Christians and the Church.
1974: 225. Adopted.

PEACE CORPS
Endorsement of.
1961: 216.

PEALE, JOHN H.
Dispensation from professorial certificate requested.
1964: 50, 53. Granted.

PEALE, REV. NORMAN VINCENT
Elected Vice President of GS.
1968: 8.
Elected President of GS.
1969: 9.

PEEKE, MRS. VESTA GREER, MISSIONARY TO JAPAN, 1893–1931.
Obituary.
1959: Annual Report of the BCWM, App., 34.

PEELEN, GEORGE W.
Dispensation requested from professorial certificate.
1967: 52, 55.
No action. Constitutional requirements not met.

PELON, GRACE
Retiring after 21 years of service to the RCA.
1971: 288.

PENSION RIGHTS IN CASE OF MERGER
See MERGER PROBLEMS.

PENSIONS, BOARD OF
Report (by OHR).
1970: 162–163. 1972: 123.
1971: 155–156. 1973: 156–157.
Report (by GSEC)
1974: 162–165. 1976: 138–139.
1975: 154–155. 1977: 152–153.
Prior to 1969 the annual reports appeared in the Appendix or Appendix 1.
1969: 106–109.
During the transitional period of change in denominational structure reports will come through GSEC and ultimately in the report of the Office of Human Resources.
1969: 170.
Overture regarding women on the board.
1959: 122, 128. Not approved.
Overture requesting the raising of pensions to ministers and widows who reached the age of 65 before January 1, 1957, to $2400 and $1200 respectively.
1963: 107, 112. Adopted.
Overture requesting a review of the adequacy of benefits.
1967: 112–114, 125, 128. Adopted.
Study Committee reports RCA pensions compare favorably with PCUS and UPCUSA.
1968: 137–138, 153–156. BP to search for ways to improve livelihood of current retirees.
Overture requesting that ministers who withdraw from the RCA may do so with pension funds contributed by them and by the churches they served.
1969: 135, 148, 153. No action.
GSEC special report on the History and Organizational Development and Integration of the Board of Pensions.
1971: 159–162.
Overture requesting the Pension information in the office be kept confidential.

1971: 109-116. No action.
Recommended that members of GSEC be nominated to the BP as terms expire until all fifteen members of the BP are also members of GSEC.
1971: 171. Approved.
Recommended amendments.
1972: 167-173.
The BP remains a separate, legal board. The working relationship with the other boards is functional.
1972: 128.
Overture requesting a study of the possibility of the formation of an Ecumenical Pension Fund.
1972: 89. Adopted.
Overture requesting that the BP assessment of 75¢ a member be made an asking.
1973: 101-102. Referred to RCBP, which committee recommends no action since pension commitments require assessments.
Overture requesting revision of pension formula to equalize benefits of a minister who comes in later in life and retires at 65 after 25 years, and one who serves 35 years or more, but of necessity must retire before age 65—"90" magic number formula.
1973: 94-96. Referred to RCBP.
RCBP recommends no action.
1973: 174. No action.
RCBP recommends that at the end of the period of the contract with Travelers the possibility of diversification of the funds be explored for greater security.
1974: 184. Adopted.
Constitution and rules revised.
1975: 119-132. Adopted.
Overture requesting the TC undertake a biblical study of principles governing pension plans such as our own and set forth guidelines for the administration, and necessary development of such a plan.
1977: 118-119. No action.
Pension Policy for missionaries, see CHRISTIAN WORLD MISSIONS—PENSION POLICY.
For other reports see following listings.

PENSIONS, BOARD OF, STANDING COMMITTEE ON
Report.
1958: 123-129. 1964: 102-106.
1959: 116-120. 1965: 92-95.
1960: 102-106. 1966: 106-109.
1961: 124-127. 1967: 98-101.
1962: 112-115. 1968: 83-86.
1963: 99-103. 1969: 109-113.

PENSIONS, BOARD OF, REVIEW COMMITTEE ON
Report.
1970: 164-170. 1974: 184-187.
1971: 157-158. 1975: 155-158.
1972: 124-129. 1976: 139-140.
1973: 173-177. 1977: 153-154.

PENTECOST AND GENERAL SYNOD
See entry under GS.

PEOPLE'S REPUBLIC OF CHINA
The NCC attitude toward.
1959: 167.
Overture regarding NCC's attitude toward.
1960: 113, 117. Tabled.
Overture opposing Red China in the United Nations.
1961: 129-130, 132, 142. Referred to CAC.
CAC reports that this is a complicated matter; that Christians should earnestly pray for wisdom in fighting Communism.
1962: 221-222.
CAC policy statement approving admission of Red China to the United Nations so that lines can be open. Also a minority report.
1966: 226-227, 235. Report approved.

PERMANENT COMMITTEES AND COMMISSIONS
List of
1970: App. 2, 2-6.
1971: App. 2, 9-12.
1972: App. 2, 9-12.
1973: App. 2, 9-12.
1974: App. 2, 10-13.
1975: App. 2, 10-13.
1976: App. 1, 10-13.
1977: App. 1, 10-13.

"PERSONS"
Overture requesting an interpretation of the word "persons."
1975: 93-94. No action. Ruled out of order because of previous action.
Overture requesting classification of term.
1976: 115-116. No action since this will be considered in the President's Review Committee report.
See also ORDINATION OF WOMEN.

PETZ, WILLIAM J.
Dispensation from professorial certificate requested. Graduate of Princeton Theological Seminary. Examination sustained at NBTS.
1969: 40, 44. Granted.

PHILLIPS, OSTERHOUDT
Dispensation from professorial certificate requested.

1960: 52, 53, 57. Denied.
Received from the Congregation Christian.
1961: 276.

PIET, REV. JOHN H.
Called to office of Lector in English Bible at WTS.
1960: 47.
Elected to the Office of Professor of Theology (English Bible and Missions) at WTS.
1962: 53, 58.

PIET, JOHN J.
Requested a dispensation from the professorial certificate. A graduate of Union Theological Seminary with examination sustained at NBTS.
1966: 46. Granted.

PLAAS, RICHARD E.
Dispensation from professorial certificate granted.
1976: 146, 148.

PLACE OF MEETING AND THE RACIAL QUESTION.
1965: 431. Adopted.

PLAN CALENDAR
1963: 367-368. 1966: 328.
1964: 355. 1969: 181.
1965: 292, 297.

PLAN FOR UNDERSTANDING
See COMMITTEE OF EIGHTEEN.

PLANNED PARENTHOOD
1960: 180-182.
1961: 214.
CAC report.
1962: 217-218.
See also BIRTH CONTROL.

PLEA FOR UNDERSTANDING
A reply to the RCA. See AFRICA, SOUTH.

POLITY IN THE RCA.
General statement.
1965: 152-154.

POLLUTION
See ENVIRONMENT.

POPULATION CONTROL
1973: 213-216.
See also PLANNED PARENTHOOD and BIRTH CONTROL-DEATH CONTROL.

PORNOGRAPHY
Overture requesting RCA to protest the "findings" of the Commission and suggest support of the passage of legislation such as that introduced by the late Sen. Everett M. Dirksen.
1971: 103, 114. Referred to CAC.
Report of the CAC.
1972: 203-206.

POVERTY, THE CHURCH AND
1966: 230-233. 1968: 211-214.
1967: 210-211, 212. 1969: 245-246.
CAC urges all efforts in the war against poverty and encouragement of the Office of Economic Opportunity.
1966: 232-233, 236. Adopted.
See also CHURCH WORLD SERVICE.

PRADERVAND, DR. MARCEL
Tribute upon retirement from Secretary of World Alliance of Reformed Churches for 22 years.
1970: 229, 243.

PRAYER AMENDMENT
CAC recommends (1) RCA request Congress to retain the historic relation between church and state and to oppose any proposed prayer amendment; (2) Churches re-examine the meaning of prayer in terms of Christian faith; (3) encourage local churches to study creative ways in which an objective study of religion can be introduced into the public schools.
1972: 213-215. (1) not adopted; (2) and (3) adopted.
See also RELIGION AND THE PUBLIC SCHOOLS and BIBLE READING AND PRAYER IN THE PUBLIC SCHOOLS.

PRAYER CALENDAR
President suggests a RCA Prayer Calendar for Missions.
1965: 341-343, 347-348. Referred to Committee on Education for Mission.

PRAYER FOR NATIONAL LEADERS
Overture requesting the NCC to urge weekly prayers in the churches.
1962: 121, 127. No action because of the many requests that might come.

PREACHING-TEACHING-REACHING MISSION (PTR)
Department of Evangelism venture.
1962: 97-104. Recommended that each church in the RCA participate in this mission.
Prospects bright—130 churches expect to participate in 1964.
1964: 93.
Cut-off date, January 1, 1968.
1965: 89.

PRE-MARITAL COUNSELING
Report.
1958: 202.
1959: 208-209.

PRESBYTERIAN CHURCH, U.S.
Overture regarding conversations on merger or union.
1962: 122–124, 127. Steps looking forward to merger with PCUS are being taken and other union possibilities are to be held in abeyance. Adopted.
President suggests this be pursued.
1963: 376, 438, 439. To be referred to BNAM.
Recommended that RCA accept invitation to become full members in PCUS-UPUSA discussions.
1971: 253-254. Lost.
Two observers from the RCA continue to attend meetings of the Presbyterian Joint Committee on Union.
1973: 231.
See also MERGER; MERGER PROBLEMS; and CHURCH UNION (PCUS).

PRESIDENT OF GENERAL SYNOD
President suggests beginning in 1968 each PS submit names for president and vice president from delegates at Synod.
1966: 339, 352, 355. Referred to GSEC for study and report.
GSEC report recommends no action at this time for several reasons, one being danger of politicking.
1967: 150–151. No action.
President suggests that the retiring president, General Secretary, and Executive Secretary communicate their willingness to meet with the new president and the president's employer (consistory, board, business) in order to outline and interpret current demands of the office.
1974: 273, 283. Adopted.

PRESIDENTS OF GENERAL SYNOD
See entry "Recent Officers of" under GENERAL SYNOD.

PRESIDENTS OF PARTICULAR SYNODS, MEETING OF
President recommends that the President of GS convene a meeting of Presidents of PS's for sharing common concerns.
1966: 343, 353, 355. Approved. Referred to SCBD for financing.
Meeting of.
1967: 175–176.
Stated Clerks of PS's included in meetings.
1968: 171–173.
Field Secretaries also included in meetings.
1969: 208-209.

PRESIDENT'S OFFICE AND DENOMINATIONAL STRUCTURE, COMMITTEE ON
Report.
1960: 333-334.

PRESIDENT'S REPORT (STATE OF RELIGION)
1958: 248-255, 257-305 (Rev. Howard C. Schade).
1959: 238-254, 259-307 (Rev. Marion de Velder).
1960: 221-235, 239-287 (Rev. Howard G. Hageman).
1961: 262-325 (Rev. Henry Bast).
1962: 278-339 (Rev. Norman E. Thomas).
1963: 372-433 (Rev. Bernard R. Brunsting).
1964: 382-389, 392-441 (Rev. M. Verne Oggel).
1965: 332-344 (Rev. Gordon L. Van Oostenburg).
1966: 336-351 (Rev. Donner B. Atwood).
1967: 300-309 (Rev. Raymond E. Beckering).
1968: 324-333 (Rev. Harold J. Schut).
1969: 317-329 (Rev. Raymond R. Van Heukelom).
1970: 253 (Rev. Norman Vincent Peale).
1971: 266-271 (Rev. Lester J. Kuyper).
1972: 271-278 (Rev. Christian H. Walvoord).
1973: 273-279 (Mr. Harry E. De Bruyn).
1974: 271-280 (Rev. Donald H. De Young).
1975: 241-250 (Rev. Raymond H. Reewerts).
1976: 24-32 (Rev. Bert E. Van Soest).
1977: 24-34 (Rev. Louis H. Benes, Sr.).

PRESIDENT'S REPORT, SPECIAL COMMITTEE ON
Report.
1958: 256.
1959: 255-258.
1960: 236-238.
1961: 328-332.
1962: 341-344.
Proposed that this be made a standing committee.
1959: 239, 255, 257. To be voted in 1960.
Committee to be changed to a standing committee.
1960: 218.
See next listing.

PRESIDENT'S REPORT, STANDING COMMITTEE ON
Report.
1963: 434-439.
1964: 390-391.
1965: 345-349.
1966: 352-356.
1967: 309-312.
1968: 333-336.
1969: 329-331.
See next listing.

PRESIDENT'S REPORT, REVIEW COMMITTEE ON
1970: 253. Not appointed.

1971: 271-273. 1975: 250-251.
1972: 278-279. 1976: 33-34.
1973: 279-280. 1977: 35-36.
1974: 281-284.
Recommendation that there no longer be an appointment of this committee.
1971: 273. Lost.

PRINS, REV. JACOB
Resignation as Minister of Evangelism. Expression of appreciation.
1959: 105, 107, 109.

PRISONS
A CAC report on prison reform.
1972: 207-213.
CAC essay to the church—"Prisoners and Agape Action."
1977: 205-206.

PROFESSOR OF THEOLOGY
See THEOLOGY, PROFESSORS OF.

PROFESSORATE AND THEOLOGICAL SEMINARIES, STANDING COMITTEE ON
Report.
1958: 54-64. 1960: 49-60.
1959: 49-57. 1961: 66-74.
Proposed that committee be made a permanent committee.
1959: 79, 356. To be voted on in 1960.
Permanent Committee established.
1960: 59-60.
See next listing.

PROFESSORATE, PERMANENT COMMITTEE ON
Report.
1962: 53-62.
1963: 47-54.
Committee dissolved. Permanent Committee on Theological Education to be constituted.
1963: 138.

PROFESSORATE, SPECIAL COMMITTEE ON
Report.
1960: 58-60.
1962: 63-65.

PROFESSORIAL CERTIFICATE
Overture regarding a uniform policy as to the number of years to be spent in our denominational seminaries in order to qualify for the professorial certificate.
1960: 51, 53, 57. Referred to PCP for study.
A valid and important instrument.
1964: 54.
Change in wording in the Constitution.
1965: 44, 47. Adopted.
Change in Constitution approved.
1966: 196, 201. Adopted and sent to classes for approval.
Classes approved.
1967: 172.

PROGRAM, COMMITTEE ON
Report.
1958: 143. 1961: 154.
1959: 150. 1962: 144.
1960: 126. 1963: 337.

PROGRAM AND DEVOTIONAL EXERCISES, COMMITTEE ON
Report.
1964: 345. 1971: 264-265.
1965: 288. 1972: 269-270.
1966: 317. 1973: 271-272.
1967: 282. 1974: 269-270.
1968: 310-312. 1975: 239-240.
1969: 314-316. 1976: 250-251.
1970: 251-252. 1977: 321-322.
See also DEVOTIONAL EXERCISES AT GS.

PROJECT EQUALITY
A program developed by the National Catholic Conference for interracial justice and an effort to end employment discrimination. CAC recommends membership.
1969: 244-245, 249, 194-195. Deferred, but later adopted.
Overture asking GS to rescind 1969 action regarding RCA participation.
1970: 95, 108. No action.
See also RACE RELATIONS.

PROMOTION AND COMMUNICATIONS, OFFICE OF
Development of.
1969: 179-183.
Report.
1970: 171-174. 1974: 155-159.
1971: 174-178. 1975: 139-143.
1972: 131-135. 1976: 79-80.
1973: 158-161. 1977: 88-89.
Media Coordinator for TRAVARCA, which also see.
1970: 172.
Secretaries for other areas named.
1974: 155, 156.

PROPERTY, RETENTION OF IF CONGREGATION SHOULD NOT BE IN FAVOR OF MERGER
See MERGER PROBLEMS.

PROTESTANTISM AS PORTRAYED IN FILMS
1958: 204.

PTR
See PREACHING-TEACHING-REACHING MISSION.

PUBLIC MORALS
See specific problems, and CAC reports.

PUBLIC PRONOUNCEMENTS
Overture suggesting matters should first be submitted to classes and be approved by a 2/3 vote.
1959: 122. No action.

PUBLIC RELATIONS
Report of Director.
1958: 121–122. 1964: 114.
1959: 114–115. 1965: 102.
1960: 100–101. 1966: 115–116.
1961: 122–123. 1967: 108.
1962: 110–111. 1968: 91.
1963: 98. 1969: 118.
Overture suggesting full-time office.
1960: 110, 117. No action.
President recommends that a trained layman or laymen work on publicity for the denomination.
1965: 337.
SCPR recommends possibility of engaging a Public Relations Director.
1965: 346, 348. GSEC to study matter and report.
See PROMOTION AND COMMUNICATION, OFFICE OF.

PUBLICATION OF MATERIALS BY BOARDS, INSTITUTIONS, OR COMMISSIONS
Overture requesting such materials have approval of the TC so that people may see if they conform with Standards of Unity.
1965: 111, 122, 124. No action.
Overture requesting a clearing house of responsible persons to rule on publications and programs to be recommended for use or reading.
1969: 132–133, 145–146, 152. NDWW and GPC have set up self-governing actions. No action.

QUICK MEMORIAL FUND (MARTHA ANTOINETTE QUICK MEMORIAL FUND)
Received in 1934 in the amount of $572,500, income of which is to be allocated annually by the sub-committee on allocations. Some share usually goes to scholarships and student aid. Allocations listed.
1958: 18–21. 1968: 22–23.
1959: 18. 1969: 21–22.
1960: 16. 1970: 20–21.
1961: 18. 1971: 21–22.
1962: 17. 1972: 17–18, 164–165.
1963: 25–26. 1973: 22–23.
1964: 19. 1974: 23, 129–130.
1965: 19–20. 1975: 25.
1966: 21. 1976: 60, 93.
1967: 21. 1977: 60, 101.

QUORUMS
Overture suggesting requirement of at least a simple majority in all church judicatories.
1969: 134–135, 147, 153. Adopted. Referred to CRC.
In regular sessions of classes a majority of ministers and of elders is required to constitute a quorum at classis.
1970: 195–196. Adopted and sent to classes for approval.
Approved by classes.
1971: 152.
At a special session of classis, the presence of three minister delegates and three elder delegates shall constitute a quorum in a special meeting of classis.
1970: 199. Adopted and sent to classes for approval.
Approved by classes.
1971: 152.
These words added by amendment: "those ministers of the Word who are actively serving in ministries under the jurisdiction of classis. . . ."
1971: 199. Adopted and sent to classes for approval.
Approved by classes.
1972: 120.
Overture requesting the BCO be amended: "The presence of a majority of the members of classis is required to constitute a quorum at any regular session of classis."
1974: 102–103. Adopted.
The above action is listed in error and should read "no action."
1975: 16.
The presence of a majority of the minister delegates and the elder delegates is required to constitute a quorum of any session of PS or GS.
1970: 196. Adopted and sent to classes for approval.
Approved by classes.
1971: 152.

RACE, COMMISSION ON
BNAM suggests formation of.
1964: 99–100, 231–232.
Report.
1965: 84, 86, 90–91, 206.
Future of Commission referred to GSEC.
1968: 78–79.
Now relates to GSEC.
1969: 84–86. Referred to Sub-Committee on Denominational Structure.
GPC suggests dissolution of Commission since other committees are now equipped to handle the work.
1970: 182–183. Adopted.

RACE RELATIONS
Cooperative program designed by the NCC.
1958: 153, 201.
CAC stresses the Covenant of Open Occupancy and "Credo of Race Relations."
1959: 208.
The President calls attention to the church's responsibility.
1962: 287-289.
Report of CAC—reaffirms previous actions.
1964: 225, 227, 230-231.
CAC reports that racial inclusiveness should be one of the criteria for use of denominational funds for church extension.
1965: 206-208, 218-219, 221. Adopted.
Overture requesting that the 1965 action on "open occupancy" be among the criteria for use of denominational funds in church extension be rescinded.
1966: 123, 143, 149. Overture of 1965 was misread by classis; this overture is declared out-of-order.
Overture asking GS to rescind the action of 1965 regarding "racial inclusiveness" as a criterion for use of denominational funds in church extension. This would require new churches to set up arbitrary standards of church membership.
1966: 122-123, 143, 149. No action.
CAC suggests an added Constitutional Question, "Does your congregation have a policy of racial inclusiveness?"
1966: 225, 235. Adopted.
Overture asking "racial inclusiveness" be deleted as a criterion for use of denominational funds.
1967: 112, 124, 128. No action.
CRC does not approve of the "racial inclusiveness" question. Such a question could open the door to all kinds of questions reflecting strong opinions of various groups of the church.
1967: 182-183, 185. Received for information.
CAC reports GS has adopted the Credo, but congregations are urged to participate.
1966: 224-225, 235. Adopted and referred to classes.
Statement on race by CAC
1967: 208-209, 212, 214.
CAC recommendations: (1) RCA go on record commending the NAACP Youth Council of Milwaukee for efforts to secure fair housing; (2) that classes use their influence to secure fair housing; (3) that local congregations work with local fair housing committees.
1968: 211, 220. All adopted.
CAC urges Credo on Race Relations be republished and distributed among the churches.
1971: 225-226. Approved.

RADIO BROADCASTING
Report of RCA Committee on.
1958: 317-318. 1960: 298.
1959: 321-322. 1961: 359-366.
Overture regarding a petition sent to the Film Commission of the NCC.
1958: 134. No action.
Proposed Temple Time constitution.
1961: 359-366. Referred to western PS's.
Proposal lost. Committee dissolved.
1962: 389-390.
See also TEMPLE TIME and WORDS OF HOPE.

RADIO, VISUAL EDUCATION, AND MASS COMMUNICATION COMMITTEE
A division of the NCC.
1959: 179. 1961: 97.
1960: 145. 1962: 167-168.
1965: 250—15th anniversary.
1969: 87.

RANSOM, MISS RUTH
Retirement after 16 years as Executive Secretary of the BCWM. Words of recognition.
1959: 95.

RAVEMCO
See RADIO, VISUAL EDUCATION, AND MASS COMMUNICATION COMMITTEE.

RCYF
See REFORMED CHURCH YOUTH FELLOWSHIP.

REALIGNMENT OF CLASSES
See CLASSES, REALIGNMENT OF.

REBAPTISM
See BAPTISM, (REBAPTISM).

RECRUITMENT FOR PARISH MINISTRY
President recommends BTE and OHR study problem.
1969: 328, 330, 331. Adopted.
Study proceeding in cooperation with OHR.
1970: 34-35.
See 1972 and 1973 entries under THEOLOGICAL EDUCATION, BOARD OF.

RED CHINA
See PEOPLE'S REPUBLIC OF CHINA.

REDEKER, REV. RUSSELL
Elected Executive Secretary of the BDM.
1958: 98.

Recognition upon his retirement from the RCA staff after 19 years.
1977: 151. Adopted.

REFERENCE, COMMITTEE OF
GSEC to serve as COR.
1966: 172-173.
Report.
1966: 183-188.
1967: 171-172.
1968: 167-168.
1969: 200-201.
1970: 192-195.
1971: 195-197.
1972: 174-175.
1973: 177-178.
1974: 132.
1975: 133.
1977: 93.

REFORMED CHURCH BUILDINGS
HC initiates a new program of filing pictures of church buildings and other materials of archival interest, of all RCA churches.
1973: 270.
HC again encourages all congregations to send archival materials to Gardner Sage Library, NBTS.
1977: 238.

REFORMED CHURCH COLLEGES
Committee to study the needs of the three colleges.
1963: 73-75. Division of Higher Education of the BE to be established.
Special Committee on, report.
1964: 57, 59-60. RCA scholarship fund advertised in the CH.
A study of the needs, functions and prospects of.
1966: 57-68. Good report on our three colleges and their relationship with the RCA by a team from the Association of American Colleges.
Overture requesting a study of doctrinal positions taught in Bible and Philosophy departments of our colleges.
1966: 140, 142. Referred to SCHE.
GSEC to study a program of assessments for the budgets of our Christian Colleges.
1967: 77-78.
Before assessments can be made, "assessments" and "askings" have to be defined.
1968: 137.
President asks special effort to activate all congregations of the RCA to support our colleges.
1969: 328, 331. Approved. Referred to OPC.
SCHE's statement concerning overture regarding doctrinal teaching in our colleges: "The Church and its Colleges (a Preamble to the Covenant of Mutual Responsibilities)."
1969: 64-70.
Voted the above statement be commended to the church and colleges.
1969: 63, 64. Adopted.
Recommended that the above document be published in MGS for five years.
1969: 63, 64. Adopted, but GS was instructed to provide wider distribution.
Recommended that all ministers acquaint high school counselors with programs at our colleges.
1969: 63, 64.
Recommended that all churches take special offerings for colleges on April 12, 1970.
1969: 43, 44.
Scholarship loan funds to be restudied and publicized.
1969: 43, 44.
Recommended (1) a $1.00 GS assessment for scholarship aid for young people in RCA colleges; (2) that the colleges undertake an aggressive joint effort to raise scholarship funds.
1971: 56-57. Adopted.
Recommended that a consultation between the colleges and the GPC be held for the purpose of strengthening cooperation between the colleges.
1972: 48. Adopted.
RCHE recommends a questionnaire be developed and sent to the pastors of all RCA churches asking them to supply names of potential students.
1975: 48. Adopted.
See CHURCH (THE) AND ITS COLLEGES (A PREAMBLE) AND THE COVENANT OF MUTUAL RESPONSIBILITIES.

REFORMED CHURCH IN AMERICA
Organizational structure in need of study.
1959: 244-246, 256, 258. Study committee appointed.
Overture requesting name be changed from Reformed Church in America to Presbyterian Reformed Church in America.
1969: 139, 150, 153. Name has been changed six times in our history. Referred to GSEC for study.
GSEC report indicates that there was little enthusiasm for the change of name.
1970: 127. No action.
Overture urging GS to do everything possible to avoid the dissolution of the RCA.
1970: 100, 112. No action. See COMMITTEE OF EIGHTEEN.
Overture requesting that GSEC develop policies re superintendence of debt positions and fund-raising strategies of the

church, and that the report be made to GS in 1975.
1974: 110. Adopted.
Overture requesting study of the matter of individual Reformed Churches omitting from their popular name all reference to our denomination.
1976: 99. No action. Classes have superintendence over concerns of churches in their bounds.
350th Anniversary. A Task Force is preparing various celebrations with April 9, 1978 designated as day of special observances across the denomination.
1977: 48-50.
Resolution on the occasion of the 350th Anniversary of the RCA.
1977: 49-50.
Location of headquarters. See NATIONAL OFFICES, LOCATION OF.

REFORMED CHURCH IN AMERICA/ CHRISTIAN REFORMED CHURCH JOINT COMMITTEE ON EVANGELISM
See entry under CHRISTIAN REFORMED CHURCH.

REFORMED CHURCH IN AMERICA—EXTENSION FOUNDATION, INC.
Advisability of a holding corporation.
1958: 98, 100-101, 106.
Certificate of Incorporation.
1958: 107-111.
Proposed by laws.
1958: 112-113.
Raising of funds.
1959: 108, 247, 256, 258.
National strategy plan to be developed.
1960: 92.
1961: 105-106.
Funds needed.
1966: 100-101.
Changes in personnel. Separate corporal structure continued.
1969: 169.
Report.
1960: 88-89.
1961: 105-110.
1962: 93.
1963: 88-89.
1964: 92-93.
1965: 83.
1966: 100-101.
1970: 64 (assets total $2,517,491).
1971: 73.
1974: 62.

REFORMED CHURCH IN AMERICA, STAFF
List of.
1970: App. 2, iii-iv.
1971: App. 2, 5-7.
1972: App. 2, 5-7.
1973: App. 2, 5-7.
1974: App. 2, 5-7.
1975: App. 2, 5-7.
1976: App. 2, 5-7.
1977: App. 2, 5-7.
First list.
1969: 72-75.

(The names of the following persons and their positions were gleaned from the MGS Appendixes listed above. The dates may be off a year either way, because one cannot tell from the Minutes just when the job was taken, or when the person resigned from it. In several cases these persons have worked in RCA offices for a much longer time, but the dates begin with the organization of the GPC. There has been no attempt to bring the titles of the positions together, but rather the names are listed as they appeared in the MGS according to date.)

Rev. Marion de Velder, General Secretary, 1968-1977.
Rev. Arie R. Brouwer, Executive Secretary, 1968-1977; General Secretary, 1977-.
Rev. Russell J. Redeker, Secretary for Church Planning and Development, 1968-1977.
Rev. Arthur O. Van Eck, Secretary for Church Life and Mission, 1968-1972; Secretary for Regional Services, Eastern Metropolitan Regional Center, 1972-.
Rev. Carl J. Schroeder, Secretary for Evangelism, 1968-1972.
Rev. Joseph B. Muyskens, Secretary for Social Ministries, 1968-.
Rev. Eugene H. Durkee, Secretary for Lay Ministries, 1968-1969.
Miss Grace Pelon, Consultant for Children's Resources, 1968-1970; Secretary for Children's Life, 1969-1971.
Rev. Delbert J. Vander Haar, Secretary for Western Regional Services and Family Life, 1968-1972; Secretary for Regional Services, Western Regional Centers, 1972-.
Rev. Gordon J. Timmerman, Secretary for Midwestern Regional Services and Adult Life, 1968-1972; Secretary for Regional Services, Midwestern Regional Centers, 1972-.
Rev. Lynn T. Joosten, Secretary for Eastern Regional Services and Youth Life, 1968-1972.
Rev. John E. Buteyn, Secretary for World Ministries, 1968-.
Rev. John E. Hiemstra, Secretary for North American Ministries, 1968-1972.
Mr. Kenneth E. Warren, Jr., Overseas Secretary for Middle East. 1968-1970.
Mr. Paul A. Hopkins, Secretary for the Joint Office of Africa, 1968-1972.
Rev. Marvin D. Hoff, Secretary for Asian Ministries, 1968-1969; Secretary for Operations, 1969-.
Rev. Leonard De Beer, Secretary for Missionary Personnel, 1968-1969; Secretary for Professional Development,

1969–1973; Counseling Services, 1973–.

Rev. Isaac C. Rottenberg, Secretary for Program Interpretation and Resource Development, 1968–1971; Secretary for Program Interpretation, 1971–.

Rev. Winfield Burggraaff, Consultant for Resource Development, 1968–1971.

Mr. H. Hudson Brack, Director, General Synod Operations, 1969–1970.

Miss Milli C. Greene, Associate for Youth Life, 1969–1974; Associate for Youth Life and Black Christian Education, 1974–1976.

Miss Adeline Sybesma, Reading Consultant, 1969–1972; Consultant for Church Tutorial Programs, 1972–1974; Associate for Leadership Development, 1973–.

Rev. Alvin J. Poppen, Coordinator of Human Resources, 1970–.

Rev. Theodore F. Zandstra, Secretary for Remuneration, 1970–1971; Secretary for Pastoral Services to Retired Personnel, 1971–1972; Executive Secretary of the Board of Pensions, 1970–1972.

Rev. Herbert C. Schmalzriedt, Manager of Kirkside, 1968–.

Mr. Robert J. Kleiman, Director, Office of Administration and Finance, 1969–1970.

Mr. John W. Brown, Administrative Services, 1969–1972.

Mr. David G. Lambrides, Accounting Services, 1969–1972.

Miss Beth E. Marcus, Director of Promotion and Communications, 1969–1970; Secretary for Adult Voluntary Services, 1970–; Executive director of Reformed Church Women, 1972–.

Rev. James W. Baar, Promotion in Local Churches, 1969–1971.

Mr. Roland Ackerman, Secretary for Special Gifts, 1969–1971; Secretary for Development, Eastern Region, 1971–

Rev. Elmer Ansley, Production Coordinator, 1969–1973.

Rev. Peter Paulsen, Media Coordinator, TRAVARCA, 1969–.

Miss Lorraine L. Heitmann, Shares and Scholarships, 1969–1970; Assistant in Development Services, 1970–1976.

Miss Anna Baar, Speakers Bureau; Projects, 1969–1971.

Miss Dorothy Burt, Prayer Letter Editor, 1969–1971.

Mrs. Anita J. Welwood, Director, National Department of Women's Work, 1969–1972.

Dr. Choan-Seng Song, Secretary for Asian Ministries, 1970–1972.

Miss Patricia L. Stere, Associate for Lay Ministries, 1970–1973; Secretary for Young Adult Ministry and Christian Nurture, 1973–.

Mr. J. Robert R. Harrison, Director, Administration and Finance, 1970–1972.

Rev. Paul E. Mitchell, Director of Promotion and Communications, 1970–1972.

Mr. Harold Hakken, Secretary for Development, Western Region, 1970–.

Mrs. Lois Joice, Secretary for Information Services, 1971–.

Rev. William M. Howard, Jr., Executive Director, Black Council, 1971–.

Mr. Stuart Post, Secretary for Special Gifts, 1972–1973; Development Officer for RCA-related Institutions, 1973–1975.

Rev. Douglas A. Walrath, Secretary for Regional Services, Northeastern Regional Center, 1972–.

Mr. Peter Theune, Associate for Children's Life, 1972–.

Mr. Harry Profahl, Secretary for Development, Midwestern Regional Centers, 1972–.

Rev. Harold E. Brown, Secretary for Parish Life and American Indian Ministries, 1972–1976; Secretary for American Indian Ministries, Mexico, and Adult Life, 1976–.

Mrs. Wilma N. Bentzen, Annuity Fund, 1973–.

Mrs. Christina C. Wallace, Insurance, 1973–1975.

Rev. Herman E. Luben, Secretary for New Life and Evangelism, 1973–.

Mr. Vern Essenberg, Secretary for Youth Ministries, 1973–1975.

Rev. Glenn Bruggers, Secretary for Asian Ministries, 1973–.

Rev. Donald Jansma, Secretary for Evangelism and Renewal, 1973–.

Mr. Anton Mickelsen, Treasurer, 1974–.

Miss Margaret Wissel, Assistant Treasurer, 1974–.

Mr. Hugh F. Gambaro, Production Coordinator, 1974–.

Mrs. Judy Theune, Associate for Mission Education, 1974–.

Miss Grace Ridder, Manager, RCA Distribution Center, 1974–.

Mrs. Dorothy Logan, Insurance, 1975–1976.

Rev. Raymond Rivera, National Secretary, Hispanic Council, 1975–.

Mrs. Susan R. Bishop, Personnel Associate, 1976–.

Mr. John Hunt, Insurance Coordinator, 1976–.

Mrs. Margaret Schiffert, Assistant for Editorial Service, 1976–.

Mrs. Doris Ten Elshof, Speaker's Bureau, 1976–.

REFORMED CHURCH WOMEN
Formerly NATIONAL DEPARTMENT OF WOMEN'S WORK, which also see.
Report.
1973: 289–290. 1976: 149–151.
1974: 286–288. 1977: 172–173.
1975: 254–256.
By-laws adopted.
1974: 122.
Change in By-laws proposed.
1974: 141–143. Adopted.
By-laws.
1974: 144–148.
Changes in.
1976: 60–61.
Triennial (Fourth) at Cleveland, Ohio, May 4–6, 1971.
1971: 284–285.
Triennial (Fifth) at Long Beach, Cal., April, 1974 (On Queen Mary).
1975: 254.
Triennial (Sixth) at Minneapolis, Minn.
1977: 173.
Study book for 1977—"Reveal Christ Anew Through a Biblical Life Style," by Dr. Donald De Young.
1977: 172.
For the first three triennials, see entries under NATIONAL DEPARTMENT OF WOMEN'S WORK.

REFORMED CHURCH WORLD SERVICE, COMMITTEE OF
See CHURCH WORLD SERVICE, RCA.

REFORMED CHURCH YOUTH FELLOWSHIP
Program commended.
1962: 75, 78.
1963: 58.

REFORMED ECUMENICAL SYNOD
Report on.
1964: 325–328.
Recommended that IRC explore possibilities of RCA membership in.
1972: 256.
1973: 232–233, 258.
Recommended that the CCU explore the question of RCA membership in, and report in 1978.
1977: 253, 269. Adopted.

REFUGEES
Aid from WCC.
1958: 150–151.

REGIONAL CENTERS
Northeastern, Schenectady, New York.
Eastern Metropolitan, New York City.
Midwestern Centers, Lansing, Illinois and Grandville, Mich.
Western, Anaheim, California and Orange City, Iowa.
1973: App. 2, 5–6. 1976: App. 1, 5–6.
1974: App. 2, 5–6. 1977: App. 1, 5–6.
1975: App. 2, 5–6.
See also CENTERS.

REGIONAL JUDICATORIES
See LOCAL AND REGIONAL JUDICATORIES.

REGIONALIZATION
1970: 68, 69–70.
Committee for Understanding recommends word "regionalism" replace regionalization.
1970: 193. Referred to GSEC.
Reports from PS's show uneven progress in regionalization throughout the denomination, indicating that there is no overall plan or strategy. It was recommended regionalization become first priority.
1971: 149–150, 268. Adopted.
Expectations and guidelines for regionalization.
1971: 145–150. Adopted and sent to PS's and classes for concurrance.
Overture to call a moratorium on the execution of regionalization until various facts are presented to classes and PS's.
1971: 105, 115. No action, since "Expectations and Guidelines for Regionalization" have been presented.
Present Status.
1972: 141–148.
Report.
1972: 141–148.
As a result of GSEC request the President made a report on regionalization as did the General Secretary.
1972: 113, 274–275.
See also CENTERS and REGIONAL CENTERS.

RELIEF, COMMITTEE ON
See CHURCH WORLD SERVICE.

RELIGION AND THE PUBLIC SCHOOLS
Constituency of the RCA should stubbornly resist all attempts to deprive our children of religious symbols in the educational system.
1962: 219.
CAC gives reasons for recommending approval of the Supreme Court's decision.
1965: 208–211, 219, 221. Adopted.
Further study by CAC indicates that objective courses in Religion may be provided in the public schools.

1966: 222-223, 234. Received for information.
See also BIBLE READING AND PRAYERS IN THE PUBLIC SCHOOLS and PRAYER AMENDMENT.

RELIGION IN AMERICAN LIFE (RIAL)
Organization works in cooperation with 38 national religious groups (Catholics, Jews, Orthodox, and Protestant). Advertises in popular magazines, and provides spot advertising on radio and TV.
1959: 235-236. 1969: 288-289.
1962: 357-359. 1971: 249-251, 255.
1963: 280-281. 1972: 253-254.
1964: 305-309. 1973: 255-256.
1965: 262-264. 1974: 249-250.
1966: 282-284. 1975: 228-229.
1967: 256-257. 1976: 128-129.
1968: 264-266. 1977: 139-140.

RELIGIOUS EDUCATION
See EDUCATION, BOARD OF and CHRISTIAN EDUCATION.

RELIGIOUS TEST FOR PUBLIC OFFICE
Overture regarding.
1962: 118, 127. Referred to CAC.

RENEWAL
President presents need for.
1965: 340-341, 347-348, 349. Referred to Department of Evangelism.

RENSKERS, HERMAN, FORMER MISSIONARY TO CHINA, 1910-1933.
Death, April 13, 1975 at age of 92.
1976: 131.

RESOLUTIONS, STANDING COMMITTEE ON
Report.
1958: 366-367. 1964: 463-464.
1959: 371-372. 1965: 424-427.
1960: 341-342. 1966: 383-384.
1961: 401-402. 1967: 333-334.
1962: 417-418. 1968: 365-366.
1963: 446-448. 1969: 347-349.
See next listing.

RESOLUTIONS, REVIEW COMMITTEE ON
Report.
1970: 268-270. 1972: 295-296.
1971: 287-289. 1973: 291-292.
1974: 296-298 (a Litany).
1975: 265-266. 1977: 323-324.
1976: 252-253.

"RESPONSIBLE SHARES"
For support of GS benevolent budget.
1963: 368-369, 371.
Overture requesting PS and classes cease and desist from participation in the program.
1964: 128-129, 142, 151. No action.
1965: 292-293.
1966: 321, 327.

RESUMPTION AND CLOSE
See LEAVE OF ABSENCE, COMMITTEE ON and NOMINATIONS, COMMITTEE ON.

RETIRED MEMBERSHIP OF CHURCHES
President suggests churches should make an effort to help them.
1967: 308. Committee to report in 1968.

RETIREMENT PROGRAM, R.C.A.
History of the Board of Pensions.
1971: 159-162.
Outlining of an adequate retirement program, perhaps phasing out of the "contributory" aspect; cost of financing such a program; recommendations of GSEC concerning this program.
1971: 162-173. Adopted in principle.
What was approved in principle has become operational.
1972: 119.
Benefits of three groups: those who will retire after 1985; those who retire between Jan. 1, 1972 and Jan. 1, 1985; those who retire prior to Jan. 1, 1972.
1972: 125-126.
See also PASTORAL CARE OF RETIRED CAF RECIPIENTS.

REVENUE SHARING
CAC recommends GS call attention of consistories in their stewardship as servants of their communities; the need to evaluate and provide guidance for the use of funds from the Federal Revenue Sharing Program and that they develop a "citizen's lobby" on a local level to insure funding of socially responsible programs.
1975: 200. Adopted.

REVIEW COMMITTEES
List of.
1970: 10-13. 1974: 16-20.
1971: 10-15. 1975: 18-22.
1972: 10-14. 1976: 18-23.
1973: 15-19. 1977: 19-23.
Formerly STANDING COMMITTEES, which also see.

REVISION OF THE LITURGY, COMMITTEE ON
See LITURGY, REVISION OF, COMMITTEE ON.

RIAL
See RELIGION IN AMERICAN LIFE.

RICE, ALAN W.
Recommended that he be granted a dispensation from the professorial certificate.
1974: 37, 38. Granted.

RIDDER, REV. HERMAN J.
Elected Evangelism Secretary.
1960: 92.
Appointed Acting President at WTS.
1963: 48.
Became President of both seminaries
1969: 42-44.
Resigned his position as President of the Seminaries.
1971: 32.
Resolution of appreciation.
1971: 35-36.

RIGGS, MR. ARAD
Dinner honoring him for 25 years of service to the BD.
1970: 129.
Resolution upon his retirement.
1977: 103-104.

RINGNALDA, DONALD
Dispensation requested from the professorial certificate.
1973: 33, 36. Granted.

RITSEMA, JACK D.
Dispensation from the professorial certificate requested.
1973: 33, 36. Granted.

RIVERA, KENNETH P.
Dispensation from professorial certificate and academic requirements requested.
1967: 52, 55. Granted.

ROBERTSON, E. JOHN
Dispensation from professorial certificate requested—coming from another seminary.
1959: 52-53, 57. To apply to NBTS for professorial certificate.

ROBINSON, ROBERT
Dispensation from the professorial certificate requested.
1976: 147, 148. Not granted.

ROCK, REV. STANLEY A.
Appointed Assistant Professor of Pastoral Counseling at WTS.
1976: 143.

ROGERS, REV. VIRGIL M.
Elected Professor of Old Testament Language and Exegesis at NBTS.
1961: 72, 74.

ROMAN CATHOLIC CHURCH
Conversations with.
1967: 228.
1968: 232.
Presbyterian and Reformed consultations with.
1973: 244-245. Meets twice annually.

ROTTENBERG, JOHN
Dispensation from professorial certificate requested.
1977: 162, 166, 168. Granted.

ROWENHORST, H. V.
New President of Northwestern College.
1975: 46, 48.

ROZEBOOM, JAMES P.
Dispensation from professorial certificate requested.
1977: 162, 166, 168. Granted.

ROZEBOOM, ROGER
Dispensation from professorial certificate requested.
1971: 31, 36. Approved.

RULES OF ORDER
Proposed changes.
1961: 338.
1963: 138-139.
1964: 173-177.
1965: 169-170.

RUSSIAN MISSILS IN CUBA
Overture regarding the attitude of WCC.
1963: 107-108, 112. Referred to the CWCC.

RUSSIAN ORTHODOX CHURCHES
Overture regarding possible communist influence on WCC.
1963: 107, 112. Referred to CWCC.

SABBATICALS FOR CLERGY
See MINISTERS, SABBATICALS FOR.

SABBATICALS FOR SEMINARY PROFESSORS
See THEOLOGY, PROFESSORS OF.

SACRAMENTS
Overture requesting a manual on the sacraments to be used in instruction.
1964: 121-122, 140, 150. Referred to TC.
EC amends BCO as follows: "an elder may be authorized by the Board of Elders to administer the sacraments; at least one other elder shall accompany an elder administering the sacrament privately."
1973: 184. Adopted and sent to classes for approval.
Approved by classes.
1974: 119.
Further statement by TC concerning baptism.
1974: 206-207.
See also BAPTISM and LORD'S SUPPER.

SAFFORD, GUY
Dispensation from professorial certificate requested.
1973: 33, 36. Not granted.

ST. LOUIS, GENERAL ASSEMBLY, NCC.
1958: 163-164.

SALARIES OF MINISTERS
See MINISTERS, SALARIES.

SALARY ADMINISTRATION
Background information on Executive Salaries.
1969: 187-189.
Procedure for.
1969: 189-192.
Report.
1970: 174-179.
1971: 136.
Background Information.
1971: 178-184.
Procedure for administration of salaries.
1971: 170-183.
Recommendation of Liaison Committee to GSEC. Executive Staff salaries should be reported annually.
1971: 184. Approved.
Report of salary ranges.
1972: 135-141.
Report.
1973: 149-154.
Salary ranges to be reported annually by GSEC and published in MGS.
1973: 154. Adopted.
Report.
1974: 149-154.
1975: 134-139.
1976: 76-79.
Procedures of administration of salaries and salary ranges.
1977: 68.
See also EXECUTIVE SECRETARIES, SALARIES OF.

SAN DIMAS VALLEY COMMUNITY DRIVE-IN CHURCH NOTES
As a result of President's recommendation the RCPR recommends that GSEC appoint an ad hoc committee of 5 to investigate the possible ways for emergency benevolent assistance to be given in hardship cases. That a method for raising these benevolent funds be developed by this committee and that the committee report to the November, 1977 meeting of the GSEC and they be instructed and empowered to act.
1977: 30-31, 35-36. Adopted.
Two overtures (1) requesting interpretation of the supervision of classes over boards of elders and consistories; and (2) that the alleged default of the Valley Community Drive-in Church of San Dimas be referred to the CJB for study including the extent of indebtedness and responsibility if any, of the RCA to the note holders.
1977: 117, 119-120. No action.

SCHADE, REV. HOWARD C.
President of General Synod, 1958.
Elected Executive Secretary of the BDM.
1959: 108, 109.

SCHOLARSHIP AID
RCHE recommended GSEC study the matter of $1 assessment for this purpose.
1972: 113. GSEC took action not to recommend this assessment at this time.
Recommended that congregations give specifically to scholarship funds for RCA students.
1973: 54. Adopted.

SCHOLARSHIP PROGRAM FOR CLERGY
Post B.D. fellowships awarded to two men in 1967.
1968: 42-43.
BTE asks for $4,000 from fund to be used for post B.D. assistance.
1969: 41, 44. To be referred to GPC for implementation. Approved.
See also MINISTERS, CONTINUING EDUCATION OF.

SCHUPPERT, MILDRED
Resolution for upon retirement as Librarian at WTS after 24 years.
1974: 33-34, 37.
Named Librarian Emeritus of WTS.
1975: 30.

SCHUT, REV. HAROLD J.
Elected Vice President of GS.
1966: 7.
Elected President of GS
1967: 8.

SCRIPTURE, INSPIRATION OF
Overture regarding.
1959: 124-125, 128. Referred to TC.
Declaration presented by TC.
1961: 383-388.
Overture requesting the TC make a new statement on the Inspiration of Scripture.
1963: 109-110, 112. No action since this has been done.
Revised declaration of TC on Holy Scripture.
1963: 264-267. Adopted.
TC reports that 1963 statement is still adequate.
1971: 216.

SCUDDER, DR. GALEN, MEDICAL MISSIONARY TO INDIA, 1920-1956.
Obituary.
1968: Annual Report of the CWM, App. 1, 44.

SCUDDER, DR. IDA S., MEDICAL MISSIONARY TO INDIA, 1897-1936
Obituary.
1960: 83.
1961: Annual Report of the CWM, App., 48-49.

SCUDDER, DR. LEWIS R., SR., MISSIONARY TO MIDDLE EAST FOR 38 YEARS
Death, April 3, 1975.
1976: 131.

SCUDDER, MRS. MARGARET BOORAEM, MISSIONARY TO INDIA 1897-1936
Obituary.
1958: Annual Report of BCWM, App., 33-34.

SEITZ, CRAIG
Dispensation from professorial certificate requested. Graduate of Princeton Theological Seminary, and has met constitutional requirements.
1970: 31. Granted.

SELECTIVE SERVICE
CAC recommends that RCA urge the abolition of the selective service system.
1971: 227. Lost.

SELF DETERMINATION OF PEOPLE
Resolution on.
1976: 254-255. Voted that TC prepare a foundation paper on "God and the Nations."
TC not able to prepare the paper because of lack of definition and clarity in the referral.
1977: 306.

SEMINARIES
See THEOLOGICAL SEMINARIES.

SEMINARY RELATIONS, SPECIAL COMMISSION ON
Report.
1962: 50-52.
1963: 55-56.
Proposed Commission be dissolved.
1963: 56.

SEMINARY STUDENTS
See THEOLOGY, STUDENTS OF.

SERVICEMEN
Motion made requesting CAC and CC to carefully study the needs of those veterans who have received less than an honorable discharge, and make recommendations at next Synod.
1974: 299. Adopted.
Statement of concern for those coming back home after the ghastly experience of the Vietnam War. Voted that the CC study the statement of concern and report what can be done.
1974: 295.

SHAFER, MRS. LUMAN (AMY), MISSIONARY TO JAPAN, 1912-1952 (Corrected date 1912-1935—M.S.)
Death.
1971: 73.

SIEGLAFF, HAROLD
Dispensation from the professorial certificate requested.
1959: 53, 57. Granted.

SIT-INS
1961: 216.

SITTSER, JERRY
BTE recommends the dispensation from professorial certificate be granted.
1975: 33, 34. Adopted.

SLAVERY, ABOLITION OF
CAC recommends ratification of this convention.
1968: 216-217. Referred back to CAC.

SMITH, PETER
Dispensation from the professorial certificate requested.
1972: 29, 33. Approved.

SMOKING IN OUR COLLEGES AND CHURCHES
Overture regarding.
1963: 108, 109, 112. No action. CAC to study problem concerning health.
CAC report.
1964: 219-220, 226, 230. Voluntary total abstinence from smoking.

SOLZENITSYN, ALEKSANDR
Resolution asking GS to engage in a public act of thanksgiving for his witness; and that GS continue to encourage its sons and daughters to give allegiance to God over the State in matters of morality and conscience.
1974: 226. Adopted.

SOUTH AFRICA, CHURCH OF
Correspondence with.
1960: 290-292.
1961: 338.
Statement of disapproval by CAC.
1967: 204-206, 211-212, 214. Item b deleted; a and c adopted.
CAC letter to Dutch Reformed Church of South Africa.
1968: 221.
Ad hoc Committee appointed.
1969: 162.
Committee report.
1969: 252-253.

CAC recommends the RCA concur with the NCC regarding unjust conditions in South Africa.
1971: 220-221. Adopted.
Recommended that RCA also enter into exchanges with the Gereformeerde Kerk van Afrika and the Nederduitse Hervormde Kerk.
1972: 256-257. Adopted.
Recommended that a South African student attend one of our RCA seminaries each year.
1972: 233-234, 256-257. Adopted.
1973: 232.
Ad Hoc report.
1974: 257.
1976: 226-227.
Delicate negotiations to be worked out by the Committee on Christian Unity with the Church in South Africa (Nederduitse Hervormde Kerk)—Black.
1976: 214-215, 229. Adopted.
Letters sent to Government of South Africa and Mr. Henry Kissenger.
1976: 256-257.
Recommended that the CCU be encouraged to explore all ways to communicate with the Nederduitse Gereformeerde Kerk in order to assist and support them in these difficult days of conflict.
1977: 252, 269. Adopted.

SOUTH AMERICAN MISSION PROPOSED
See CHRISTIAN WORLD MISSION and LATIN AMERICA and VENEZUELA.

SOUTHERN NORMAL SCHOOL
See BREWTON.

SOUTHEAST ASIA, WAR IN
A paper prepared at the Ecumenical Witness meeting.
1972: 216-221.
CAC recommends (1) withdraw from all participation in the hostilities still going on in Laos and Cambodia immediately after prisoners of war are released and/or lists are made available; (2) Seek release of all persons currently in prison for political reasons in South Vietnam and the U.S.; (3) render all possible aid to rebuild and reconstruct damage done to people and property in Indo China, consistent with the self-determination of the recipients.
1973: 218-219. (1) adopted; (2 and 3) not adopted.

SPEAKING IN TONGUES
See CHARISMATIC MOVEMENT.

SPECIAL APPEALS
Policy on.
1970: 139-140.

SPECIAL DAYS, CALENDAR OF

1958: xvi.	1968: xiii.
1959: xvi.	1969: xiii.
1960: xvi.	1970: xiii.
1961: xvi.	1971: xiii.
1962: xvi.	1972: xiv.
1963: xv.	1973: xiv.
1964: xv.	1974: xiv.
1965: xv.	1975: xii.
1966: xv.	1976: xii.
1967: xiii.	1977: xii.

SPECIALIZED MINISTRIES
See MINISTRIES, SPECIALIZED.

"SPIRIT BAPTISM"
See BAPTISM (SPIRIT BAPTISM).

SPIRITUAL LIFE COMMISSION
Recommended that GSEC study the possibility of instituting such a commission.
1971: 289-290. Adopted.
Recommended that a study be made of the feasibility of instituting such a commission.
1972: 114. GSEC took no action and suggested it be referred to the Secretary of Evangelism.
GPC has informed GSEC that it is prepared to authorize the appointment of a Task Force on Evangelism and Renewal.
1974: 61.
See EVANGELISM AND RENEWAL, TASK FORCE ON.

STAFF AMENABLE TO RCA JUDICATORY
Overture requesting each GPC executive staff person including Executive Secretaries of Minority Councils to be amenable to RCA classes and that each Minority Council be accountable to GPC in the use of funds.
1976: 114-115. Referred to Joint Committee on Relationship and Responsibilities of Minority Councils and Denominational Policy Bodies for study and report.

STAFF CONFERENCE
Report.

1958: 240-244.	1963: 287.
1959: 229-233.	1964: 454.
1960: 213-217.	1965: 415.
1961: 333-337.	1966: 373.
1962: 361.	1967: 323.

STAFF CONSULTING GROUP
Met in January with 30 representatives from PS's, Colleges, BTE, GPC, together with GSEC attending, discussing (1) definition of assessments, askings, and offerings; (2) procedures for judicatory ap-

proval of RCA programs, (3) fund raising in local RCA churches.
1973: 123-126. Adopted.
Report on three meetings.
1974: 127-128.
Continuing constructive meetings.
1975: 109-110.
1976: 50.
GSEC reports a brochure "Supporting the Whole Denominational Program" available.
1976: 36.
Action taken on various requests for drives by the several educational institutions.
1977: 50-52.

STAFF, RCA, LIST OF
See REFORMED CHURCH IN AMERICA, STAFF.

STANDARDS OF THE CHURCH
See DOCTRINAL STANDARDS.

STANDARDS OF UNITY
Overture requesting the rewriting of the Standards to make them current language with today's usage.
1972: 104. No action. Attention is called to the new translation of the Liturgy and Psalms.
See also DOCTRINAL STANDARDS and CONFESSION OF FAITH.

STANDING COMMITTEE
Term changed to REVIEW COMMITTEE, which also see.
1969: 226-227, 230. Adopted.

STANDING COMMITTEES
Listing of.
1958: 6-8. 1964: 8-10.
1959: 7-9. 1965: 9-11.
1960: 8-9. 1966: 8-11.
1961: 7-8. 1967: 9-12.
1962: 7-8. 1968: 9-12.
1963: 8-9. 1969: 10-13.
President suggests method of choosing committees be studied.
1963: 375, 437. Referred to GSEC.
Referred to the Committee on the Study of Boards and Agencies.
1964: 164.
Number of members of committees.
1969: 165.

STAPERT, JOHN
Dispensation requested from the professorial certificate. Graduate of Fuller Theological Seminary with examination sustained at WTS.
1966: 46. Granted.
Rev. John Stapert appointed Editor of the CH.
1975: 78.
Contract as Editor of CH renewed for four more years.
1977: 184.

STATE OF RELIGION—PRESIDENT'S RE REPORT
Overture asking for a change in this title to "President's Report."
1967: 112, 124, 128. Adopted and referred to GSEC.
"State of Religion" dropped in 1968.
1968: 137.
All reports are listed under PRESIDENT'S REPORT, which see.

STATED CLERK (GENERAL SYNOD)
Report of Special Committee on.
1961: 341-345.
Rev. Marion de Velder called to serve for a 5 year term subject to reappointment.
1961: 345.
Report.
1958: 246-247. 1963: 278-286.
1959: 234-237. 1964: 178-181.
1960: 218-219. 1965: 141-149.
1961: 338-340. 1966: 189-195.
1962: 357-360. 1967: 172-177.
Duties of, redefined.
1961: 342, 343-345.
Manual for.
1964: 201.
Office of to be restudied.
1966: 168-169.
SC becomes GENERAL SECRETARY, which also see.

STATED CLERKS
Manual indicating responsibilities of all clerks.
1964: 201.
Revision to be made in the manual: "Overtures to General Secretary must be postmarked no later than April 30."
1977: 121.

STATED CLERKS' MEETINGS (STATED CLERK AND CLERKS OF PS's)
Overture suggesting.
1962: 124, 127. Approved.
Report.
1963: 283-286.
1964: 182-203.
1965: 150-161. Meetings discontinued.

STATED MEETINGS
PS's, Classes, and GS.
1958-1965: Inside front cover of MGS.
1966: Inside back cover of MGS.
1967-1968: Outside back cover of MGS.
1969-1971: Inside back cover of MGS.
Classical Stated meetings only.
1972-1975: Inside back cover of App. 2.
1976-1977: Inside back cover of App. 1.

STATISTICAL BLANKS
Overture requesting blanks be sent to Stated Clerks of classes before January 5.
1962: 116, 127. Adopted.

STATISTICAL HEADINGS
Changes.
1962: 137.
Overture regarding reinstatement of ministers' addresses.
1960: 110, 116. Not adopted.
Changes regarding baptized members.
1962: 284, 341. Referred to GSEC.
Overture requesting a column for Parish benevolences for such items as aid to needy families, scholarships, etc.
1963: 108, 112. No action.
Overture requesting "disciplined" be changed to "excommunicated."
1966: 141, 144, 149. Adopted.

STATISTICAL REPORTS OF CLASSES
1958: 258-305.
1959: 268-305.
1960: 240-287.
1961: 277-325.
1962: 291-339.
1963: 383-433.
1964: 392-441.
1965: 351-399.
1966: 442-497.
1967: App. 2, 57-112.
1968: App. 2, 58-113.
1969: App. 2, 15-71.
1970: App. 2, 14-71.
1971: App. 2, 23-86.
1972: App. 2, 21-85.
1973: App. 2, 21-84.
1974: App. 2, 22-125.
1975: App. 2, 22-125.
1976: App. 1, 22-115.
1977: App. 1, 23-115.

STEDGE, JOYCE
Dispensation from professorial certificate requested. Motion to consider this dispensation separately lost.
1973: 33, 36-37. Dispensation granted.
Overture requesting GS to rescind 1973 action of granting a dispensation from the professorial certificate to Mrs. Stedge.
1974: 95. No action.
Overture requesting a special committee to study the legality of the ruling of the President of Synod, 1973, and the legality of classes in ordaining, installing, and giving Mrs. Stedge a license to preach.
1974: 95. No action.
Three overtures requesting GS to declare null and void the licensing, installation and ordination of Mrs. Stedge.
1974: 94, 96-97. No action.
History of the case.
1974: 123-124.
CJB declines to consider the complaints against the classis for licensing Mrs. Stedge since complaints must come from minorities or individuals who are under the jurisdiction of the same judicatory.
1974: 113.
Overture requesting that the dispensation from the professorial certificate and her subsequent licensure and ordination as minister of the Word and her installation as pastor be declared null and void.
1975: 91. No action.

STEGENGA, PRESTON J.
Resigned from Presidency of Northwestern College.
1966: 80.

STEWARDSHIP ADVANCE
Plan for implementation of.
1958: 236-239.
1960: 205, 207.
1961: 231-232.
A brochure.
1962: 240-241.

STEWARDSHIP COUNCIL
Report.
1958: 226-235.
1959: 222-228.
1960: 204-212.
1961: 229-261.
1962: 239-268.
1963: 340-366.
1964: 347-352.
1965: 291-295.
1966: 320-324.
1967: 285-288.
1968: 313-317.
1969: 181-183.
Standing Committee on suggested.
1960: 108.
1961: 338, 340. Adopted.
Relation to other boards.
1962: 280, 341.
Overture requesting that the Council publish a record of expenses and cost of operation in the Orange Book, as do other boards.
1965: 103, 116. Referred to Standing Committee of SC.
Council's reply to overture.
1965: 299. Such report has been published each year except 1962. No action.
Subsequent reports will be a part of the PC report.
1970: 253.
1971: 175-176.
CAC paper "A Crisis in Stewardship" considers the stewardship of natural resources and power.
1973: 208-213.

STEWARDSHIP COUNCIL, STANDING COMMITTEE ON
Report.
1962: 269-277.
1963: 367-371.
1964: 353-381.
1965: 296-301.
1966: 325-329.
1967: 289-297.
1968: 318-320.

STORM, MRS. W. HAROLD (IDA), MISSIONARY TO ARABIA FROM 1936-1966
Death.
1972: 65.

STUDENT VOLUNTEER MOVEMENT
1959: 179.

STUDENTS IN THEOLOGICAL SEMINARIES
See individual seminaries.

STUDENTS OF THEOLOGY, SUPERVISION OF
See THEOLOGY, STUDENTS OF, CLASSICAL SUPERVISION OF

STUYVESANT (N.Y.) PROTESTANT REFORMED DUTCH CHURCH
Funds place with Board of Direction for investment.
1959: 17-18.

SUDAN
1973: 59.

SUNDAY OBSERVANCE
See LORD'S DAY OBSERVANCE OF.

SUNDAY SCHOOL CURRICULUM MATERIALS
See CURRICULUM, SUNDAY SCHOOL.

SUPERINTENDENTS, BOARD OF
See THEOLOGICAL EDUCATION, BOARD OF.

SUSPENSION
Overture requesting clarification of word "suspension."
1975: 87. No action. Dealt with in revision of 1974.

SYMBOL, RCA
See CHURCH EMBLEM.

SYMBOLS USED AT SYNOD
Description of.
1966: 386.

SYNODICAL ASSESSMENTS RECEIVED

1958: 25-26.	1968: 24-25.
1959: 24-25.	1969: 23-24.
1960: 21-22.	1970: 23-24.
1961: 21-22.	1971: 23-24.
1962: 20-21.	1972: 23-24.
1963: 19-20.	1973: 26-27.
1964: 21-22.	1974: 26-27.
1965: 21-22.	1975: 27-28.
1966: 22-23.	1976: 86-87.
1967: 23-24.	1977: 94-95.

SYNODICAL MINUTES AND REFERENCES, STANDING COMMITTEE
Report.

1958: 137.	1967: 129.
1959: 129.	1968: 125.
1960: 118.	1969: 154.
1961: 143.	1970: 114.
1962: 129-130.	1971: 118.
1963: 114-115.	1972: 107.
1964: 154-156.	1973: 115.
1965: 125-127.	1974: 111.
1966: 152.	1975: 94.

SYNODICAL LEGISLATION
See DIGEST OF SYNODICAL LEGISLATION.

TABULAR STATEMENT, CONSOLIDATED
1961: 237-255.
1962: 247-266.
See BENEVOLENCE RECEIPTS.

TAIWAN
1970: 60.
1974: 64.
1975: 59.

TANIS, REV. EDWARD H.
Elected Field Secretary of BWM for Western Synods.
1961: 98-99.

TAX EXEMPTIONS FOR CONTRIBUTIONS TO INDIVIDUAL CONGREGATIONS
Overture regarding.
1959: 125, 128. No action.

TAYLOR, MISS MINNIE, MISSIONARY TO JAPAN, 1919-1937
Death.
1971: 72.

TE PASKE, MAURICE
Thanksgiving expressed for his life and memory.
1977: 255, 270.

TEACHING ELDER
See ELDER, TEACHING.

TELEVISION AND VIOLENCE
CAC urges letters be sent to the President of the U.S. and the networks stating RCA's concern regarding detrimental effects of excessive depiction of violence; and a pastoral letter from the CAC to families of the RCA and that the director of mass media present a list of programs helpful for children.
1971: 224. Adopted.
Recommended that the CAC and OPC take responsibility for presenting to the church a list of programs helpful to children in the coming TV season.
1971: 197. Adopted.

TEMPLE TIME
Suggested a committee be appointed to approach Temple Time Committee to make it the official voice of the RCA.
1958: 317-318. Referred to Committee.
Suggestion that a new board be established in the 3 western synods to make Temple Time the official voice of the RCA.
1959: 321-322. Referred back to Committee.
Study continued.
1960: 298.

Name changed to BOARD OF BROADCASTING OF THE RCA.
1961: 359, 366. To be referred to the three western synods for adoption.
Proposed Constitution.
1961: 359-366.
Proposal lost. The committee dissolved.
1962: 390.
See also RADIO BROADCASTING, RCA, COMMITTEE ON; and also the new name for the program WORDS OF HOPE.

TEN CLAY, REV. HENRY
Appointed Dean of Students at WTS.
1961: 61.
Resigned as Dean of Students at WTS.
1967: 43.

TEN PERCENTER FELLOWSHIP
1959: 225, 241-242.
1960: 205, 207.
1961: 230.

TENT-MAKER MINISTRY
Overture requesting an amendment be made in the BCO including a definition of "tent-maker" ministry and as concerning a minister of the Word duly installed under classis.
1975: 88-89. No action.

TER LOUW, SIMON
Mr. Ter Louw, a preaching elder requests dispensation from all academic requirements and professorial certificate.
1966: 46-47. Ordination not deemed necessary for his work, Denied.
Second request for dispensation. He has worked faithfully in two congregations and there are many testimonies in his behalf.
1969: 40-41, 44. Granted.

TEUSINK, REV. HOWARD G.
Resolution for work as Executive Secretary of Stewardship Council.
1962: 277.

THEOLOGICAL COMMISSION
Report.
1960: 325-327. 1969: 233-237.
1961: 383-388. 1970: 203-211.
1962: 399-403. 1971: 211-217.
1963: 263-270. 1972: 197-201.
1964: 208-212. 1973: 191-201.
1965: 171-173. 1974: 203-209.
1966: 205-212. 1975: 162-189.
1967: 187-199. 1976: 231-245.
1968: 185-198. 1977: 272-307.
Commission was suggested for the purpose of producing a document outlining the Christian Faith of the RCA.
1958: 355.
Overture requesting the Commission.
1959: 123. Commission constituted.
References to such a commission.
1959: 249, 257, 363-367.
Appointment of Commission.
1959: 367.
Overture expressing concern over TC's report on the Historicity of Genesis.
1961: 138-140, 142. No action.
Overture opposing TC's report on Inspiration of Scripture.
1962: 124, 127. No action. Classes and consistories urged to submit their deliberations to TC before February 1, 1963 for their study.
No response to overture pending reaction of classes.
1962: 399-400.
Structure of Commission.
1970: 209, 210.
Contact has been made with the committees of other Reformed bodies and the World Alliance of Reformed Churches, etc. to exchange minutes and various studies.
1973: 201.
Considering possibility of publishing some of the papers written in the last fifteen years.
1974: 209.
Plans to be presented concerning printing of.
1975: 189.
See also CONFESSION OF FAITH—NEW; OUR SONG OF HOPE; and CONFESSIONAL INSPIRATION, COMMITTEE ON.

THEOLOGICAL EDUCATION, BOARD OF
List of.
1967: App. 2, 10.
1968: App. 2, 12.
1969: App. 2, 10.
1970: App. 2, 11.
1971: App. 2, 18.
1972: App. 2, 18.
1973: App. 2, 18.
1974: App. 2, 19-20.
1975: App. 2, 20.
1976: App. 1, 20.
1977: App. 1, 20.
Report.
1968: 38-40. 1973: 28-31.
1969: 36-44. 1974: 28-37.
1970: 27-36. 1975: 29-33.
1971: 27-34. 1976: 142-147.
1972: 25-30. 1977: 158-171.
President suggests one board for the two seminaries.
1960: 230. Referred to Permanent Committee on Professorate.
Suggested by PCTE that GS appoint a committee to frame a plan for creation of a

single Board of Theological Education to replace the two boards of the seminaries.
1966: 45, 49. Adopted. Referred to COR.
Overture opposing a single board for the two seminaries.
1967: 122, 126, 128. No action since 1966 GS had approved.
Procedure of reporting to GS referred to Sub-committee on Denominational Structure.
1969: 160.
Relationship with GS and other boards.
1969: 170-171.
Overture requests GS to instruct the BTE to present the full plan of Theological Education for Synod ratification.
1970: 85, 105, 200. Review Committee recommended. Referred to EC.
Recommended that there be a Review Committee.
1971: 143. Adopted.
RCTE recommends that the CHR and DPD study the following: (1) the validity of the contention that RCA theological education is unique enough that it is difficult to duplicate elsewhere; (2) a survey of the motives involved in the choice of a seminary and in the decision to seek a plan of service in the RCA.
1971: 31, 36.
Two overtures requesting classical representation on the BTE.
1972: 96-97, 105. No action. This would make an unwieldy board.
Study presented by Coordinator of HR and the Director of PD on (1) the uniqueness of theological education in RCA seminaries; (2) responsibility of classis for providing employment; (3) criteria for dispensations, etc.
1972: 165. Referred back for further study.
Report of the study by OHR and BTE (Alvin J. Poppen and Robert A. Nykamp). A comprehensive study giving 12 tables showing probable retirements in the next 10 years; number of churches without pastors now; students available for ministry; reasons for non-RCA students choosing other seminaries; contributing factors in choosing ministry; new opportunities for, etc.
1973: 139-148. See RECRUITMENT FOR PARISH MINISTRY.
New opportunities available for ministry.
1974: 118.
Overture requesting GS to include in the GS budget beginning in 1976, the cost of the operation of the BTE.
1975: 83. Adopted.
New Constitution.
1977: 70-76, 161.
Revised By-laws. When they were approved in 1968 it was envisioned there would be one president for the two seminaries.
1977: 43. Adopted.

THEOLOGICAL EDUCATION, BOARD OF, REVIEW COMMITTEE ON
Report.
1971: 35-38. 1975: 33-36.
1972: 30-33. 1976: 147-148.
1973: 34-38. 1977: 166-171.
1974: 37-40.

THEOLOGICAL EDUCATION IN THE RCA (prior to the formation of the BTE)
One hundred seventy-fifth anniversary committee on the founding of the first Theological Seminary in America (NBTS).
1958: 346-349.
1959: 349-354.
Four year seminary course suggested.
1958: 253, 256. Referred to Special Committee on Curriculum.
Permanent Committee on Theological Education proposed.
1962: 64.
1963: 52, 55, 138-139. Committee constituted.
Overture requesting committee for study of Theological Education, RCA.
1966: 126, 144, 150. Study already being made by PCTE. No action.
Overture suggesting a special committee be appointed which will give specific attention to the possibility of merger of the seminaries.
1966: 127, 144, 150. Referred to SCBE.
See also CURRICULUM, SEMINARY, SPECIAL COMMITTEE ON; and entries under NBTS and WTS; and THEOLOGICAL SEMINARIES.

THEOLOGICAL EDUCATION, PERMANENT COMMITTEE ON
Duties.
1964: 173-174, 178-179.
Because of overlapping of the Standing and Permanent Committee, it is recommended that the Rules of Order be changed, and that the present Permanent Committee be dissolved and new personnel appointed, the new committee then to be responsible to GS.
1964: 51-52. Adopted. Must be approved by GS of 1965.
Membership and functions of the Committee (Revision).
1965: 142.

Report.
1966: 44–50.
1967: 50–56.
1968: 41–43.
Committee dissolved because of overlapping.
1968: 43.

THEOLOGICAL PROFESSOR, OFFICE OF
See THEOLOGY, PROFESSOR OF, OFFICE OF, and FOURTH OFFICE.

THEOLOGICAL QUARTERLY OF THE REFORMED CHURCH
Suggested the two seminary publications be combined.
1960: 230, 236. Approved and referred to Department of Evangelism.
(Note: Beginning with the fall issue of 1969, *The Reformed Review* which had been published for 14 years by WTS became a joint project of the two seminaries (NBTS and WTS) and thus became "A Quarterly Journal of the Seminaries of the RCA." M.S.)

THEOLOGICAL SEMINARIES
Merger possibilities.
1961: 39.
Relationship to Stewardship Council.
1962: 51. Referred back for study.
Relationship to GS.
1962: 51. Referred back for study.
Relationship to the BE, SC, etc. Suggest a Permanent Committee on Ministerial Education be established.
1962: 50–51, 52, 60. Referred to Special Commission for further study.
Merger proposals.
1965: 46, 47, 48. Proposal withdrawn; suggested the study of other opportunities for more effective unification and coordination of theological education.
In regard to merger possibilities, the President suggests a special panel gather factual material on the question of whether or not we need two seminaries.
1966: 344, 353, 355. Referred to COR for consideration.
Seminary merger to be the subject of study at Seminary Faculty Convocation.
1966: 43. Recommended thorough study of the task of theological education and asked that GS hold in abeyance the idea of a single board of theological education for the two seminaries. Referred to GSEC.
Recommended by GSEC that (1) GS set up a single board of superintendents for the two seminaries for purpose of establishing a single theological seminary; (2) that 27 persons serve on the board and that no permanent faculty be set up until the board is formed and that this structure be continued annually until the legal problems incident to the merger of the seminaries have been resolved; (3) process of nominations of board members be outlined.
1967: 165–166. (1) "Single theological seminary" amended to "unification of the program of theological education," adopted; (2) "merger of the seminaries" amended to "unification of the program of theological education," adopted; (3) "single seminary concept" amended to "the unified program of theological education," adopted.
Board of Superintendents and Trustees to become one Board of Superintendents. GSEC will appoint convener.
1967: 55, 56.
To be convened in September, 1968.
1968: 137.
Unified administration of the two seminaries in three steps: (1) both presidents resign; (2) Dr. Herman Ridder be appointed president of both seminaries; (3) Dr. Ridder appoint administrative personnel needed.
1969: 42–44.
The Program Design Committee is presenting a "Two-Level, Two-Site Design" to use creatively both sites without duplication.
1969: 37.
The unified program (Bi-level, Multi-site): First two years at NBTS, which is to teach men to live and act in the world with theological understanding; transfer to WTS for professional skills level for two years. Each school to operate its own BD program until fall of 1971.
1970: 27–28.
Seven overtures on Bi-level, Multi-site program: 2 to restudy and reconsider; 2 to make it voluntary; 3 opposing it for a variety of reasons.
1970: 86–90, 105–106. No action since BTE has removed the cut-off date of the three year program.
Overture asking GS to instruct the BTE to continue to offer a three-year course (with optional internship) at both seminaries, in addition to the BLMS optional program.
1970: 101, 112. No action.
Report on progress of the BLMS program.
1971: 27–28.

Degree nomenclature changed: Master of Divinity Degree (M. Div.) replaced Bachelor of Divinity Degree (B.D.). Those holding a B.D. degree may apply to the seminary from which they were graduated and receive a new M. Div. certificate for a fee of $25.00. The MCE program is not being offered to new students.
1971: 29.
Dr. Lester J. Kuyper becomes Interim President of the two seminaries upon the resignation of Dr. Herman Ridder.
1971: 32.
GSEC recommends one seminary and that in close proximity to a new location for the National Offices.
1971: 137–138.
Overture urging the RCA to re-establish separate boards of trustees for NBTS and WTS.
1971: 108, 115. No action.
Rev. Arie Brouwer invited to become President of the seminaries.
1972: 25. Declined.
BLMS is the preferred program of the BTE but it needs further study because of unanticipated practical problems.
1972: 26.
Guidelines for consultations on seminary location.
1972: 32.
BTE recommends that a series of consultations among BTE, GPC, GSEC, Seminary Faculties, local church representatives, seminary students and RCA college representatives be held.
1972: 28, 32. Adopted. Definitive recommendations to be presented for action next year.
In seeking further unification of the seminaries, a unified budget has been developed.
1972: 27.
BLMS program a knotty problem. The BTE still considers it an exciting program which needs continued study, but they also allow for the conventional three-year program.
1973: 30.
BTE chooses a president for each seminary—Rev. Howard G. Hageman, as President of NBTS, and Rev. I. John Hesselink, Jr., as President of WTS.
1973: 28–29, 32.
Recommendation that both seminaries remain wholeheartedly committed to the BLMS program until all presently enrolled students have completed the program or have phased into alternate programs. That some of the positive components of the program be integrated into a single new curriculum at each site with the option that there could still be movement between sites.
1974: 36.
Special Committee on the Location of National Offices and Seminaries recommends that the two present locations in Holland, Michigan and New Brunswick, N.J. be retained as primary locations of our program of Theological Education.
1973: 188. Adopted.
Overture requesting that it be mandatory for those coming from other seminaries to have one year at one of the RCA seminaries.
1974: 99–100. No action.
Recommended that the BTE report next year on how training of ethnic minority students could be implemented in the seminaries, looking to the American Indian Council, Black Council, and Hispanic Council for insights.
1974: 40. Adopted.
BTE reports that both seminaries have Hispanic students; NBTS has two black students.
1975: 31.
The RCBTE reacted with surprise and unbelief that GS does not in any way support the seminaries financially, even though GS is the calling agent for engaging qualified faculty. Recommended that BTE reexamine the basis of funding, and develop plans for expanded support.
1977: 170–171. Adopted.
See also NATIONAL OFFICES, LOCATION OF and THEOLOGICAL EDUCATION IN THE RCA, and NBTS and WTS.

THEOLOGICAL SEMINARY PRESIDENTS, ELECTION OF

Overture asking GS to initiate action to cause the appointment of a Seminary President to be subject to a vote of ratification by GS.
1970: 86, 105, 201. Referred to EC and COCG.
COCG reports this would necessitate changing the by-laws of NBTS and WTS and that the present by-laws were approved by GS within the last four years.
1971: 208.
Motion made that the two seminaries be asked to amend the by-laws.
1971: 209. Lost.
Overture asking GS to instruct the BTE to amend its by-laws to cause the appointment of the president of the seminaries to be subject to a vote of ratification by GS.
1972: 93–94. Not adopted.
Presidential situation: An invitation to become President of the seminaries was ex-

tended to Rev. Arie Brouwer who would remain Executive Secretary of the GPC and thus be able to unify theological education with the program of the GS.
1972: 25. After many interviews with faculties and students. Mr. Brouwer declined.
Overture requesting GS to instruct the BTE to refrain from implementing the Executive Secretary-President of the Seminaries arrangement because of basic difference in theological education and general program of the RCA.
1972: 101. Adopted.
Overture requesting GS and the BTE to reconsider their decision to offer Rev. Arie Brouwer, the position since the administrative structure of the denomination would be under the direction of one man.
1972: 100. No action since this is no longer germane.
Overture requesting GS to instruct the BTE to select a president for each seminary.
1972: 103-104. Referred to BTE for their continued review.
Dr. Howard Hageman appointed President of NBTS and Dr. Ira John Hesselink, Jr. appointed President of WTS.
1973: 28-29.

THEOLOGY AND LITURGY
See entries under THEOLOGICAL COMMISSION and LITURGY, REVISION OF, COMMITTEE ON.

THEOLOGY, STUDENTS OF, CLASSICAL EXAMINATIONS AND SUPERVISION OF
Suggestions for change of examination, especially in Greek and Hebrew.
1958: 350.
Seminary's statement of work done in Ecclesiastical History and methods of sermonizing, deemed sufficient.
1959: 355-356.
Greek and Hebrew: (1) may accept a statement from the seminary, or (2) exegetical study prepared by student in advance of examination.
1959: 355.
Theology, Biblical Introduction, piety, views in desiring to become a minister, and adherence to Standards of the RCA—examination in accordance with constitutional requirements.
1959: 355.
Guidelines presented. Much as above, although the examination is called a dialogue between classis and candidate.
1965: 43-46, 48. Adopted.
Overture expressing disapproval of the 1965 Guidelines, and requesting action be rescinded, since authority of the classis is inhibited by it.
1966: 121, 142-143, 149. No action. Guidelines do not impair the freedom of classis.
Licensing of seminary students to preach recommended by the convocation of seminary faculties.
1966: 48-49. Adopted and referred to CRC.
Amendment of constitution regarding examinations consists of five parts: (1) examination at the end of his junior year on conducting public worship and preaching; (2) examination at the end of his middle year in order to continue his provisional license and secure the right to candidate during his senior year; (3) shall appear before his classis at the end of his seminary training for examination for licensure and ordination; (4) candidate shall be ordained by his classis to the Christian ministry after he has received a call; (5) the candidate may be examined by the calling classis at its discretion, before his call is approved.
1967: 178-179. Sent to classes for approval.
Classes approved.
1968: 169.
Overture asking that certain examinations of the above be deleted; or that another classis may be substituted for the home classis.
1969: 126-128, 143, 144, 152. No action.
COCG's proper wording of the above.
1969: 214-216, 228, 229. Adopted and referred to classes.
Approved by classes.
1970: 141.
Two overtures asking for an amendment concerning examinations: (1) examinations do not allow for ministries other than the parish; (2) a simplified system of examiniation preferred.
1970: 83, 85, 103-104. A special committee to study after consulting with the two classes.
Recommended that a classis may request another classis to act in its behalf with respect to examinations.
1970: 198-199. Defeated.
Overture requesting classes have sole prerogative to certify a candidate for ministry to any secular authority which required certification; (stems from the fact that seminaries have given information to draft boards).
1969: 125-126, 143, 152. No action.

Suggested that term "in preparatory training for the ministry" be changed to "seminary training for the ministry."
1970: 198. Referred to classes for approval.
Approved by classes.
1971: 152.
Confusion caused because 1st, 2nd, and 3rd year, or junior, middle and senior year can no longer be used on account of the BLMS program, year of internship, etc. A complete rewriting of articles 8 and 9 is requested.
1971: 199-203. Adopted and sent to classes for approval.
Classes approved.
1972: 120.
Overture requesting the COCG formulate appropriate amendments to *Government* to bring said *Government* into harmony with present trends: examination for chaplaincy, examination after a year of internship, etc.
1972: 94. Referred to BTE and COCG.
EC's amendment: the candidate shall be examined by his classis at the conclusion of each year of seminary training; his classis may also require the candidate to appear at the conclusion of any period of internship.
1973: 184. Adopted and referred to classes.
Recommended EC make amendment to the BCO providing for the appearance of all seminary students before classes. This makes provision for interns.
1973: 36. Adopted.
Position letter sent to BTE.
1973: 179.
Overture requesting a ruling on whether it is the responsibility of classes to take women under their care for the objective of being granted licensed candidate status in the RCA since at the present time women may not be ordained.
1977: 118. No action.

THEOLOGY, STUDENTS OF, CALLING OF
Candidating and calling of.
1958: 351. No negotiations before graduation.
1959: 55.
1960: 55, 60.
Overture requesting promises of calls be issued after Apr. 1.
1960: 111, 117. Referred to Permanent Committee on Professorate.
Overture suggesting this terminology be changed to "provisional call."
1968: 94, 117. Referred to ECRC.
Overture asking that *Government* be amended so that "provisional call" replace "promise of a call."
1969: 125, 143, 152. Last year same overture was referred to ECRC for study and referral to classes. Adopted.

THEOLOGY, PROFESSOR OF, OFFICE
Rules for nomination of.
1958: 61.
Report of Committee to Study Nature and Offices of Ministries.
1960: 315-317.
President suggests Office be dropped.
1961: 268, 329, 331. Referred to PCP for study.
Office to be retained; CRC to prepare amendment.
1962: 54-55, 58-59, 63-64.
Report of CRC.
1963: 133-134, 136. Amendment adopted.
See also FOURTH OFFICE.

THEOLOGY, PROFESSORS OF
Proposed meeting of.
1960: 55, 229-230, 236.
Convocation of.
1961: 69-70. 1964: 54-55.
1962: 54, 55. 1966: 42.
Recommended that 1:3 of each faculty be delegates to GS.
1960: 55.
Voted that two members of each faculty be delegates to GS.
1960: 57.
Commission suggests study of relationship of professors to GS and boards.
1961: 70. Approved.
1962: 51-52.
Sabbaticals declared beneficial to the whole church.
1962: 54.
Permanent Committee on TE suggests all installed professors be asked to attend GS.
1965: 44, 47. Referred to GSEC for study.
Suggested by PCTE that all Professors of Theology of the seminaries attend GS.
1965: 44. Referred to GSEC.
Referred to Sub-committee on Denominational Structure.
1966: 163, 182. No action.
BTE recommends amendment to BCO: "Upon reaching the age of 65 years the Professor of Theology shall elect to be declared Professor Emeritus or to be dismissed to the classis or other ecclesiastical body he chooses. The previous retirement age of 70 years shall continue to

apply to those professors elected by GS prior to July 1, 1977.
1976: 143, 147. Adopted.

THOMAS, REV. NORMAN EDWIN
Elected Vice President of GS.
1960: 6.
Elected President of GS.
1961: 5.
Appointed Dean at NBTS.
1970: 30.

THOMPSON, ROBERT
Dispensation from professorial certicate requested.
1971: 31, 36. Approved.

TIHANEY, LESLIE CHARLES
BTE recommends that dispensation from certain educational requirements and professorial certificate be granted.
1975: 33, 34. Adopted.

TITHING
1958: 234.
1959: 225, 241.
1961: 230.
1962: 243.
1963: 341.
1964: 348.
1965: 291-293.
1966: 320.
1968: 318.
Resolved that GS reaffirm its approval and urge members of the RCA to practice tithing.
1975: 17. Adopted in 1974 and referred to GPC for implementation.

THOMS, DR. W. WELLS, MISSIONARY TO ARABIA (MUSCAT) FROM 1931-1970.
Death.
1972: 66.

TRANSFER OF A CHURCH MEMBER, CERTIFICATE FOR
Word "transfer" is recommended in place of "dismission."
1966: 197, 201. Referred to classes.
Approved by classes.
1967: 172.
See also DISMISSION CERTIFICATE.

TRANSFER OF CHURCHES TO OTHER PARTICULAR SYNODS
Overture regarding.
1960: 112, 117. No action.

TRAVARCA (TELEVISION, RADIO, AUDIO VISUALS, RCA)
1970: 172.
1971: 174-175.
1972: 133.
1973: 159-160.
1974: 156-157.
1975: 141-142.
Report of 300 films per month processed; 3600 film bookings in a year.
1977: 88-89.

TRAVEL, STANDING COMMITTEE ON
Report.
1958: 306-307.
1959: 308-309.
1960: 288-289.
1961: 346.
1962: 375.
1963: 440.
1964: 442.
1965: 400.
1966: 357-358.
1967: 313.
1968: 337.
See next listing.

TRAVEL AND LEAVE OF ABSENCE, REVIEW COMMITTEE ON
Report.
1969: 332-333.
1970: 254-255.
1971: 274-275.
1972: 280-282.
1973: 281.
Recommended that GSEC take proper steps to disband this Review Committee.
1972: 281. Adopted.

TRAVEL POLICY
Mileage allowance increase from 10¢ to 13¢ a mile.
1974: 121. Adopted.

TRAVER, BARRY
Dispensation from professorial certificate requested.
1976: 146, 148.

TRINDLE, JOSEPH W.
Dispensation from professorial certificate requested. Graduate of Fuller Theological Seminary. Examination at NBTS not sustained.
1967: 52-53, 56. Denied.

TSIANICLIDES, NICOLAS
Dispensation from A.B. degree requested because training in Greece was more than that of an A.B. degree.
1967: 52-53, 56. Granted.

TURKSTRA, CLIFFORD P.
Dispensation from professorial certificate requested.
1968: 41, 43. Granted provided he complete his CPT course.

T.V. CODE FOR FAMILY VIEWING
1962: 219-220, 224.

UNDERSTANDING, COMMITTEE FOR
Another name for COMMITTEE OF EIGHTEEN, which see.

UNION CHURCHES
Overture requesting an amendment to the Constitution to provide more adequately for union churches.
1966: 133-136, 147, 150. Referred to CRC.
CRC will report next year.
1967: 180.
Proposed amendment on.

1968: 181.
Committees from RCA, UPCUSA, and PCUS.
1968: 134.
CRC presents proposed chapter for BCO.
1968: 235-238.
COCG recommends this term be continued instead of "cooperating churches."
1972: 186. Adopted.

UNIFICATION CHURCH
See MOON, SUN MYUNG.

UNION CLASSES, PRESBYTERIES AND SYNODS
Overture asking permission be provided for Union congregations, Classes, Presbyteries, and Synods.
1968: 96-97, 118, 123. Referred to IRC.
Proposed chapter for BCO.
1968: 238-241.
Proposed chapter for *Government.*
1969: 267-270.

UNION, FUTURE PLANS OF
Overture requesting a statement in the BCO expressing the historic Calvinistic Commitment to visible unity and truth; and (2) to appoint a committee to draw up minimum term for a union plan with the historic Reformed position.
1970: 81-82, 103. Working out statement might cause disunity. Historic statements of faith already seek to do this. No action.

UNION JUDICATORIES
A three man RCA committee to work with similar committees from PCUS and UPCUSA.
1968: 234-235.

UNION SYNODS
Proposed chapter for BCO.
1968: 241-243.
Proposed chapter for *Government.*
1969: 270-272.
Overture requesting GS not to take any action on proposals allowing such unions.
1969: 137, 149, 153. A simplified form will be presented in a year. No action.
Four overtures requesting GS to clarify the position on such synods, legality, rights of individual churches not involved in union, etc.
1970: 90, 100-101, 112. The action of PSNJ is already before CJB, therefore no action will be taken pending their judgment.
Overture asking for rule on legality of Union Synods.
1970: 90, 106-107. Referred to COCG.
COCG is not ready to make a recommendation on this referral.
1971: 199.

UNITED CALVINIST WITNESS IN WASHINGTON, D.C.
1962: 353-354.
1963: 210.
1964: 329.
A permanent committee was suggested to develop a "Joint Presbyterian-Reformed Witness" in Washington, with membership from the Hungarian Reformed Church, RCA, PCUS, and UPCUSA.
1965: 274-275. Adopted.
See also CALVINISTIC WITNESS IN WASHINGTON, D.C.

UNITED CHURCH WOMEN
1959: 170-171.

UNITED FARM WORKERS
See BOYCOTTS, ECONOMIC.

UNITED JUDICATORIES
Three man RCA committee to work with similar committees from PCUS and UPCUSA.
1968: 234-235.
Five overtures opposing in various ways and degrees the forming of union judicatories.
1971: 94-96, 107-108, 110, 112, 115, 116. No action. Matter will come up in the report of the PSNJ.
Motion requesting COCG to study the matter whether to retain in the *Church Government* terminology of Union Churches, Synods, etc. or whether to change to "cooperating churches" and "cooperating synods."
1971: 124. Adopted.

UNITED NATIONS
CAC recommends RCA endorse the UN and membership in it.
1976: 183. Adopted.

UNITED PRESBYTERIAN CHURCH, U.S.A.
Overture regarding merger.
1961: 136.
Conversations with.
1966: 245.
Letter in response.
1966: 173-175, 182. Approved.
Conversations with.
1967: 228.
1968: 232.
See also MERGER, and MERGERS PROPOSED.

UNITED SYNOD OF NEW JERSEY
Plan for.
1970: 123-124.

Report of Joint Committee on.
1970: 121-122.
Plan of operation for, see NEW JERSEY, PARTICULAR SYNOD OF.

UNITY, QUEST FOR
Prapat, Indonesia.
1958: 151.
Oberlin, Ohio.
1958: 151, 155.

URBAN CHURCHES AND MINISTRIES
GPC to appoint a Committee of Urban Mission
1969: 83.
Recommended that GPC and the PS's analyze the current state of urban churches and ministries and give priority to it.
1975: 68. Adopted.
Overture urging the designation of $500,000 annually for the next 10 years to be used for Christian Ministry in metropolitan areas.
1976: 109-110. Referred to GPC for study and report.
Urban Field Secretary added to the staff of Synods of Michigan and Chicago.
1976: 124.
RCA growth in Urban Ministries. Recommended priority.
1976: 122-125.
GPC reports that Urban work will have major emphasis at the November, 1977 meeting.
1977: 140.

UTICA (N.Y.) CHRIST REFORMED CHURCH
Dissolution of.
1958: 18.
Overture regarding transfer of funds.
1959: 123. Received for information.
Funds to be transferred to the new Christ Community Church.
1960: 15.
Proceeds of sale turned over.
1961: 18 (total of $35,232.82).

VAN BEEK, ELDER GILBERT
Dispensation requested from academic requirements.
1973: 33, 36. Granted.

VAN BEEK, RAYMOND
Dispensation from the study of Hebrew and Greek requested.
1964: 50-51. Premature, therefore denied.
Dispensation from biblical languages and professorial certificate requested.
1966: 47. Granted.

VAN BRONKHORST, DOUGLAS
Dispensation from professorial certificate requested.
1972: 29, 33. Granted.

VAN BUNSCHOOTEN BEQUEST
Summary read.
1958: 9.
1959: 7.
1960: 7.
1961: 6.
1962: 6.
1963: 7.
1964: 7.
1965: 8.
1966: 8.
1967: 8.
1968: 9.
1969: 10.
Request that the summary of the bequest be read at annual congregational meetings, classis, PS, and GS meetings giving the information that the bequest now provides $10,000 a year for use of ministerial students at Rutgers and NBTS. Also requested that an article on the bequest appear in the CH.
1959: 29.
Overture expressing opposition to reading of the summary at all ecclesiastical assemblies.
1961: 131, 142. No action.
Overture asking to relieve the classes of the necessity of reading the summary at stated meetings of classis as set forth in 1959.
1969: 133, 147, 152. GSEC to inform lower judicatories that it is no longer necessary. Adopted.

VANDE BERG, THEODORE KENNETH, JR.
Dispensation from professorial certificate requested.
1977: 162, 166, 168. Granted.

VANDEN BERG, REV. RICHARD J.
Retirement from the office of Executive Secretary of the BDM.
1958: 98, 100.

VANDEN BERGE, REV. PETER.
Resigned as Librarian of NBTS.
1967: 36.
Resolution for serving 11 years as Librarian at NBTS and taking responsibility for the publication of the *Historical Directory of the RCA, 1628-1965.*
1967: 334.

VANDER BILT, ELDER HENRY
Dispensation from academic requirement requested.
1973: 33, 36. Granted.

VANDER KOLK, REV. JUSTIN
Elected President of NBTS.
1959: 38-39.
Elected Vice President of GS.
1963: 7.

Resigned from the Presidency of NBTS
1963: 34.
Resolution.
1963: 51-52.

VANDER LINDEN, LEONA, MISSIONARY TO CHINA, 1901-1941
Obituary.
1964: Annual Report of the BWM, App., 71.

VANDER LUGT, REV. GERRIT T.
Called to be Professor of Theology at NBTS.
1960: 50, 54, 57.
Resigned his position as President of Central College.
1960: 70.
Retired from the Chair of Systematic Theology at NBTS and named Professor Emeritus.
1967: 36, 37.
Resolution for.
1967: 53-54.
A tribute to Dr. Vander Lugt for serving 18 years on the Revision of the Liturgy Committee was given by Dr. R. C. Oudersluys. Dr. Vander Lugt died the day before the *Liturgy and Psalms* came off the press. A specially bound copy was presented to Mrs. Vander Lugt.
1968: 200-201.

VANDER MEER, ELDER JACOB
Dispensation requested.
1973: 32, 36. Denied.

VANDER WERF, DR. CALVIN
Elected 8th President of Hope College.
1963: 67, 142.

VAN DOREN, MISS ALICE BOUCHER, MISSIONARY TO INDIA FOR 47 years.
Obituary.
1963: Annual Report of the BWM. App., 56.

VAN ENGEN, CHARLES
Dispensation from professorial certificate requested.
1973: 33, 36. Granted.

VAN ESS, MRS. DOROTHY, FORMERLY WITH THE ARABIAN MISSION
Death at 90.
1976: 131.

VAN HEUKELOM, REV. RAYMOND R.
Elected Vice President of GS.
1967: 8.
Elected President of GS.
1968: 8.

VAN KEMPEN, FREDERICK
Recommended that he be granted a dispensation from the Hebrew language and be granted the professorial certificate.
1974: 37, 38. Approved.

VAN OOSTENBURG, REV. GORDON L.
Elected President of GS.
1964: 7.

VAN SOEST, REV. BERT
Elected Vice President of GS.
1974: 15.
Elected President of GS.
1975: 16.

VAN VRANKEN, NELLIE SMALLEGAN, MISSIONARY TO INDIA 1917-1960
Obituary.
1966: Annual Report of the BWM, App., 16.

VAN WYLEN, DR. GORDON
Elected President of Hope College.
1972: 37.

VEENSCHOTEN, MRS. STELLA GIRARD, MISSIONARY TO THE CHINESE IN CHINA AND THE PHILIPPINES, 1917-1951.
Obituary.
1963: Annual Report of the BWM, App., 56.

VENEREAL DISEASE
CAC paper.
1973: 217-218.

VER BEEK, CARL
Enthusiastic appreciation for his leadership as GPC chairman.
1974: 70.

VER WYS, RONALD
BTE recommends that dispensation from professorial certificate be granted.
1975: 33, 34. Adopted.

VENEZUELA
Rev. and Mrs. Samuel Solivan become first RCA missionaries to Venezuela.
1977: 150.
See also LATIN AMERICA.

VIETNAM
CAC resolution
1965: 220-221. Adopted.
CAC urges a cease-fire agreement and a phased withdrawal of troops.
1966: 227-229, 235-236. Adopted.
Overture asking for days or week of prayer.
1967: 122, 126, 128. Adopted.
Recommendations of CAC: (1) that GS call for the U.S. to find at once a non-military solution to Vietnam; (2) that literature be printed or purchased concerning moral concerns of military involvement for study and debate in the churches leading up to

election; (3) that there be a day of prayer and offering for people caught in this tragic struggle.
1968: 202-204, 219. (1) returned for rewriting; (2) lost; (3) adopted.
The War, the Draft, and Conscience—a CAC paper: six recommendations (#4-9) asking the church to be supportive of those in service, counsel those who are conscientious objectors, and asking those who conscientiously dissent to be respectful of the rights of others, etc.
1968: 204-205, 219. 4,5,6,7,9 adopted; 8 lost.
CAC statement on.
1969: 247-248. Much as above; asking the church also to work as an agent of reconciliation as opportunities present themselves. Adopted.
CAC statement on: (1) favor an accelerated withdrawal of troops; (2) adopt the NCC statement on receiving a list of the estimated 1250 prisoners of war; (3) continue in prayer and efforts toward peace.
1970: 214-218. Approved.
CAC recommends that a communication be sent to the North Vietnamese peace negotiators requesting they live up to the rules of the Geneva Convention in treatment of prisoners of war.
1971: 228. Adopted.
Overture recommending GS urge President and Congress to take steps to remedy the plight of the bi-racial children; that this be referred to GPC for implementation; and that GPC explore plans whereby our own people would consider adopting these children.
1973: 113-114. Adopted.
1974: 69.
CAC recommends that every congregation participate in a public act of remembrance and reconciliation, recognizing the suffering of those who lost their lives in the Vietnam War.
1975: 193. Adopted.
Recommended that relocation of refugees and orphans be promoted by RCA churches.
1975: 66-67.
CAC recommends that RCA membership be alert to possibilities of assisting refugees in any way.
1976: 183, 184. Adopted.
See also SOUTHEAST ASIA.

VISIT-IN-PERSON PROGRAM
A project of the Evangelism Committee.
1965: 89.
1967: 93, 96.

VOLUNTARY SERVICE, ADULT
See ADULT VOLUNTARY SERVICE.

VOTING AGE (CHURCH)
Overture to amend Constitution regarding voting age.
1967: 110, 124, 127. Not adopted.
Overture requesting voting age be lowered to 16.
1968: 94-95, 117, 123. Adopted. Referred to ECRC.
ECRC presents the following to be sent to classes: They shall be elected by the communicant members of the church who have attained the age of 18 years, or at the discretion of the consistory, 16 years.
1968: 181, 182. Adopted and referred to classes for approval.
Classes approved.
1969: 205.
Overture requesting restrictions on voting age be removed; that the words, "who have attained the age of eighteen, or at the discretion of the consistory, 16 years" be deleted, and that it read "elected by the communicant members of the church."
1972: 91, 194. Adopted and sent to classes for approval.
Approved by classes.
1973: 128.

VOTING AGE (NATIONAL)
Recommended that GS encourage its membership to support legislation to amend the Constitution of the U.S. to allow 18 year-olds to vote in national elections.
1970: 218. Adopted.

VOTING RIGHTS (CHURCH)
Overture requesting a definitive statement as to the right of a higher judicatory to deprive a lower judicatory of voting and representative rights while still allowing that lower judicatory to hold membership.
1974: 100. No action.

WALVOORD, REV. CHRISTIAN H.
Appointed Executive Secretary of the BE.
1964: 61, 63.
Elected Vice President of GS.
1970: 9.
Elected President of GS.
1971: 9.

WALVOORD, MISS FLORENCE, MISSIONARY TO JAPAN FOR 35 years.
Obituary.
1968: Annual Report of the BWM, App. 1, 44-46.

WAR, CONSCIENCIOUS OPPOSITION TO
Overture concerning.
1968: 114, 122, 124. Referred to CAC.

WARD, RICHARD L.
Dispensation requested from Professorial certificate. After one course is completed at Union Theological Seminary, Richmond, the BTE asks authority to grant the dispensation.
1969: 41. Approved.
GSEC report: Since requirements were not completed by April, 1970, the matter was referred to BTE for recommendation.
1970: 126.
Dispensation from professorial certificate requested. Examination by NBTS.
1970: 33. Adopted.

WARNSHUIS, REV. ABBE LIVINGSTON
In Memoriam.
1958: 22.

WASHINGTON, JONAS
Dispensation from professorial certificate requested.
1958: 57-58. Granted.

WEEK OF PRAYER FOR CHRISTIAN UNITY
See CHRISTIAN UNITY, WEEK OF PRAYER FOR.

WEITZ, MARTIN
Dispensation from professorial certificate granted.
1976: 146, 148.

WELCKER, STANFORD
Dispensation requested from the academic requirements and the professorial certificate.
1971: 31, 36. Approved.

WELLER, DR. KENNETH
Appointed President of Central College.
1970: 53.

WESTERN THEOLOGICAL SEMINARY
Report.
1958: 45-53. 1963: 38-46.
1959: 45-48. 1964: 39-45.
1960: 44-48. 1965: 37-42.
1961: 58-65. 1966: 36-42.
1962: 41-49. 1967: 42-49.
Board of Trustees, list of.
1958: 377-378. 1963: 457-458.
1959: 382-383. 1964: 474-476.
1960: 353-354. 1965: 437-439.
1961: 412-413. 1966: 395-397.
1962: 428-429.
Degrees conferred.
1958: 46-47. 1966: 39.
1959: 45-46. 1967: 45.
1960: 45. 1968: App. 2, 174-175.
1961: no list. 1969: App. 2, 150-151.
1962: 43-44. 1970: App. 2, 142-144.
1963: 40. 1971: App. 2, 239-240.
1964: 42. 1972: App. 2, 243-244.
1965: 38-39. 1973: App. 2, 220-221.
1974: App. 2, 265-267.
1975: App. 2, 280-282.
1976: App. 1, 282-285.
1977: App. 1, 292-294.
Professors and Lectors.
1958: 373. 1967: App. 2, 11-12.
1959: 378. 1968: App. 2, 11-12.
1960: 349. 1969: App. 2, 11.
1961: 408. 1970: App. 2, 12.
1962: 425. 1971: App. 2, 19-20.
1963: 454. 1972: App. 2, 19-20.
1964: 472. 1973: App. 2, 19-20.
1965: 435. 1974: App. 2, 20-21.
1966: 393. 1975: App. 2, 20-21.
1976: App. 1, 20-21.
1977: App. 1, 20-21.
Students, list of.
1958: 46-48. 1967: 45-46.
1959: 46. 1968: App. 2, 176.
1960: 45-46. 1969: App. 2, 152.
1961: 59-60. 1970: App. 2, 145-146.
1962: 42-44. 1971: App. 2, 241.
1963: 40-41. 1972: App. 2, 245.
1964: 41-42. 1973: App. 2, 222.
1965: 37-39. 1974: App. 2, 268.
1966: 38-39.
Overture requesting GS to maintain WTS as a separate seminary and that there should not be a single board for both seminaries.
1967: 122. 126, 128. No action, since the previous GS approved.

WIDER ECUMENICITY, SPECIAL COMMITTEE ON
Report.
1964: 325.
1965: 271-273. Committee discharged.

WILLS, CHRISTIAN
Important part of stewardship.
1958: 234. 1965: 292.
1961: 229-230. 1966: 320-322.
1962: 242. 1967: 285.
1963: 341. 1968: 318.
1964: 348.
Clinics on wills.
1972: 132.

WILLIAMS, DICK (RICHARD)
Dispensation requested, but incomplete.
1971: 31. No action.
BTE recommends dispensation from professorial certificate not be granted.
1975: 33, 34. Dispensation not granted.

WILTERDINK, REV. GARRET
Called to become Director of Field Education and Assistant Professor of Theology at WTS.
1968: 40.
Elected Professor of Preaching at WTS.
1977: 165, 167-168.

WINNEBAGO
1970: 60.
Children's Home referred to American Indian Council for study.
1973: 64-65, 71. Adopted.
Exploring possibility of the sale of the Children's Home buildings. Miss Bernice Tegelar remains to work with children and families.
1974: 65, 68.

WISSINK, REV. CHARLES
Appointed Instructor of Religious Education at NBTS.
1963: 32.

WITNESSING ELDERS, ORDER OF
Recommended with "Faith at Work" approach.
1966: 387-388. Adopted.
Elders already have a witnessing responsibility, therefore not warranted—report from the Minister of Evangelism.
1967: 154.

WOMEN IN THE RCA
Overture with recommendation that the BP be enlarged to 18 members, at least three of them women.
1959: 122, 128. Lost.
Overture requesting larger representation of women on GSEC.
1974: 93. No action. Implementation would require some other means to provide these seatings.
Task Force on Women suggested by RCW.
1975: 105-107. Adopted.
A special committee presented the report of "The Committee on Sexist Bias in the RCA Liturgy."
1975: 97-98. Referred to WC.
Task force appointed to study (1) the extent in which women are involved in the program and policy making decisions in the church; (2) to review the language in the BCO and Liturgy in the light of the issue of the role of women in the denomination; (3) to develop an awareness of the issues of the involvement of women in the life of the denomination, and changes needed; (4) to formulate some recommendations.
1976: 51-52.
Recommended by WC that worship leaders make appropriate modifications in language where the RCA liturgy fails to take into consideration that men and women participate in the life of the church.
1976: 246-247.
Overture requesting women have equal rights with men in all organizations, boards, agencies and judicatories of the RCA.
1976: 107. No action.
Report of Task Force. Requested more representation on boards, commissions and agencies.
1977: 69.
See also FEMINISM; ORDINATION OF WOMEN; NATIONAL DEPARTMENT OF WOMEN'S WORK; REFORMED CHURCH WOMEN.

WOMEN, ORDINATION OF
See ORDINATION OF WOMEN.

WOMEN, ROLE OF IN CONTEMPORARY SOCIETY
CAC report.
1964: 223-225, 227, 230. Committee from each classis to report to CAC for further study.
CAC paper in preparation.
1965: 217.

WOMEN'S BOARD OF FOREIGN MISSIONS
Resolution by GPC on the occasion of the 100th anniversary of the WBFM.
1975: 60-61, 68. Adopted.

WOMEN'S GUILD
See GUILD FOR CHRISTIAN SERVICE and REFORMED CHURCH WOMEN.

WOMEN'S WORK OF THE MISSION BOARDS, DEPARTMENT OF, COMMITTEE
Organization charts.
1958: 340-342.
Report of Plan of Organization of the National Department of Women's Work.
1958: 334-345.
1959: 348.
See NATIONAL DEPARTMENT OF WOMEN'S WORK and REFORMED CHURCH WOMEN.

WORDS OF HOPE
Formerly TEMPLE TIME, which also see.
Recommended that GPC discuss with "Words of Hope" organization the possibility of some recognition and promotion of the radio broadcasts and related devotional publications.
1976: 136. Adopted.

WORLD ALLIANCE OF REFORMED CHURCHES
Report.
1969: 278-284.
1970: 235-239.
1972: 240-243.
1973: 241-245.
1974: 236-240.
1975: 215-216.
1976: 222-226.
Report through CIR.
1970: 225-226, 241.
1971: 233.
1972: 231.
1973: 229-230.
1977: 263-267.

Formerly ALLIANCE OF REFORMED CHURCHES HOLDING THE PRESBYTERIAN SYSTEM, which also see.

WORLD COUNCIL OF CHURCHES
Report.
1958: 150-155. 1968: 249-250.
1959: 157-162. 1969: 276-277.
1960: 134-138. 1970: 230-231.
1961: 159-164. 1971: 237-238.
1962: 155-160. 1972: 235-236.
1963: 162-164. 1973: 233-236.
1964: 268-274. 1974: 230-232.
1965: 245-247. 1975: 209-212.
1966: 254-255. 1976: 216-218.
1967: 233-239. 1977: 256-258.
Integration of the WCC and the International Missionary Council.
1960: 140.

WORLD COUNCIL OF CHURCHES, COMMITTEE ON
Report.
1958: 155-156. 1962: 149-155.
1959: 163-164. 1963: 164-168.
1960: 139-141. 1964: 263-268.
1961: 165-171.
Permanent Committee discontinued.
Report through CIR.
1966: 237-239. 1970: 223-224.
1967: 216-218. 1971: 231-232.
1968: 223-224. 1972: 229-230.
1969: 255-256. 1973: 227-228.
Overture regarding WCC
1958: 133-134. Referred to the CWCC.
Overture regarding WCC's attitude toward Communism
1963: 107, 111. Referred to the CWCC.
Overture regarding membership in.
1963: 110, 113. No action.
New Delhi Assembly Report.
1962: 155-156.
Overture suggesting membership on a voluntary basis.
1970: 95, 108. Recommended that funds now given to WCC from GS be solicited on a voluntary basis.
Two overtures requesting restoring assessment amount in the GS budget for NCC and WCC.
1971: 99-100, 109, 113, 116. No action.
Two overtures requesting retaining the present practice of non-assessment to NCC and WCC.
1971: 100-101, 113. No action.
Overture urging withdrawal of membership from WCC and NCC.
1971: 101, 113. No action.
Two overtures requesting withdrawal of membership.
1973: 88-89. No action.
Four overtures suggesting the contribution to NCC and WCC be on a voluntary basis.
1973: 85. No action.
Recommended that RCA continue membership in.
1973: 257. Adopted.
GSEC recommends as a responsible member denomination the RCA must find ways to contribute our RCA proportionate share of administrative expense.
1974: 117.
Since ways must be found to pay participating shares for interchurch bodies, outside of assessments to classes, the matter of funding was referred to the CIR, a special committee of which will make proposals to GS.
1974: 115, 117.
CIR recommends importance of affiliation with NCC and WCC be relayed to the churches; that feedback be sent to the churches about the conferences and assemblies to which we send delegates.
1974: 253. Adopted.
Overture requesting GS to maintain support of the NCC and WCC only by voluntary contributions of an individual member or church.
1975: 92. No action. Declared out of order because of previous action.
Overture requesting withdrawal from.
1976: 107-108. No action.
Recommended that all pastors study the WCC document on Evangelism and the reports on the Nairobi Assembly.
1976: 228. Adopted.
Fifth Assembly, Nairobi, 1975.
1976: 211-212, 216-218.

WORLD HOME BIBLE LEAGUE
Report.
1958: 186-189. 1967: 254-255.
1959: 192-195. 1968: 259-262.
1960: 169-172. 1969: 265-266.
1961: 197-200. 1972: 248-250.
1962: 191-193. 1973: 250-252.
1963: 304-308. 1974: 247-248.
1964: 299-302. 1975: 224-226.
1965: 261. 1976: 128.
1966: 279-281. 1977: 139.

WORLD HUNGER
1974: 71-72.
1975: 52, 66.
Motion made that Synod observe a fast during a noon meal; that delegates meet in cafeteria for devotions; that Synod meet financial obligations for the meal with the college; that each person contribute approximately price of meal and that the offering go to Church World Service.

1975: 259. Defeated.
CAC gives a series of recommendations concerning meatless days, vegetarian life, intake of alcoholic beverages because of use of grain, cut-back on coffee and tea so that land can be used for food production, fasting days on holidays, etc., etc.
1975: 199. Defeated.
CAC presents "Holy Living in Time of Famine" and asks it be printed in CH.
1975: 194-199.
CAC made a series of 10 recommendations concerning world hunger.
1976: 184-185. Adopted.
See BREAD FOR THE WORLD and CHURCH WORLD SERVICE.

WORLD MISSIONS, BOARD OF
See also GPC after 1970.

WORLD LITERACY AND CHRISTIAN LITERATURE (LIT-LIT)
1958: 171.
1959: 179.

WORLD MISSION, BOARD OF, RCA, STANDING COMMITTEE ON
Report.
1961: 93-101. 1965: 72-79.
1962: 80-88. 1966: 86-91.
1963: 80-84. 1967: 79-86.
1964: 81-90. 1968: 64-72.
The 136th annual report, and the last. World Mission Board becomes part of GPC.
1968: 64.
Work in Sudan suspended; missionaries expelled from Sudan.
1967: 80.
See also CHRISTIAN WORLD MISSIONS, BOARD OF and APPENDIX.

WORLD MISSION RELATIONSHIPS
1977: 131-135, 143-144.

WORLD ORDER CONFERENCE
Overture regarding—a call to repudiate the inclusion of the PEOPLE'S REPUBLIC OF CHINA.
1959: 122-123.

WORLD'S FAIR EXHIBIT
See NEW YORK WORLD'S FAIR.

WORSHIPBOOK
Overture requesting that GS empower the Committee on Liturgy to approach the Joint Committee on the Worshipbook (Presbyterian) with an offer of participation in its publication.
1971: 110, 116. Adopted and referred to GSEC.
GSEC reports that the Joint Committee on the Worshipbook completed its task and disbanded more than a year ago.
1972: 113. No action.

WORSHIP COMMITTEE
Report.
1975: 190.
1976: 246-247.
Chairman of committee asked to be consultant on Presbyterian Committee planning a new Service Book. Recommended by WC that as a member he explore possibility of common action in worship with PCUS and UPCUSA.
1974: 211. Adopted.
President suggests and RCPR recommends the WC revise form for the ordination and installation of Ministers of the Word to include description in BCO (enablers).
1976: 26-27, 33. Adopted.
Sample of a Directory of Worship with recommendation that it be made available to the ministers and consistories during the coming year.
1977: 309-312. Adopted.
For earlier reports see LITURGY, REVISION OF, PERMANENT COMMITTEE ON.

WYCKOFF, CHARLOTTE C., MISSIONARY TO INDIA, 1915-1960.
In Memoriam.
1967: Annual Report of the BWM, App. 1, 19-20.

YEARBOOK OF MINISTERS AND CHURCHES
Not to be published pending updating of Corwin's Manual.
1959: 125, 128.
Corwin's Manual, revision of.
1959: 126.
Overture requesting yearbook.
1960: 113, 117. Approved in principle.
Overture regarding.
1962: 121-122, 127. No action.
See also CORWIN'S MANUAL and HISTORICAL DIRECTORY.

YEH, CHIA-HSING
Dispensation from professorial certificate requested. Graduate of Tainan Theological College.
1970: 32. His work not equivalent to our BD degree. The need was not indicated. Denied.
Subsequent recommendation was adopted, granting the dispensation.
1970: 31.

YOUTH AND YOUTH WORK
Recommended representation on GPC be given to youth in the RCA of high school

age and college age, and that one high school and one college youth have voting privileges.
1971: 65, 76. Adopted.
Amendment suggested to the above motion—that four high school and four college youth shall be additional members.
1972: 118. Not adopted. One of each approved.
Suggested the relationship between youth and GS be studied by a Sub-Committee and the GSEC consider bringing youth into planning the Communion service and Devotional services of GS.
1971: 131. Referred to Task Force for Designing GS of 1971.
Overture requesting Youth Ministry as a national priority.
1976: 110-111. Referred to GPC for study and report.
GPC reports they will consider a Secretary for Youth Ministries at their July, 1977 meeting.
1977: 141.
Report.
1964: 56.
1965: 50-51.
1966: 54-55.

YOUTH EVANGELIST CORPS
President suggests college graduates take up this work for one or two years.
1965: 340, 347, 348. Referred to BNAM and Youth Division of the BE.
BNAM's reply to President's suggestion.
1966: 99-100. Complete plan will be presented next year.

ZIONISM AND RACISM
CAC deplores and condemns the United Nations resolution equating Zionism with racism and urges GS to convey this resolution to the appropriate leaders of the Jewish community, the United Nations, and the U.S. Congress.
1977: 199-200. Adopted.